COLOR IT CHIC

COLOR IT CHIC

Color It Chic by You and Nancy Riegelman

Published by 9 Heads Media | www.fashionfinishingschool.com

Design work - Stefani Greenwood

First Edition: 2013

Printed in China

Pulisher's Cataloging-In-Publication Data

Riegelman, Nancy

Color It Chic/Nancy Riegelman First Edition
256 Pages 28.28 x 21.7 cm
ISBN –978-0-9702463-7-0

Nancy Riegelman was born in San Francisco. She attended the University of California at Berkeley, UCLA and Art Center College of Design in Pasadena Ca, where she studied drawing and fine arts.

Nancy teaches fashion drawing at the Fashion Institute of Design and Merchandising (FIDM) in Los Angeles and international style at Art Center College of Design. She has been visiting professor at the University Premila Polytechnic in Bombay, India, Seibu University in Tokyo, Japan, the Paris Fashion Institute and the Central Academy of Art & Design in Beijing, China.

Nancy is also a fine artist who has exhibited in museums in the USA and overseas. Nancy lives in Los Angeles.

SOME IDEAS FOR THE COLORING BOOK

1. Polka Dots
2. Zig Zags
3. Use a ruler
4. Use a graphite pencil
5. Stripes
6. Use watercolors
7. Try different shades of a single color
8. Neon
9. Draw on a train
10. Try different styles of art (i.e. Pointillism, Pop Art)
11. Use markers
12. Use colored pencils
13. Try something funny
14. Listen to music
15. Paint it black
16. Write a love letter
17. Look at patterns from other cultures
18. Color in half and then have a friend color in the rest
19. Turn it upside down
20. Textures

PS. All of the images are printed twice for a second chance!

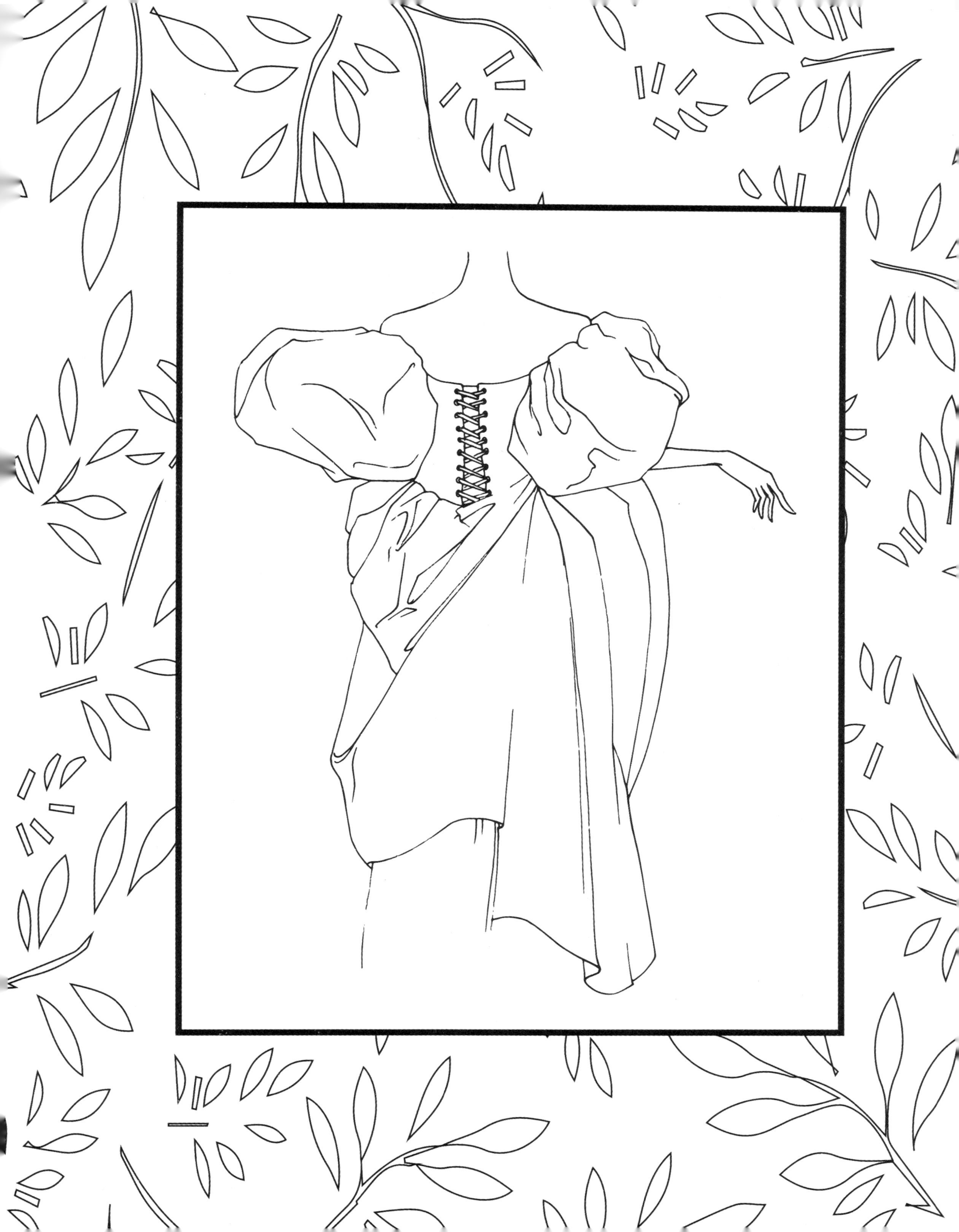

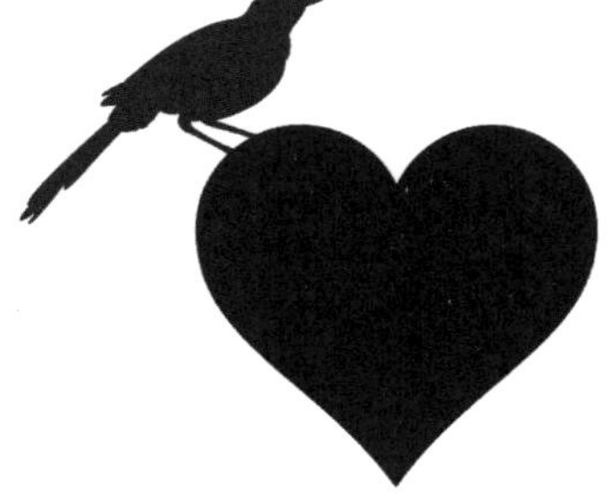

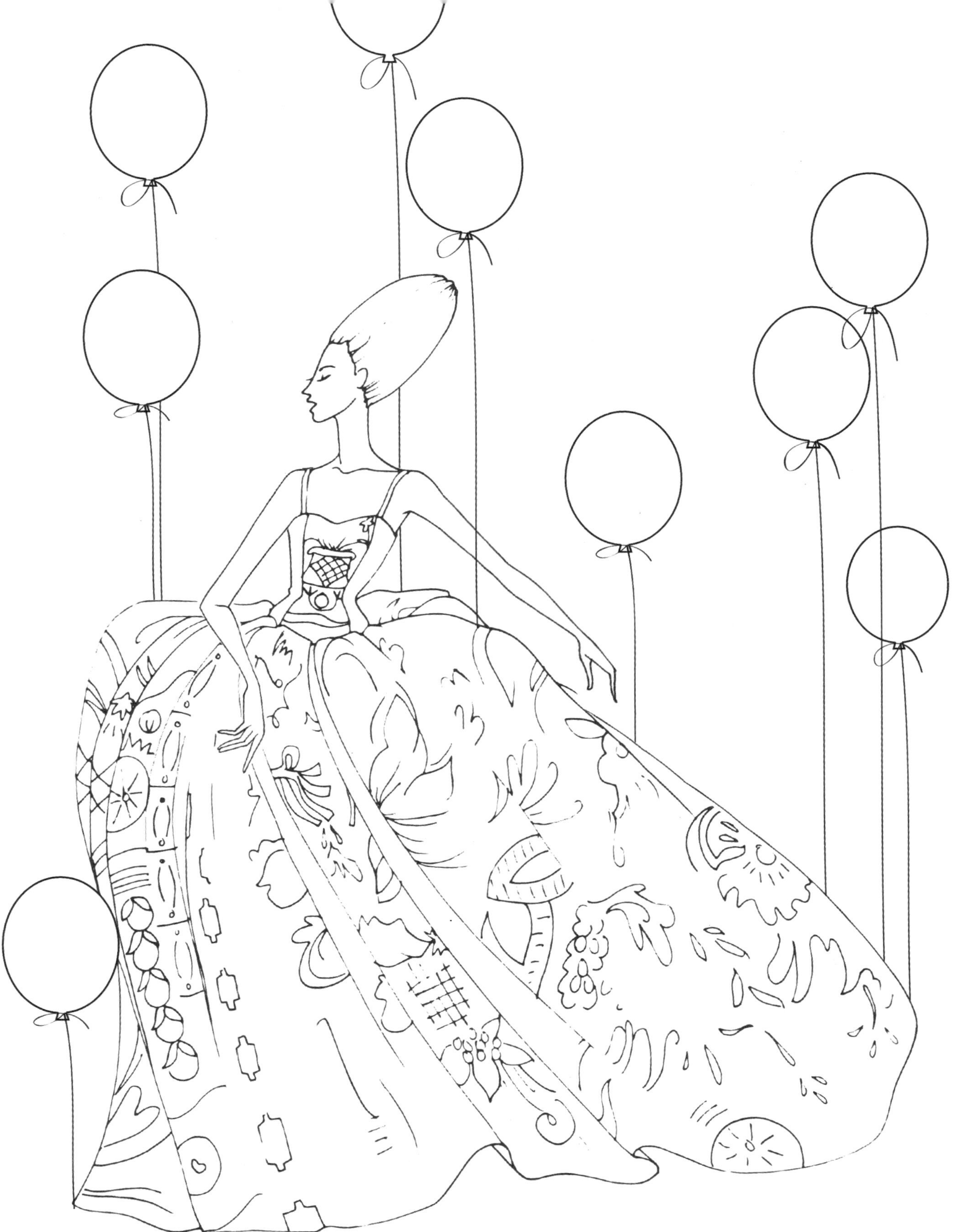

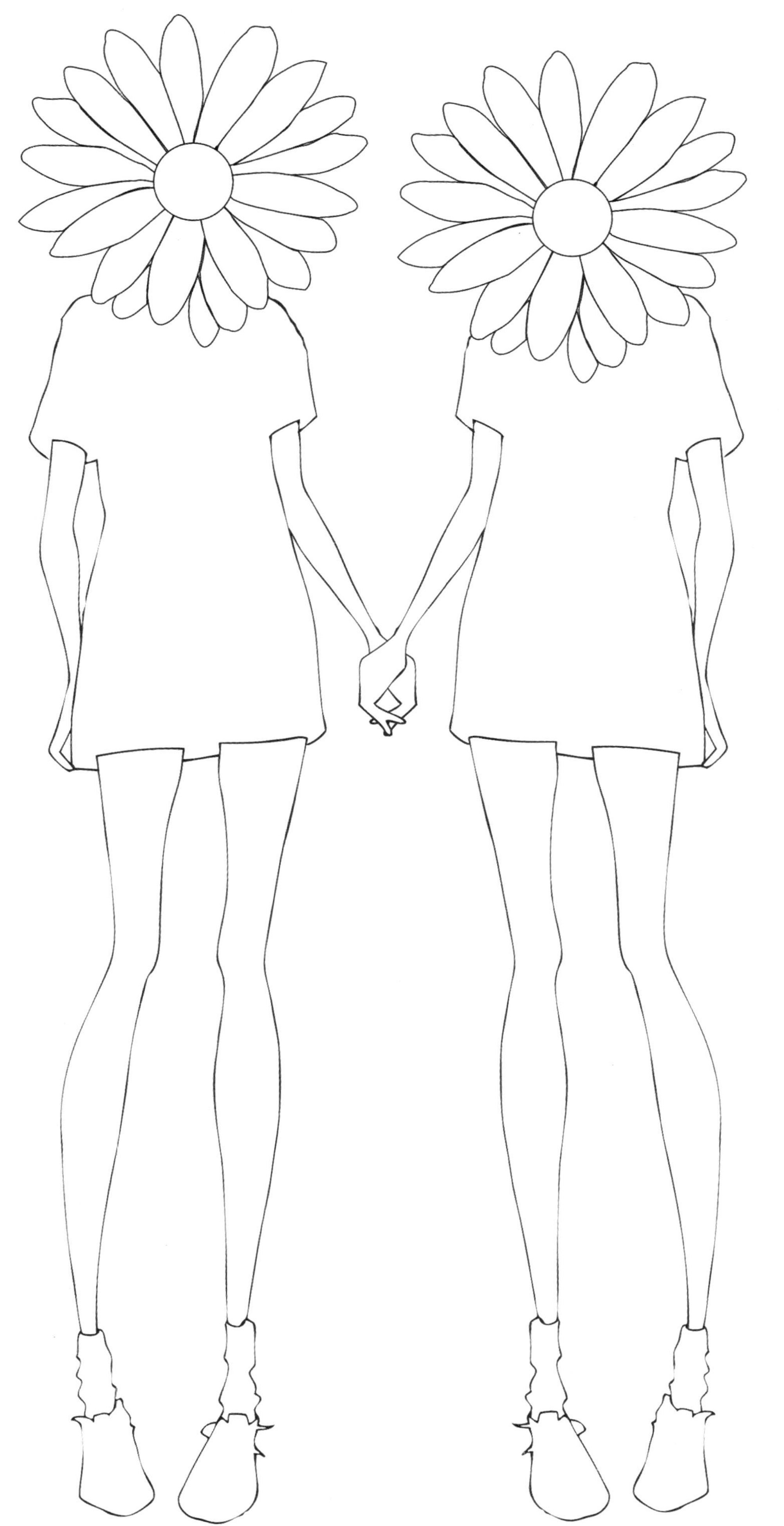

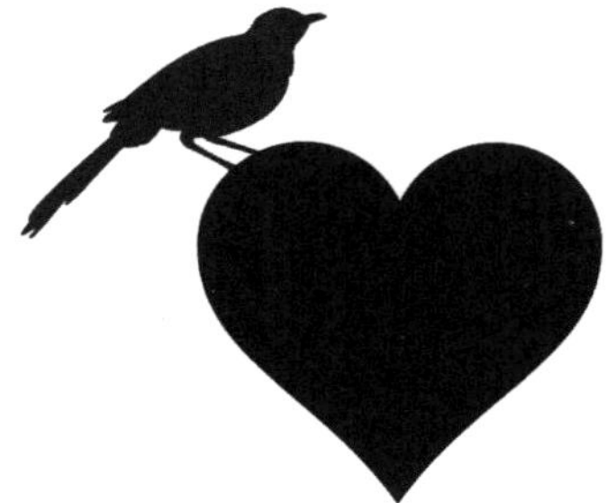

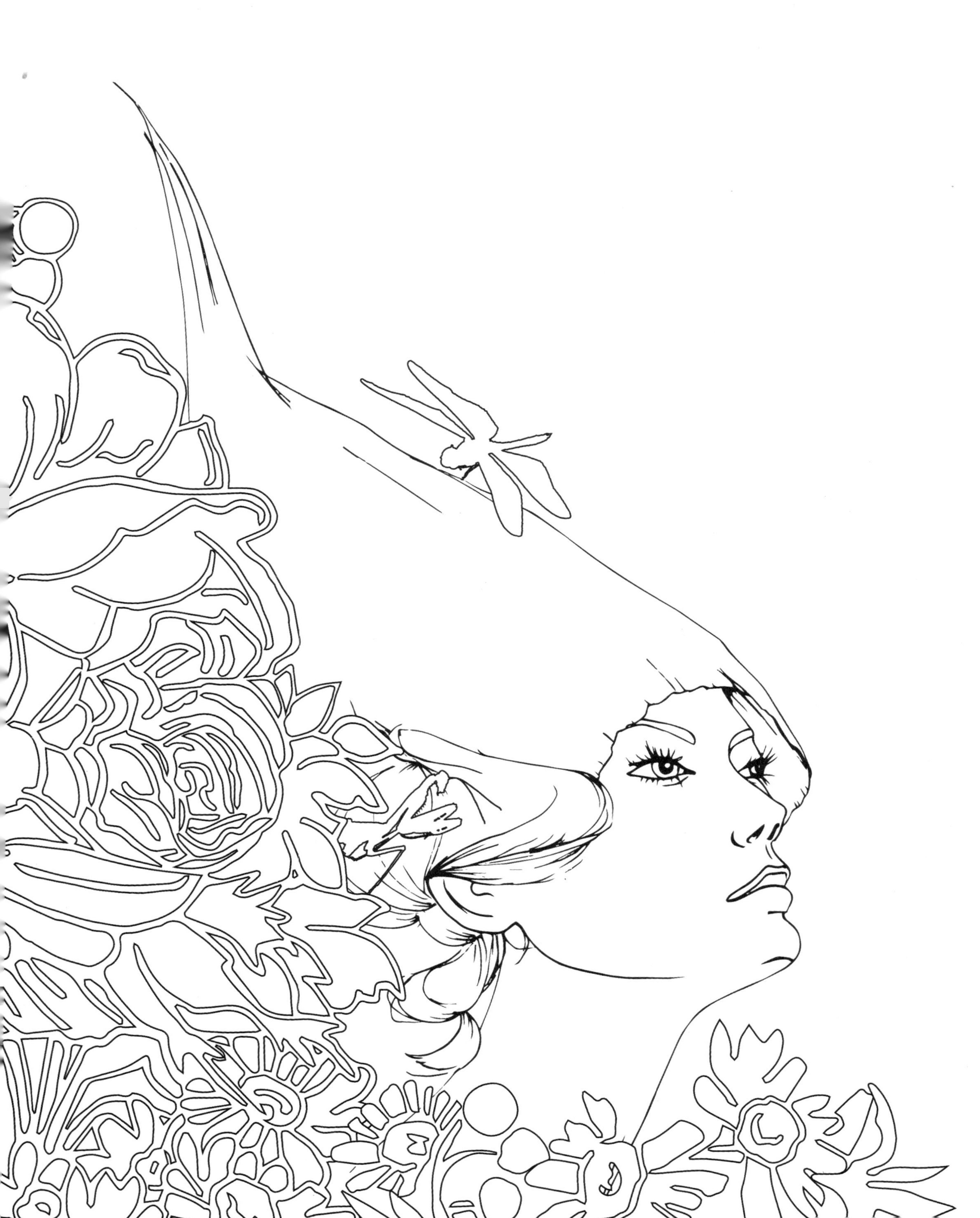

Drawing is still basically the same as
it has been since prehistoric times.
It brings together man and the world.
It lives through magic.

— Keith Haring

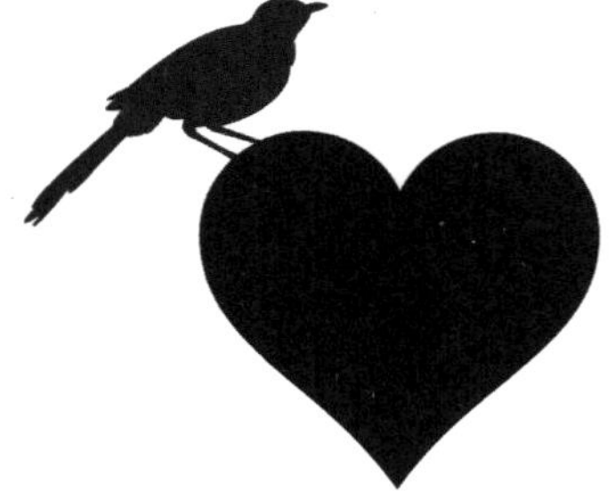

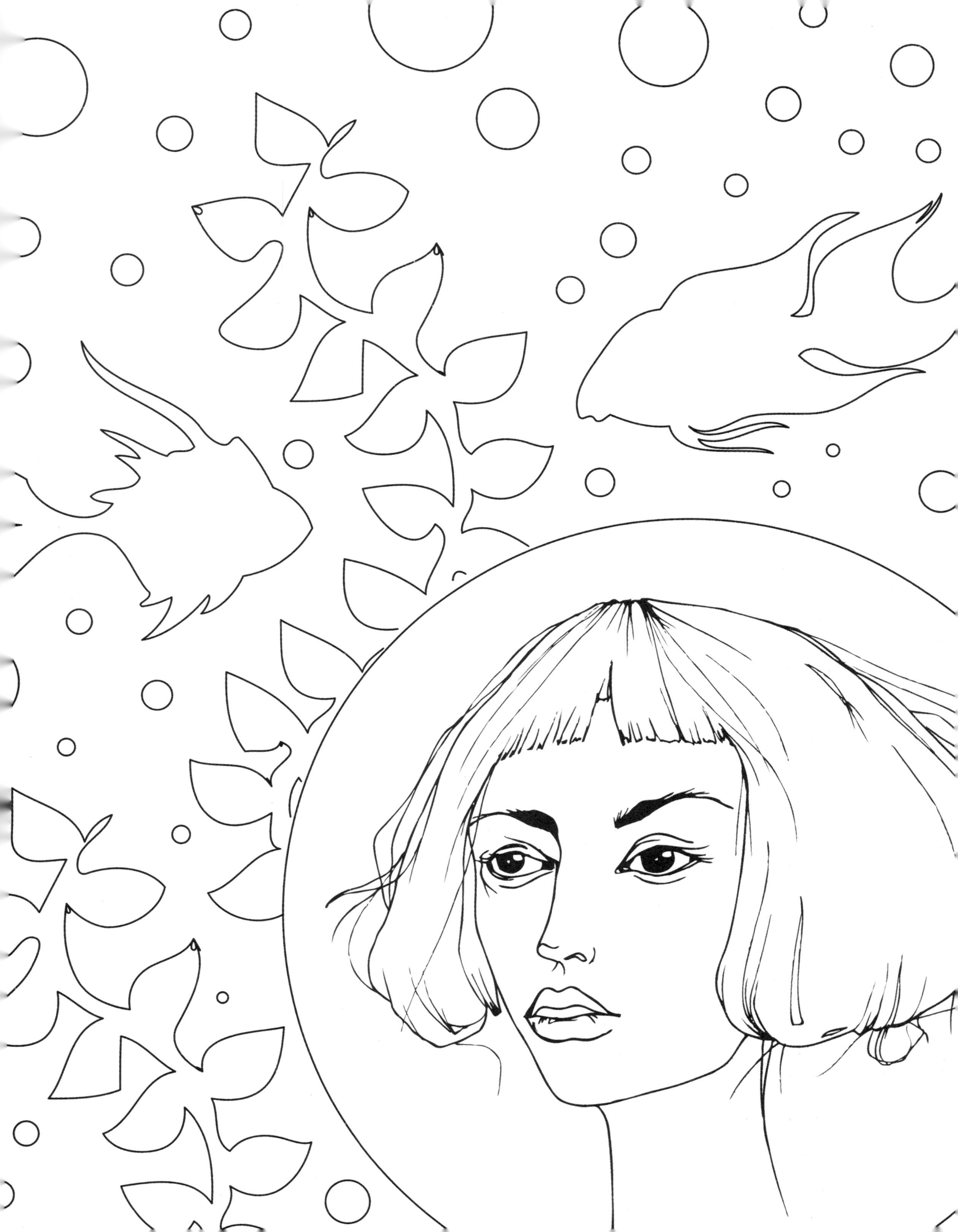

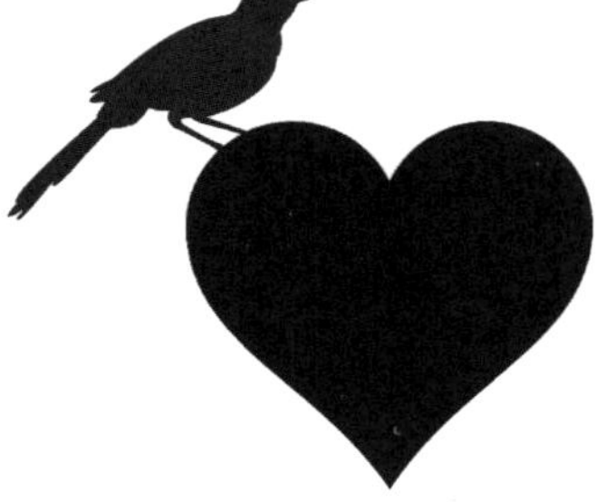

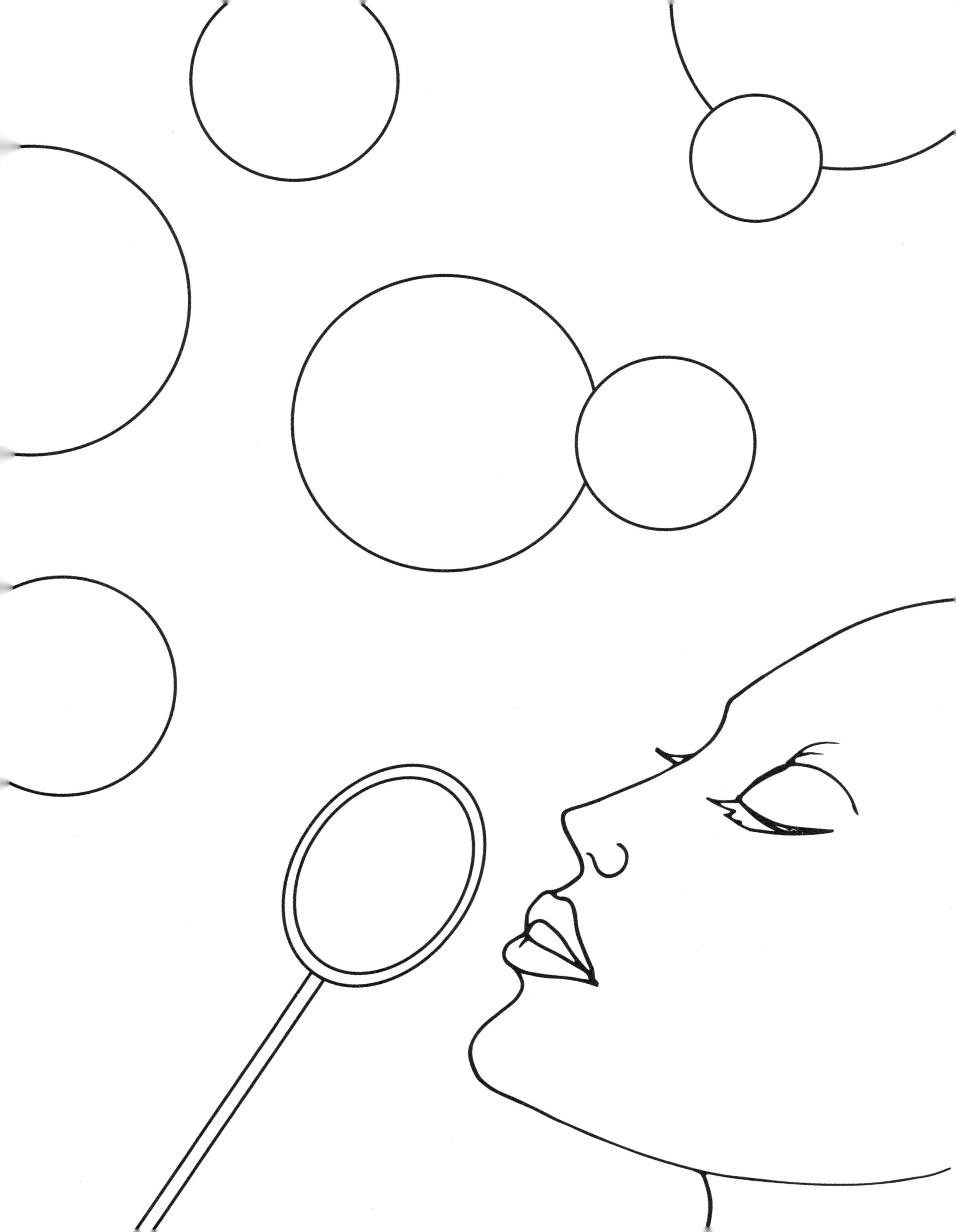

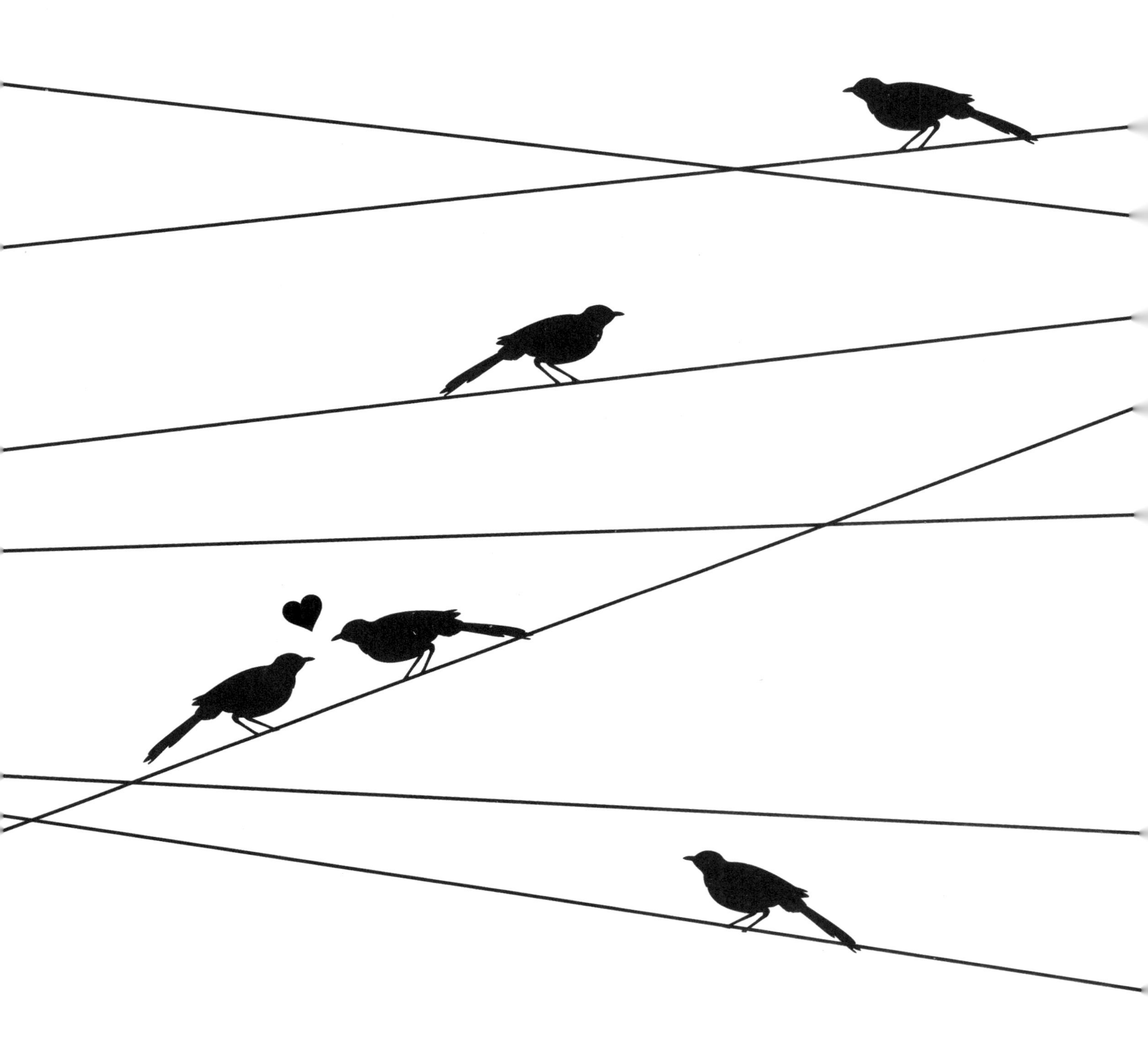

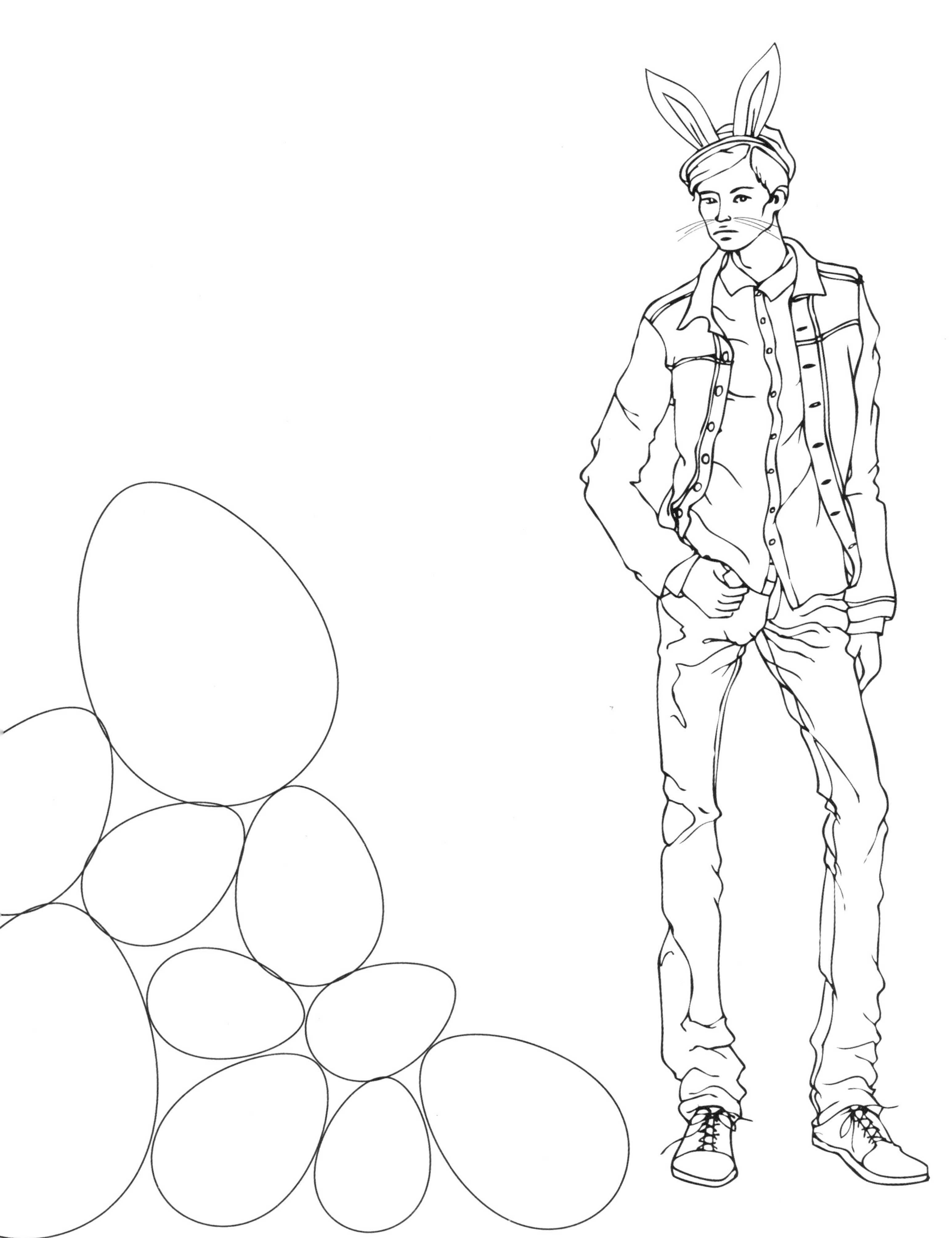

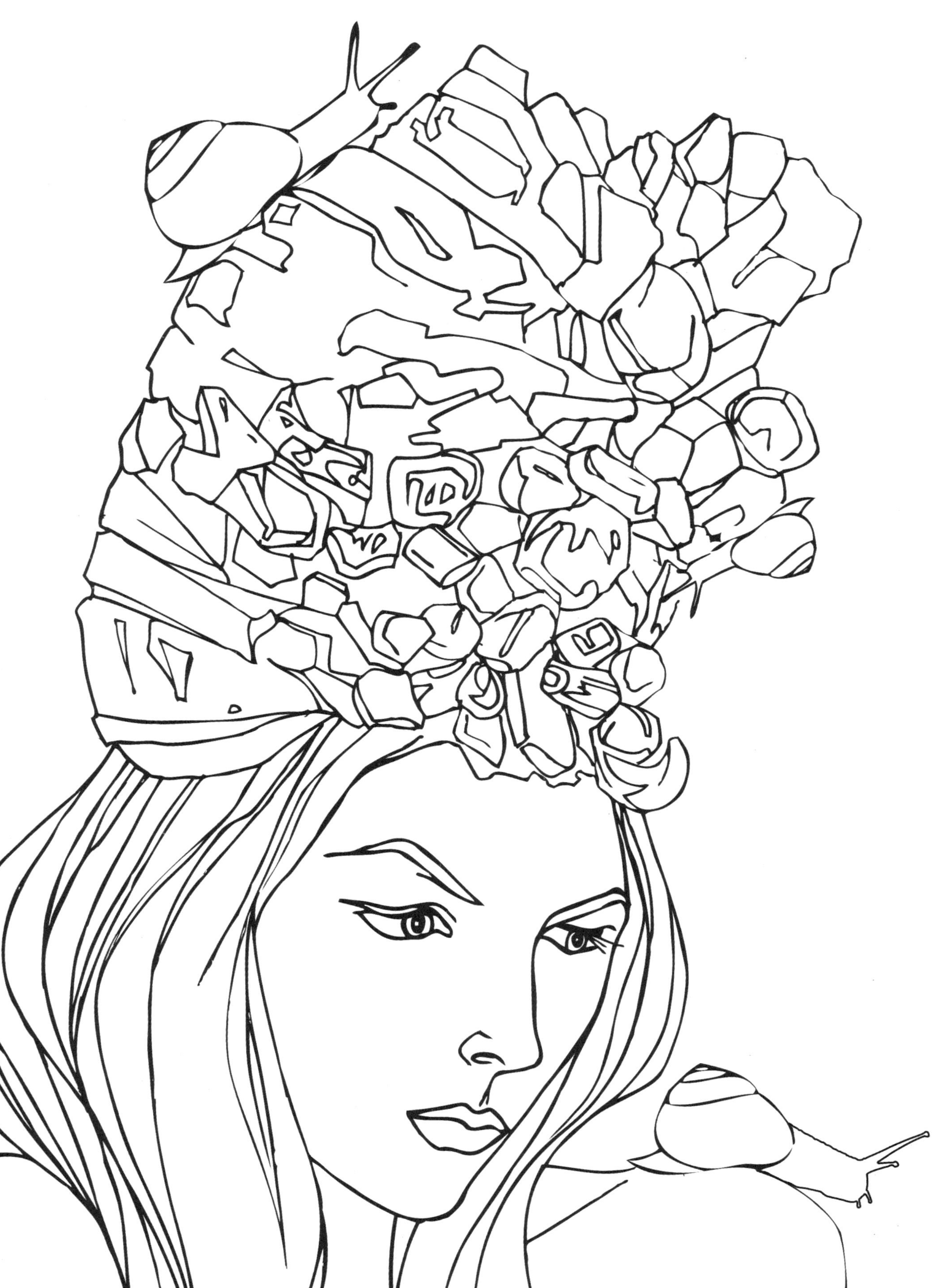

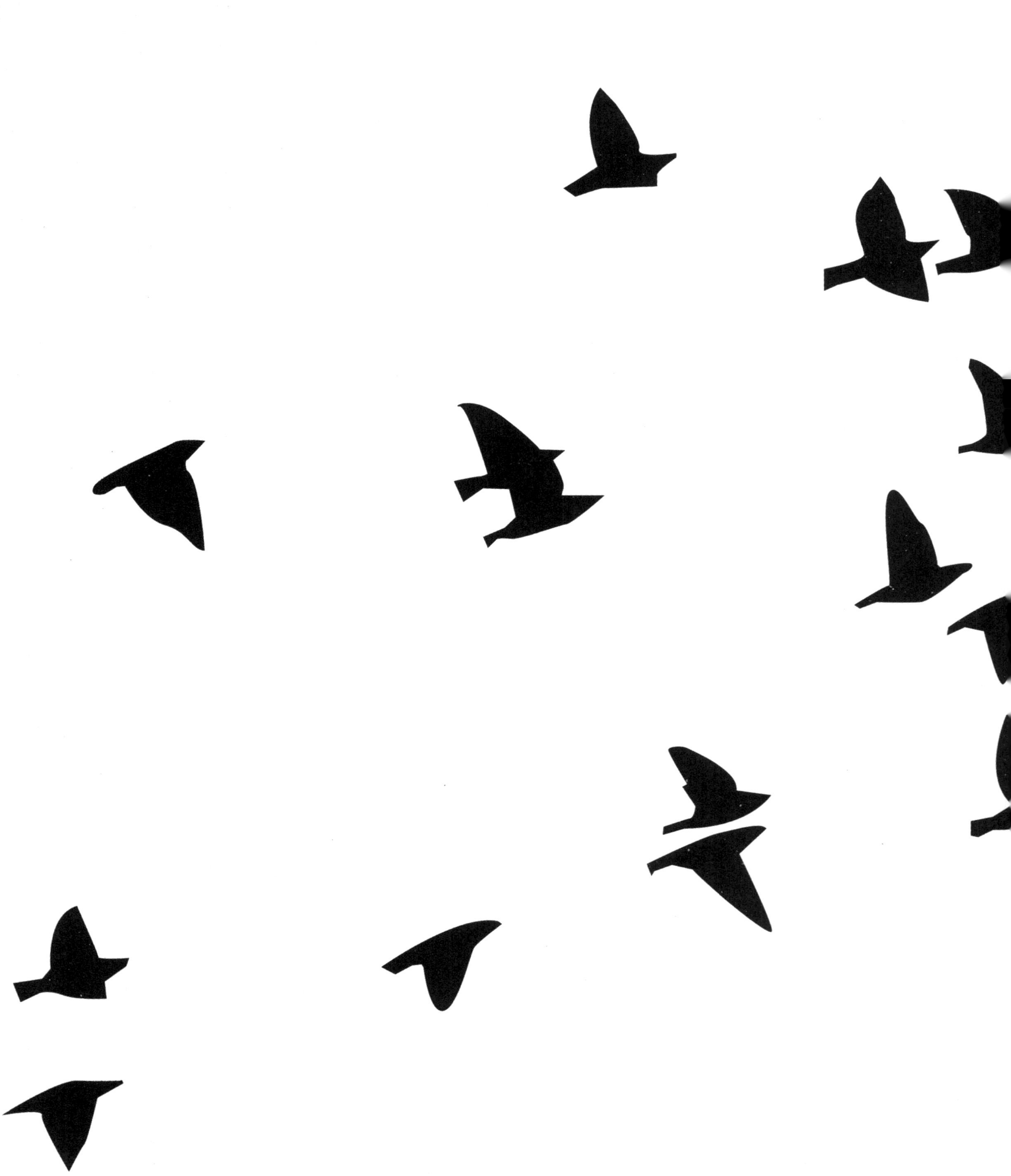

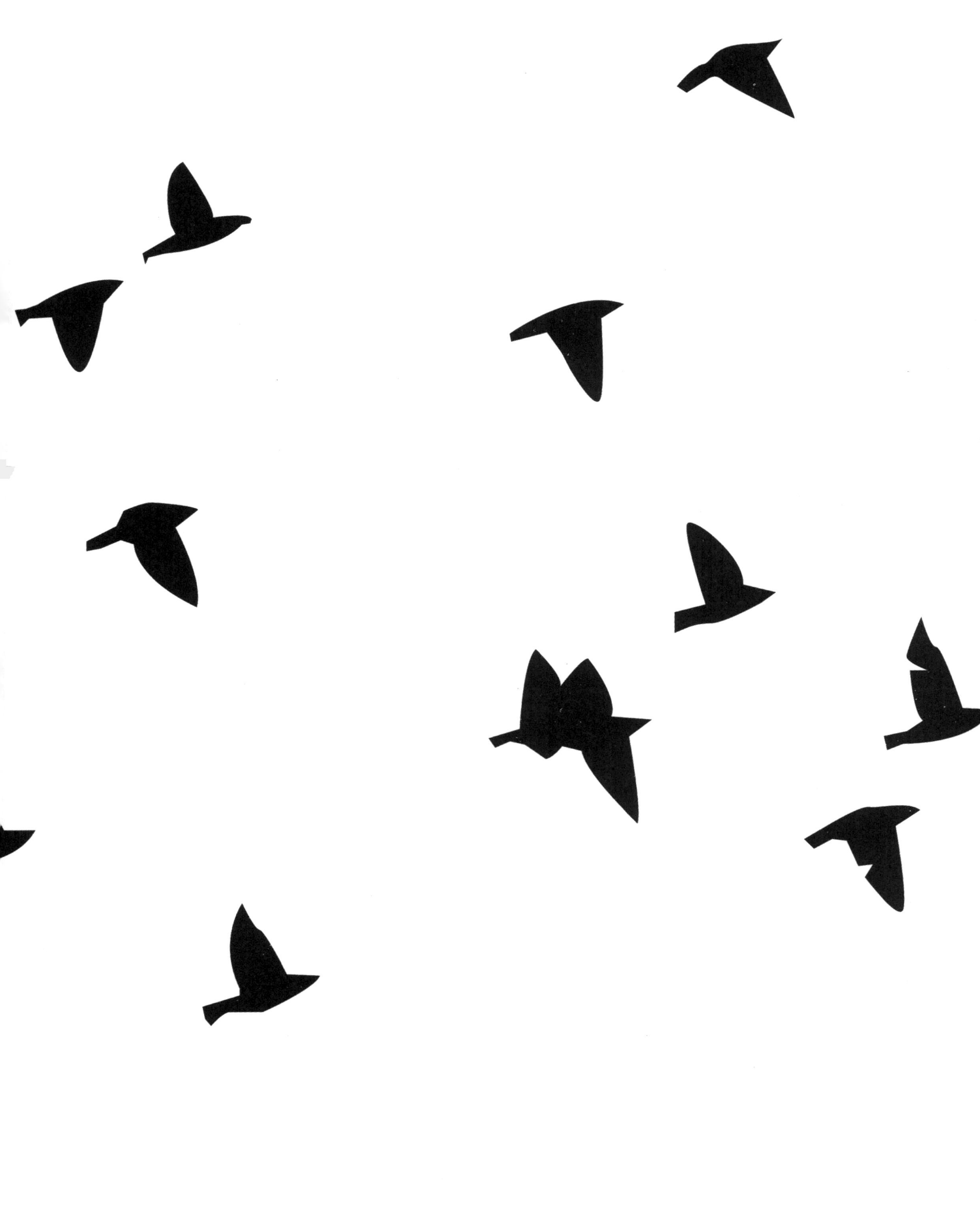

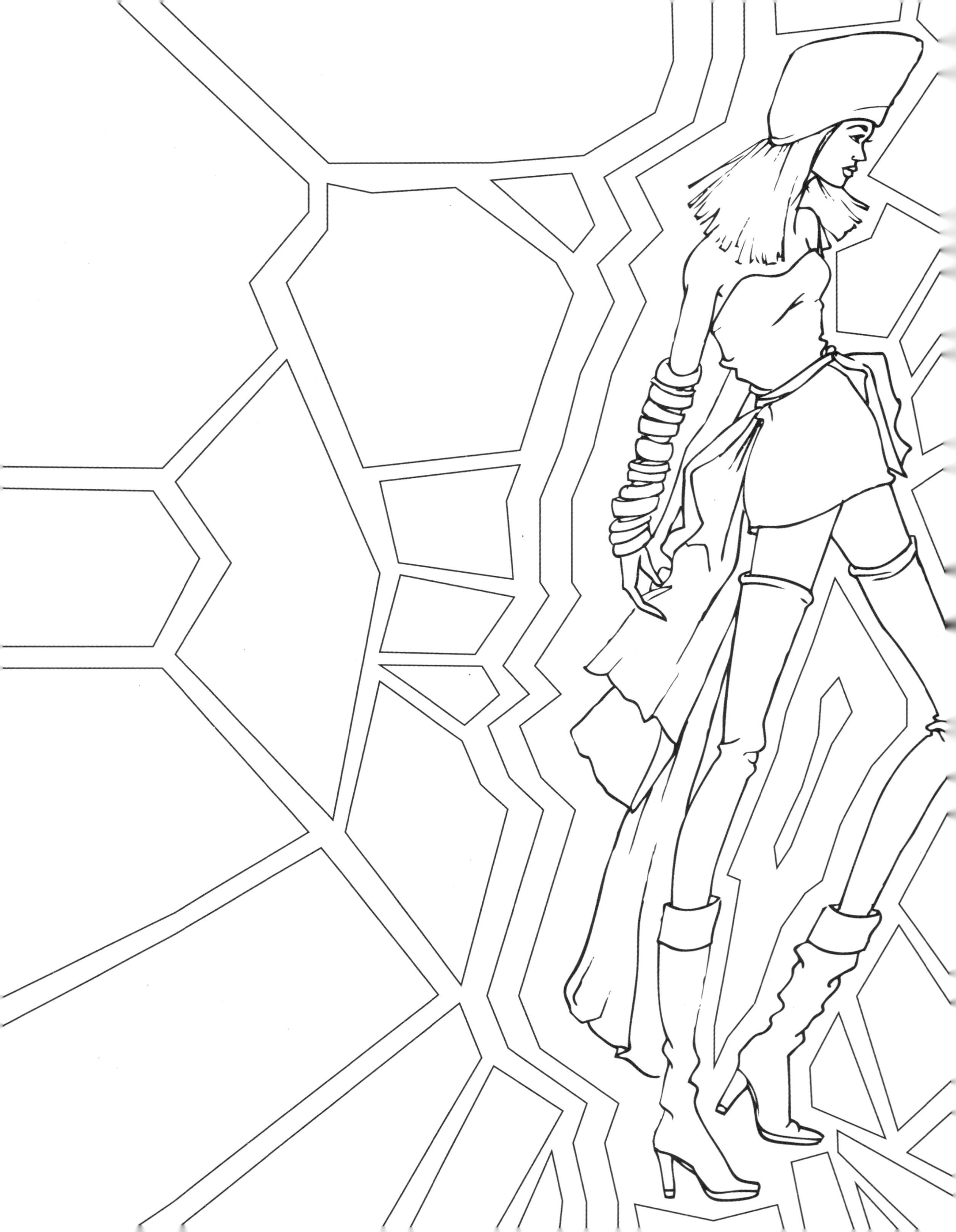

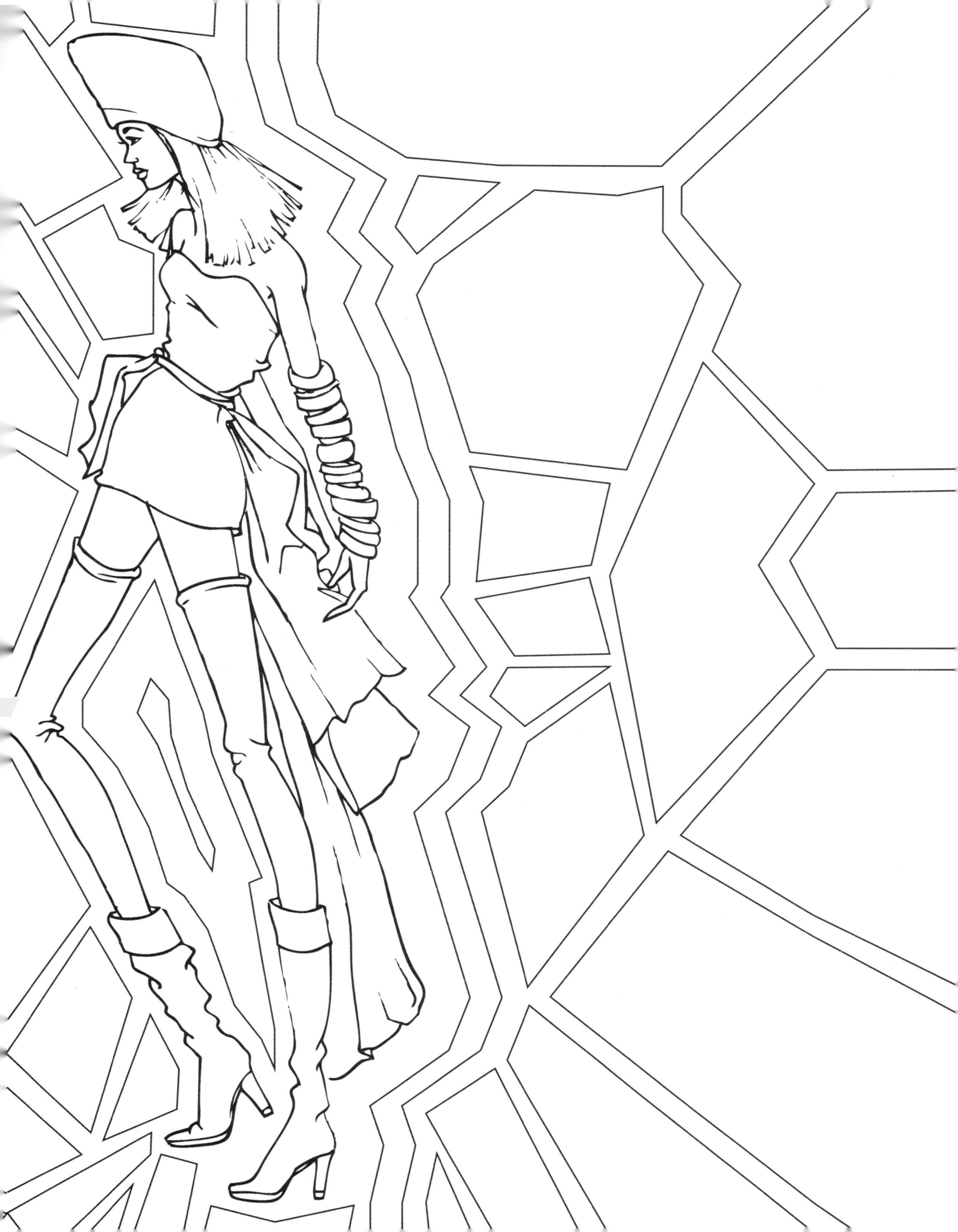

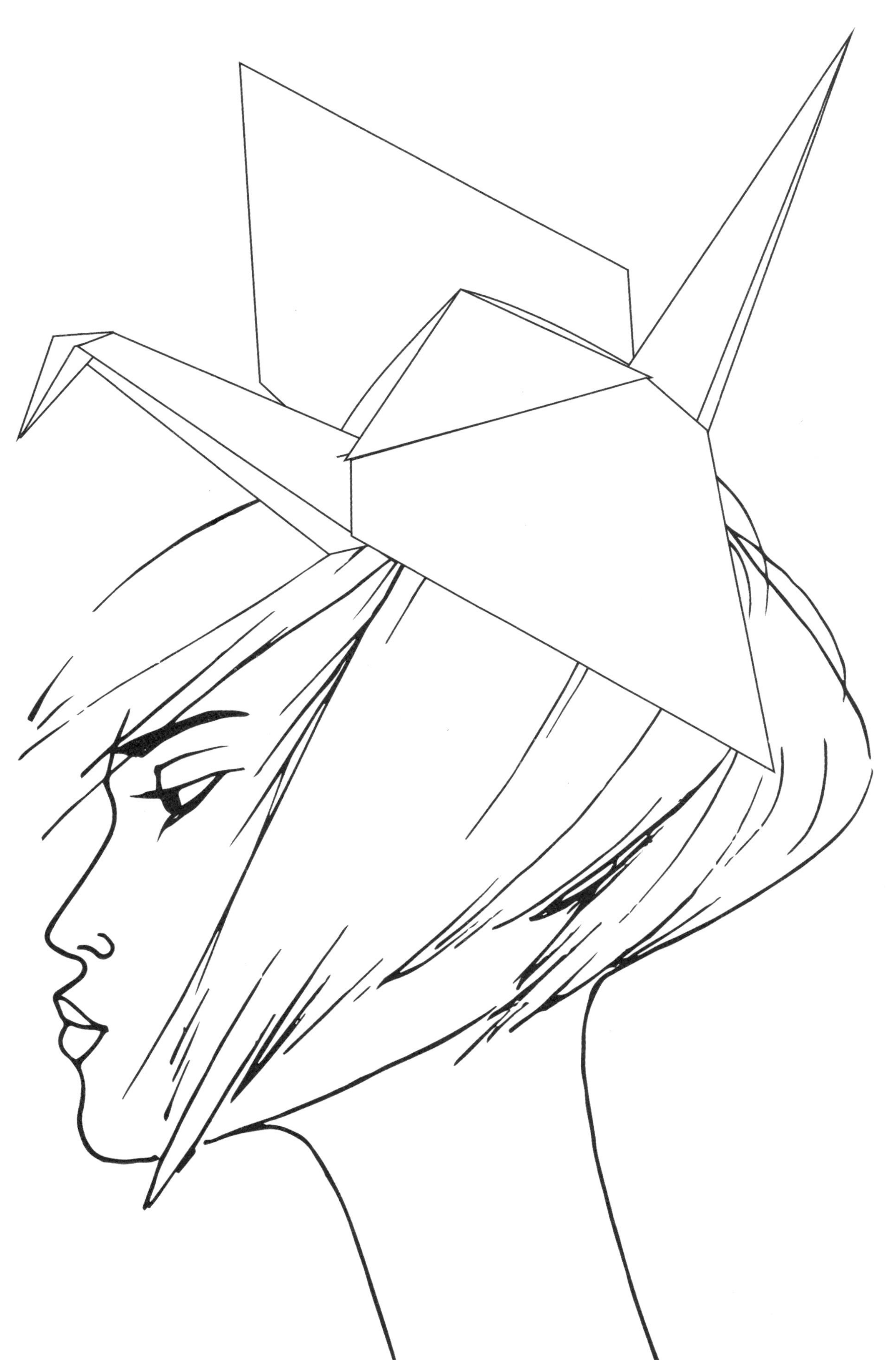

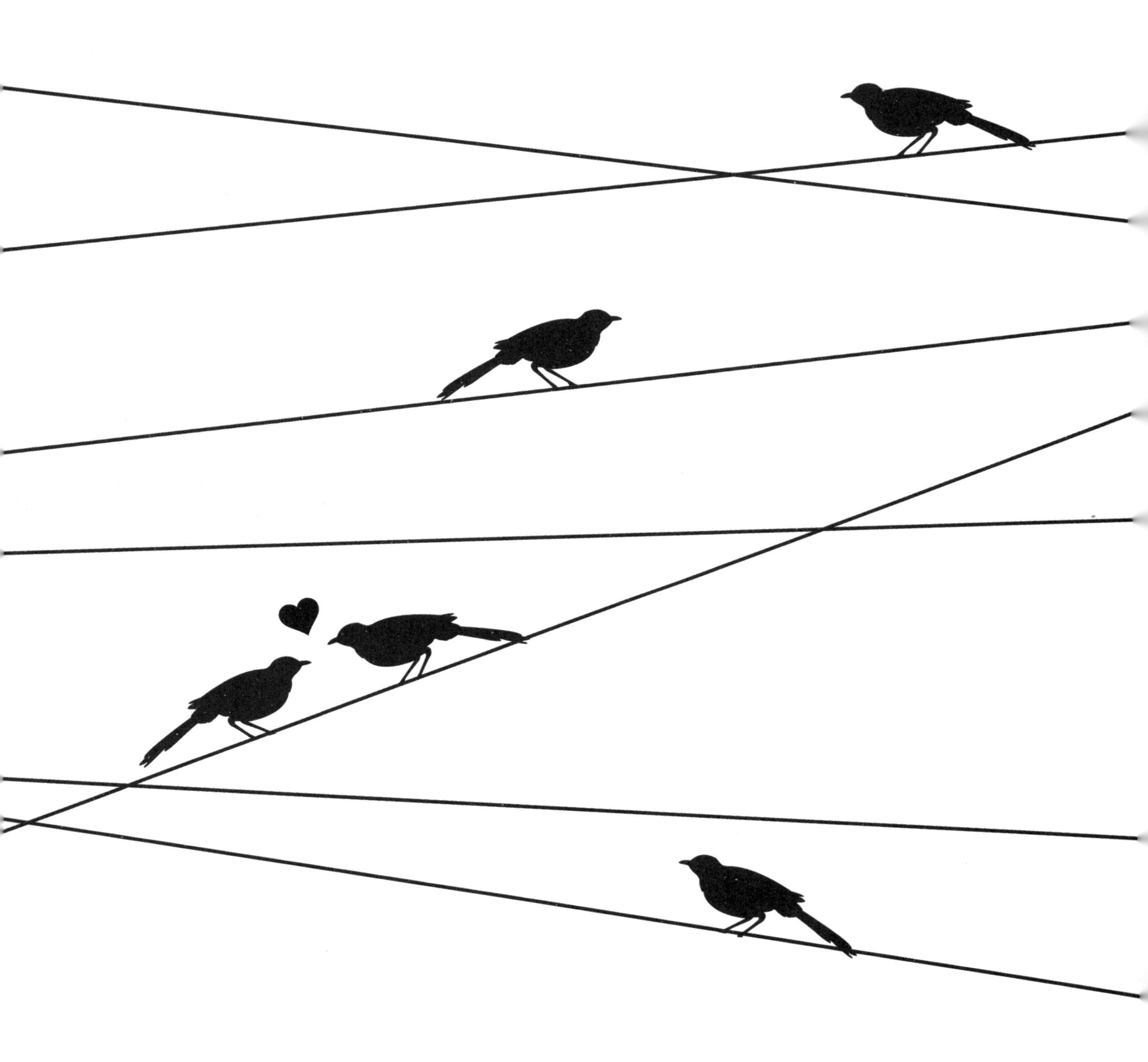

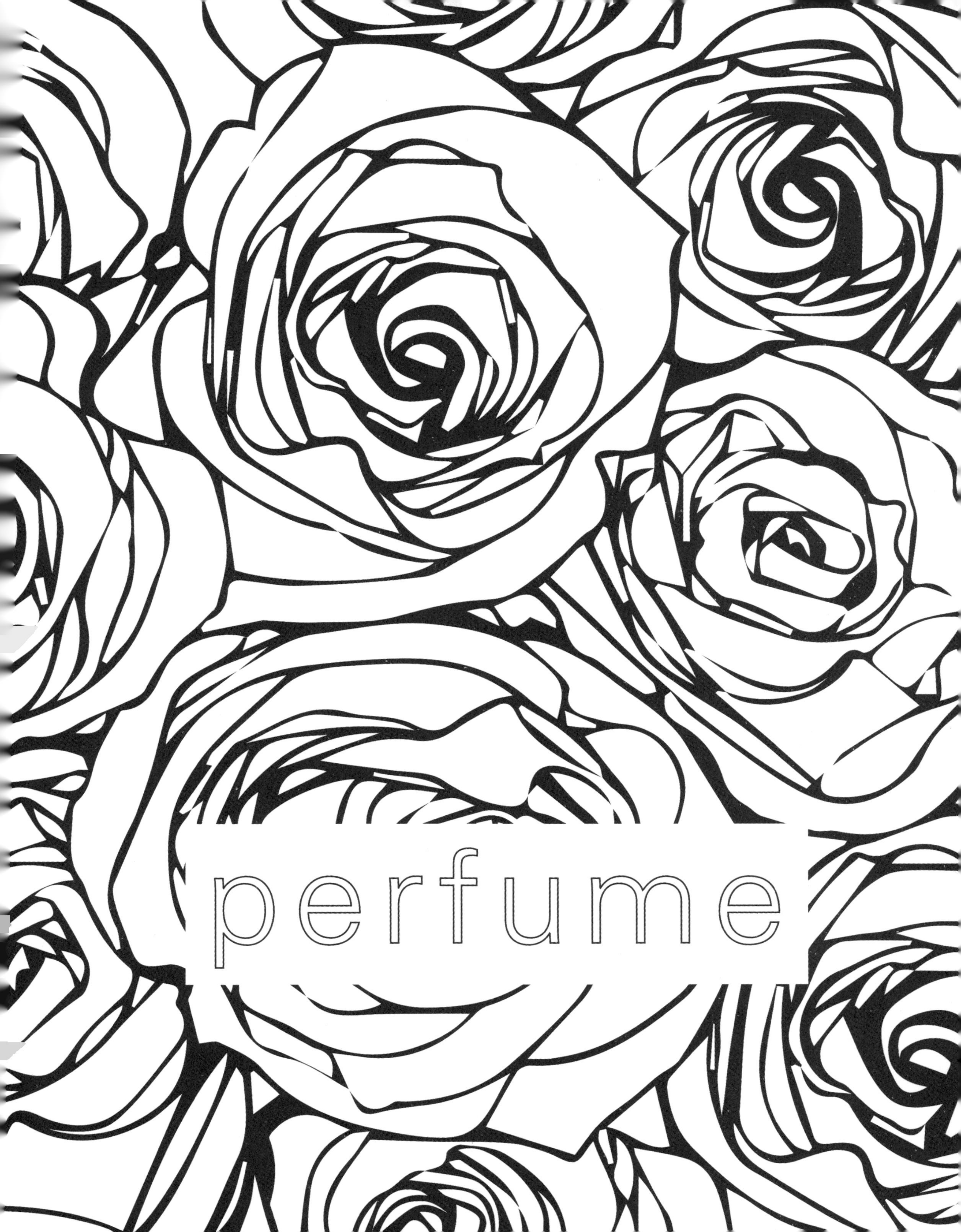
perfume

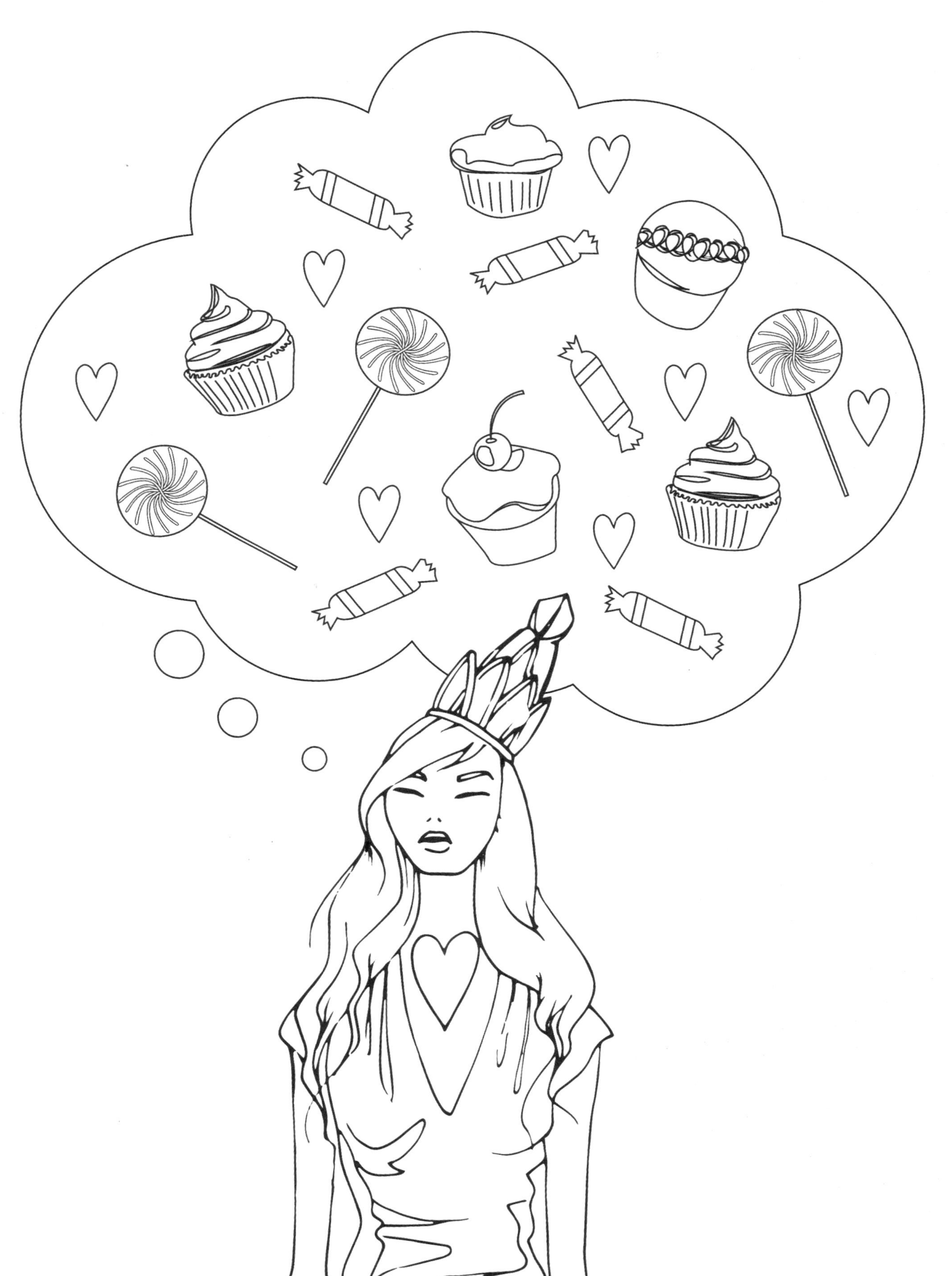

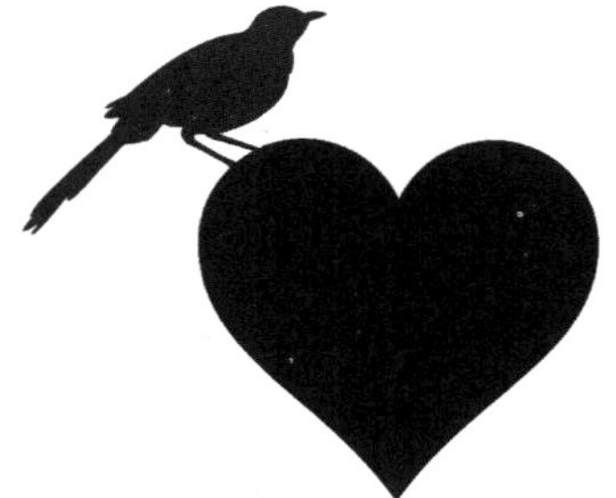

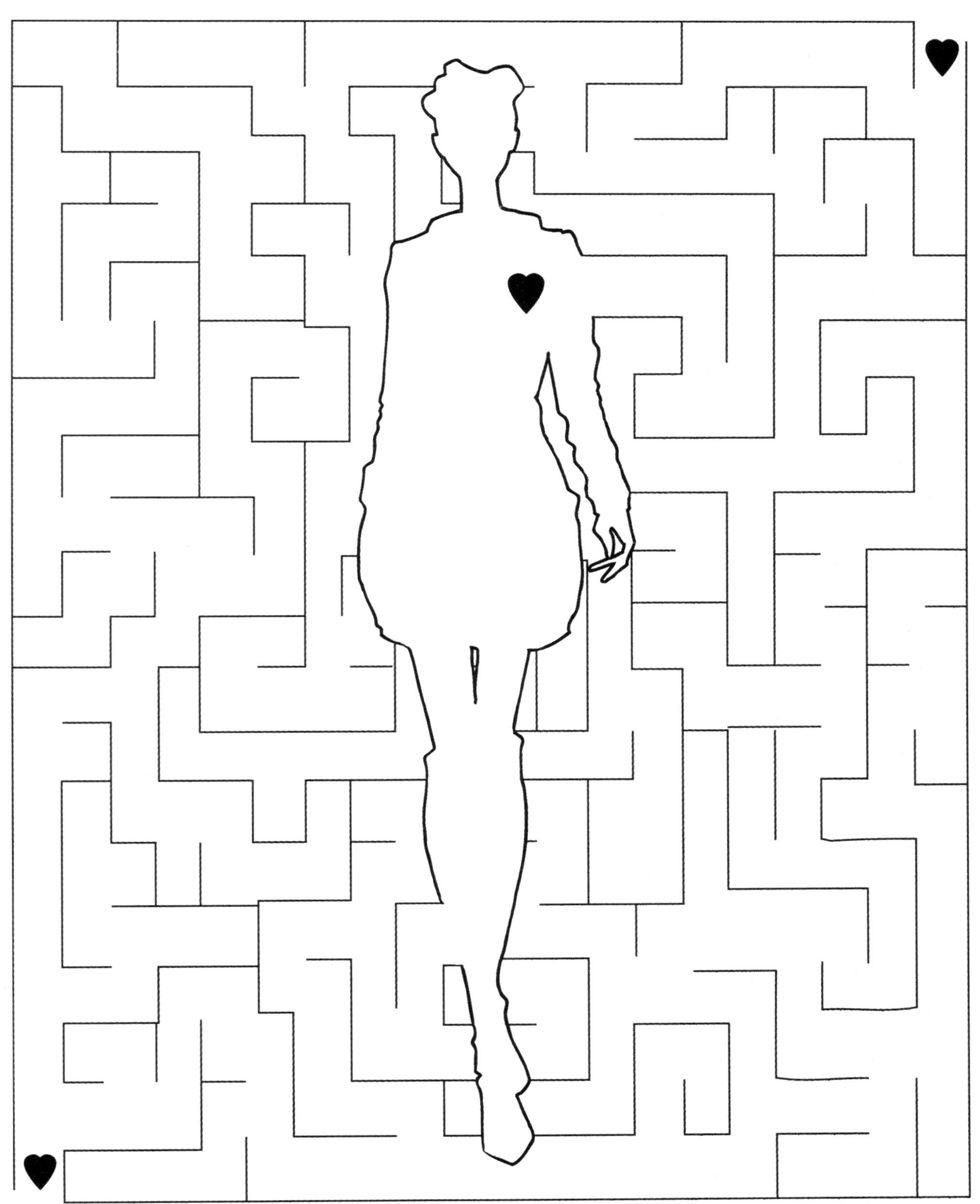

I was
three years old
when I started
drawing. I did it all my
life. - Alexander McQueen

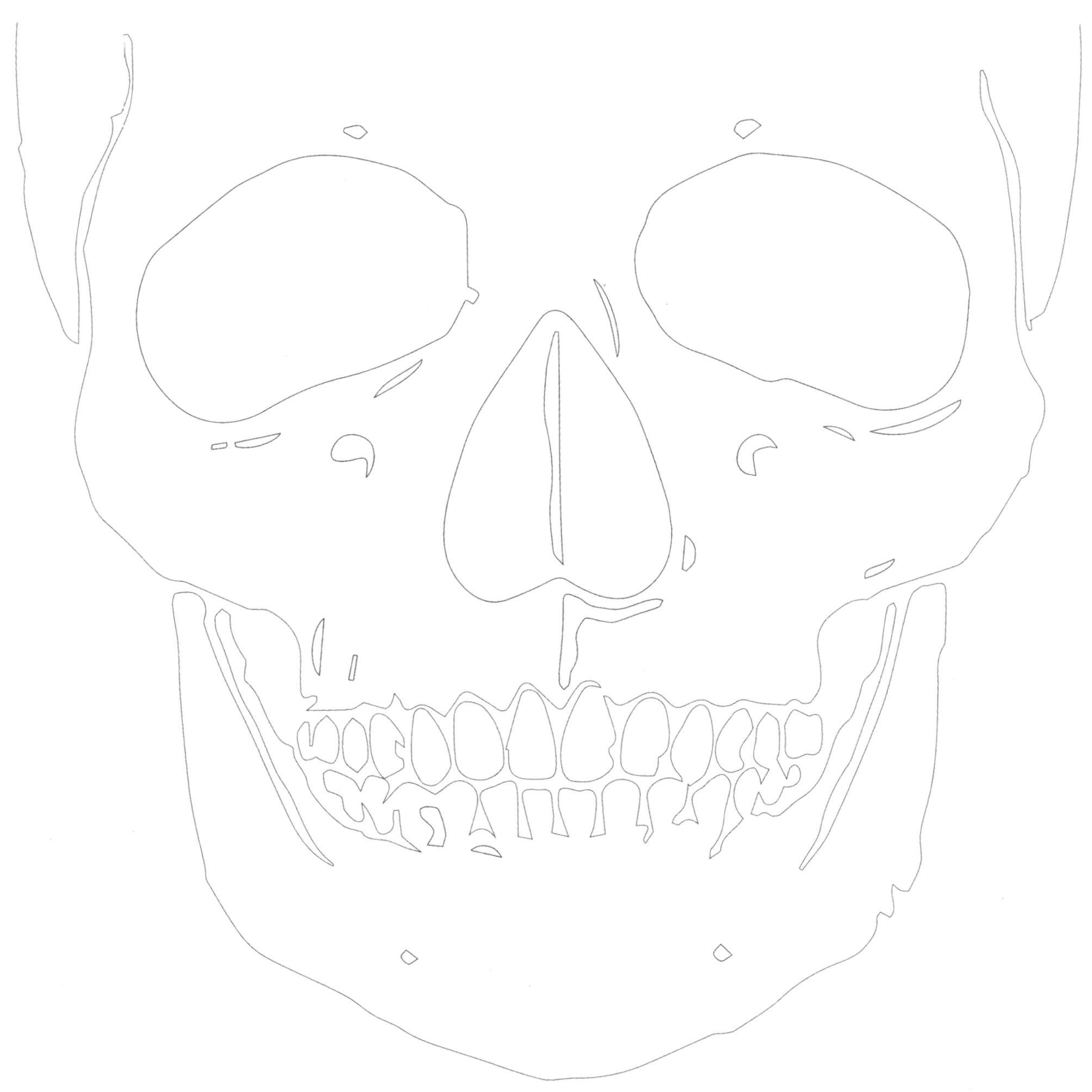

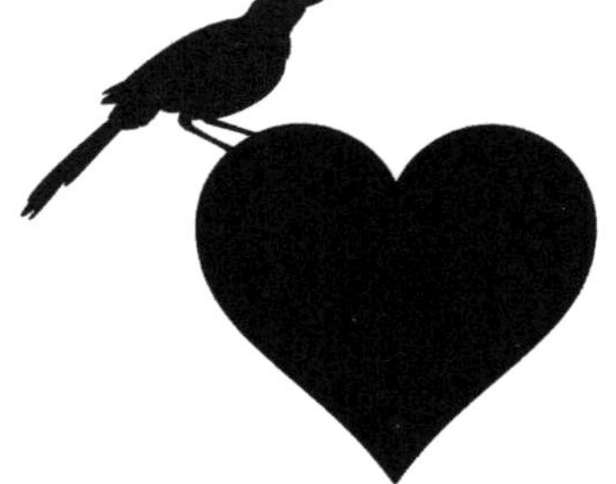

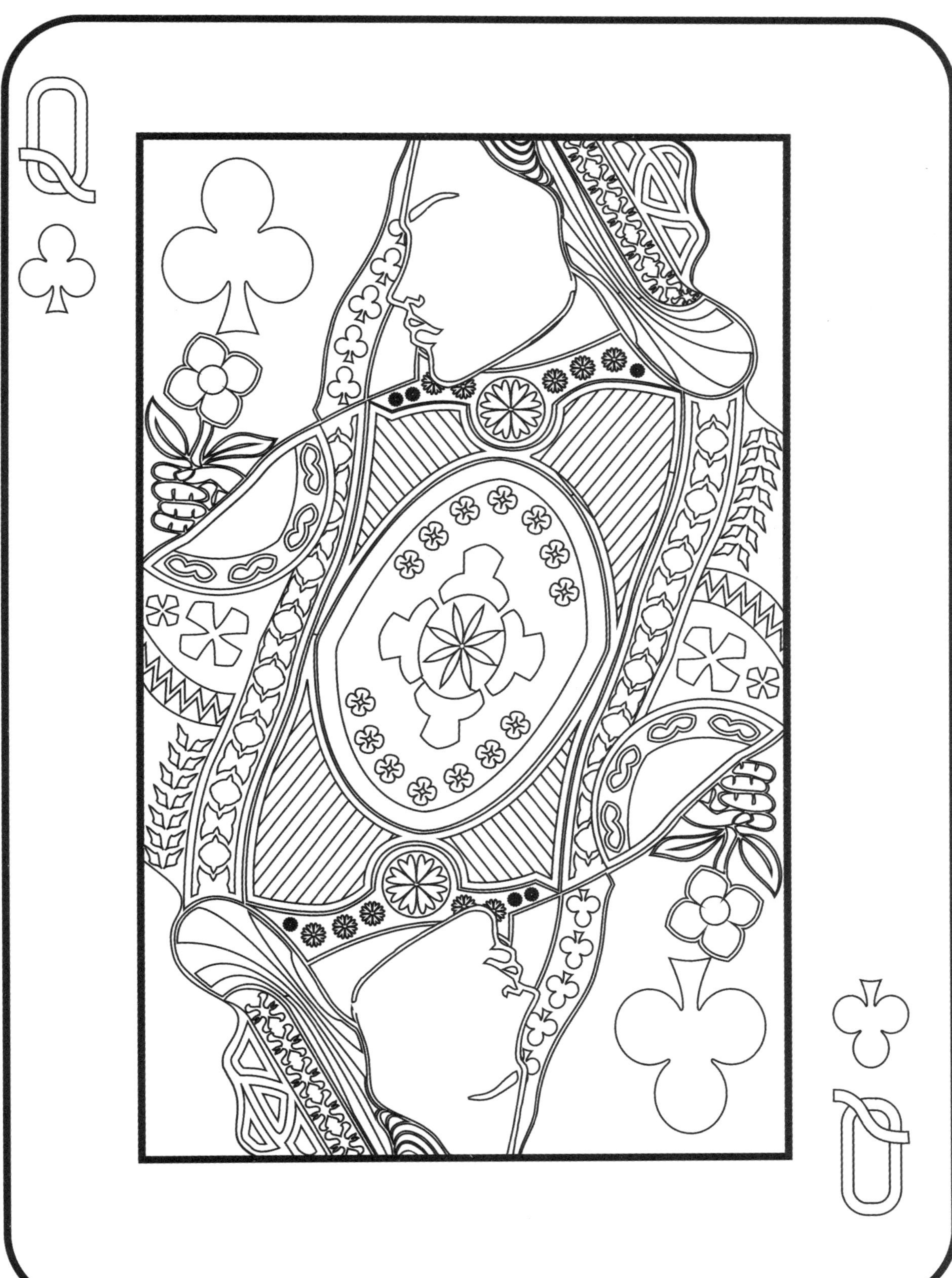

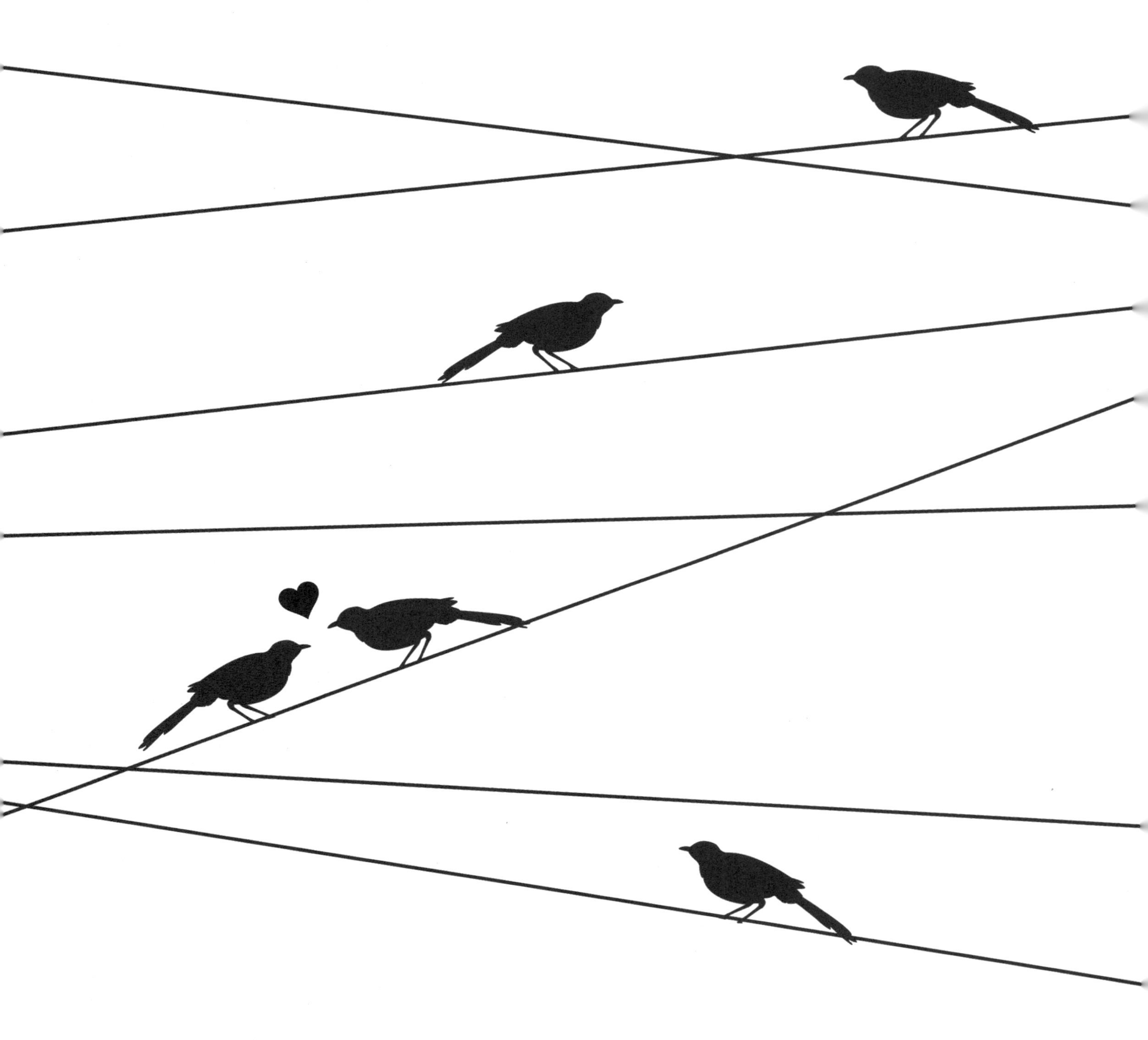

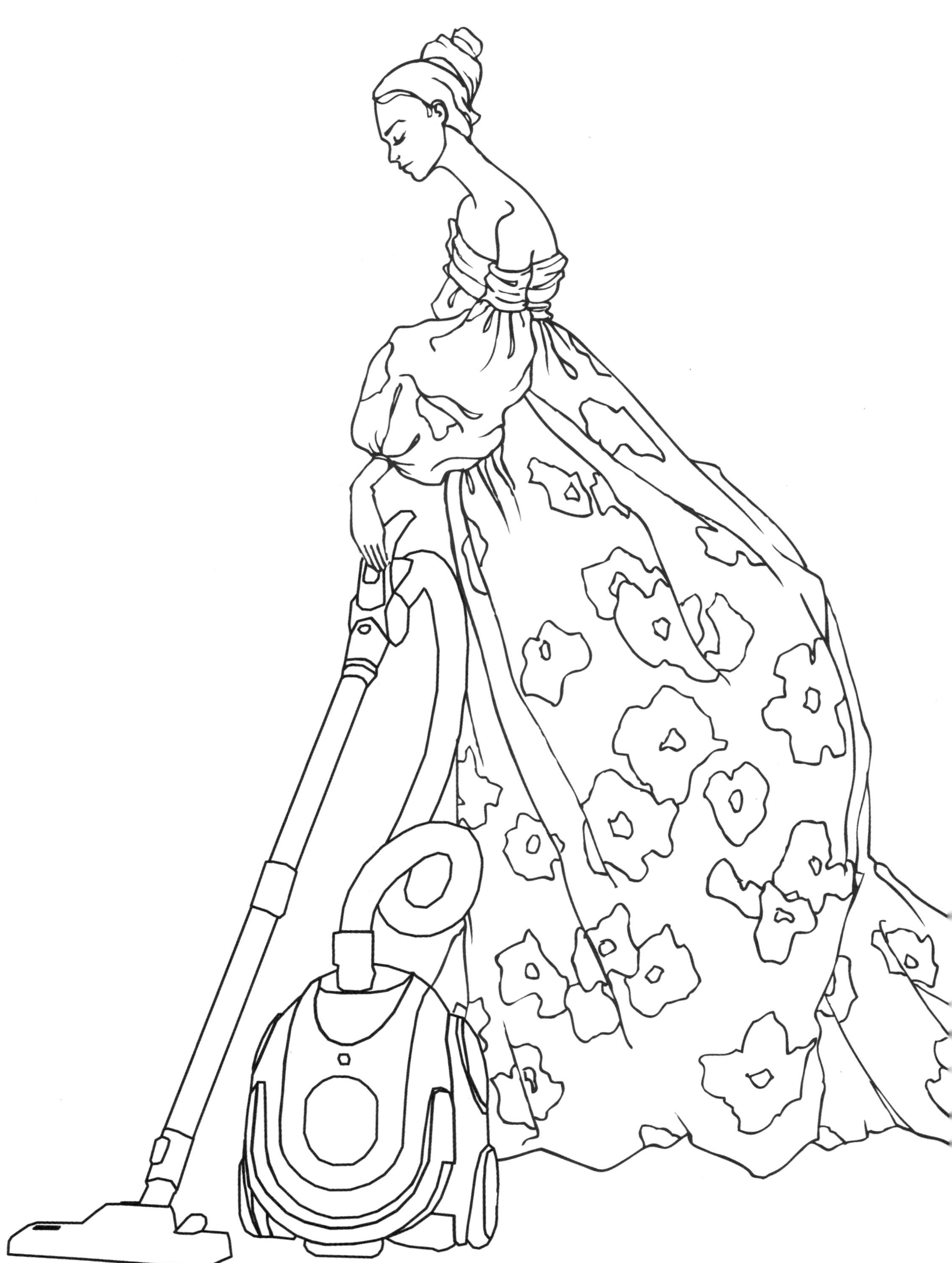

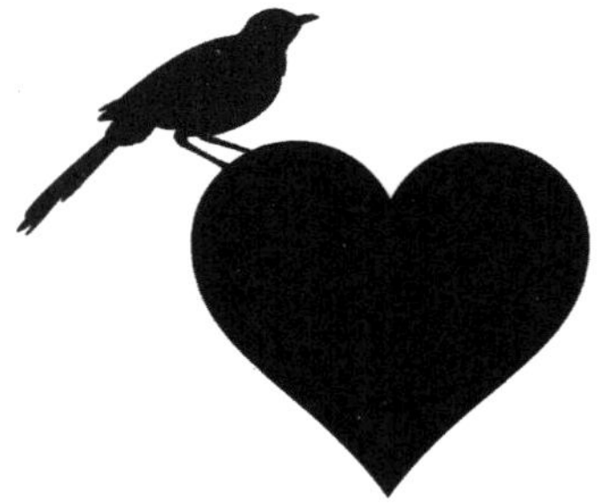

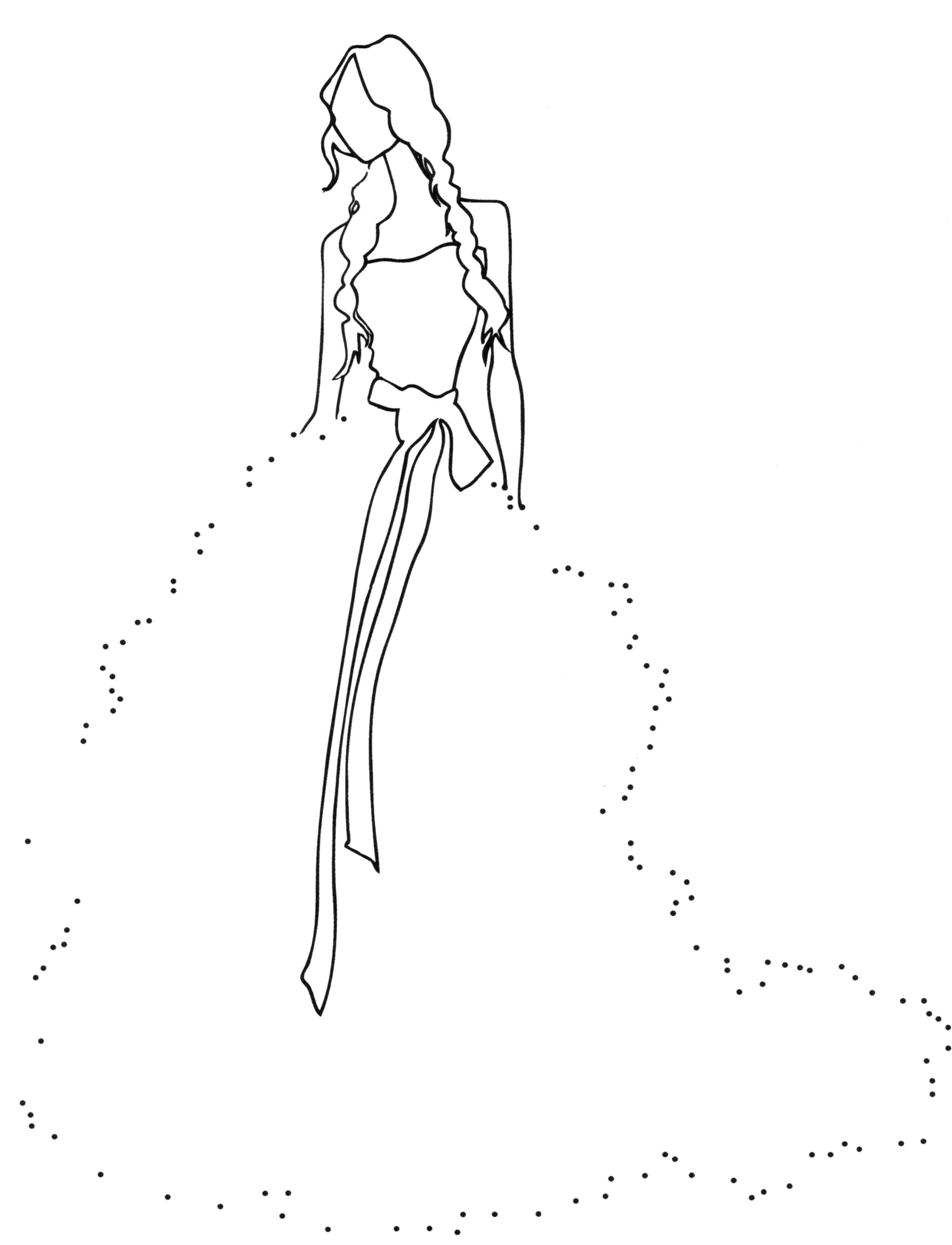

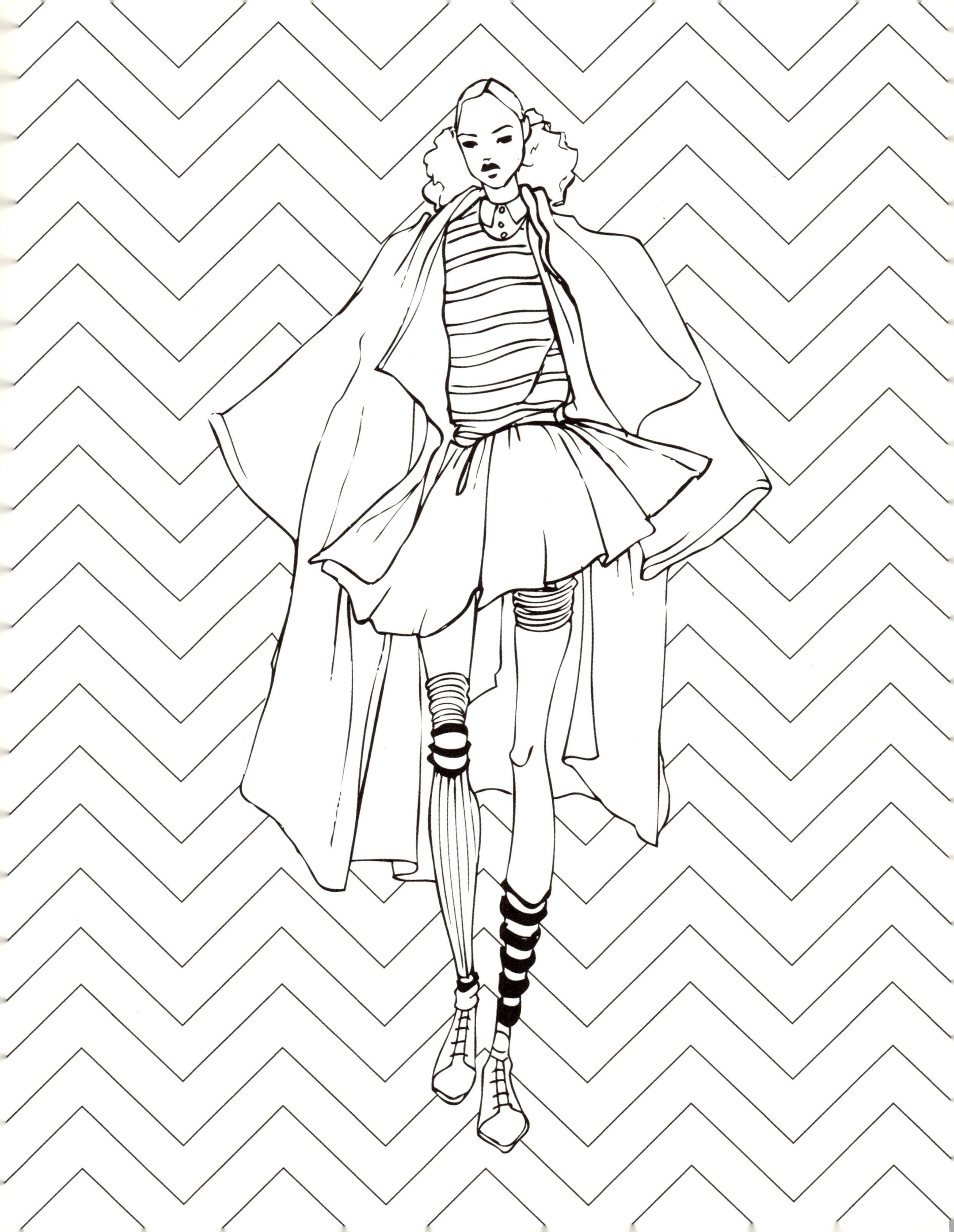

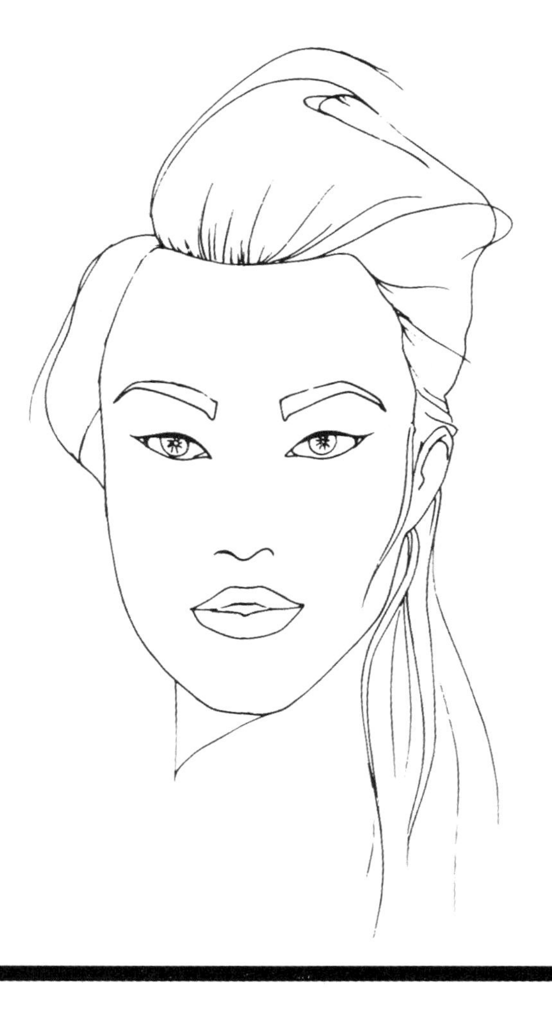
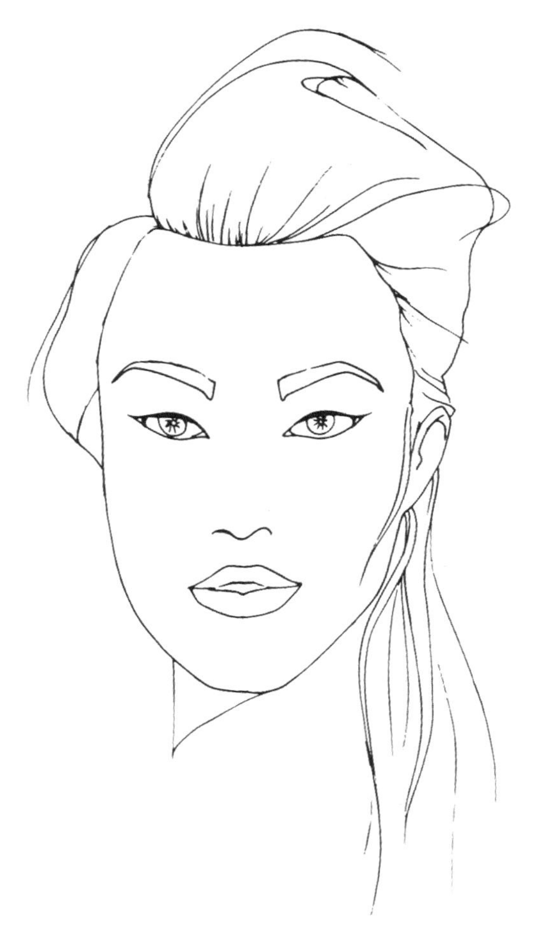
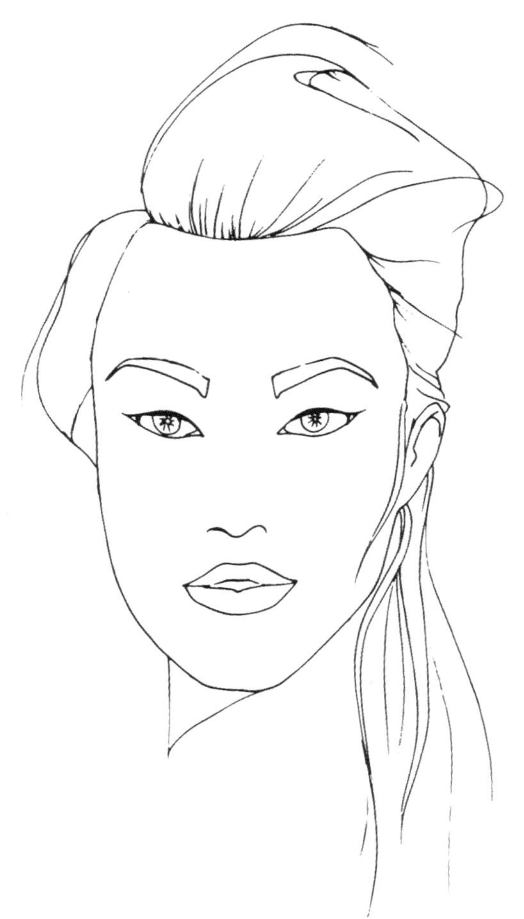
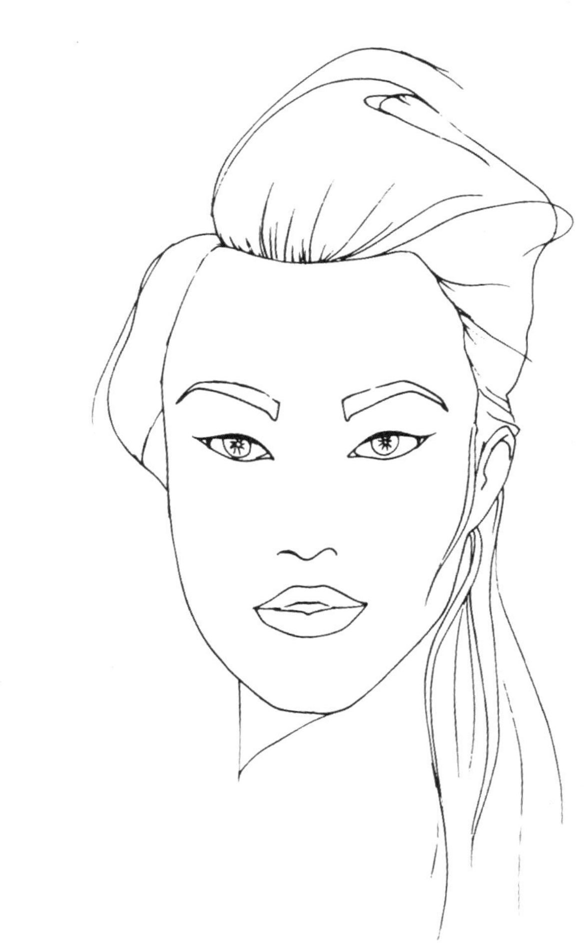

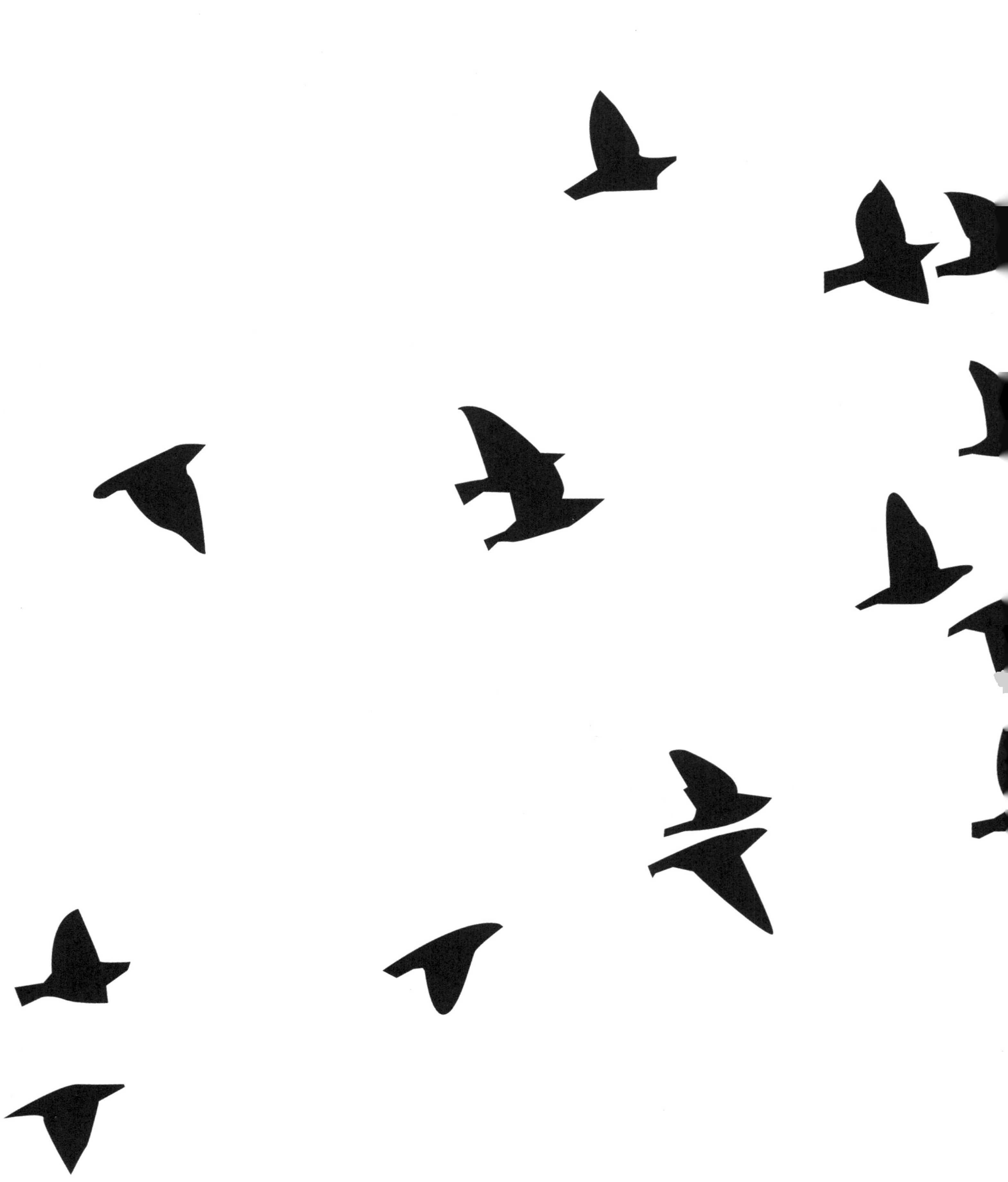

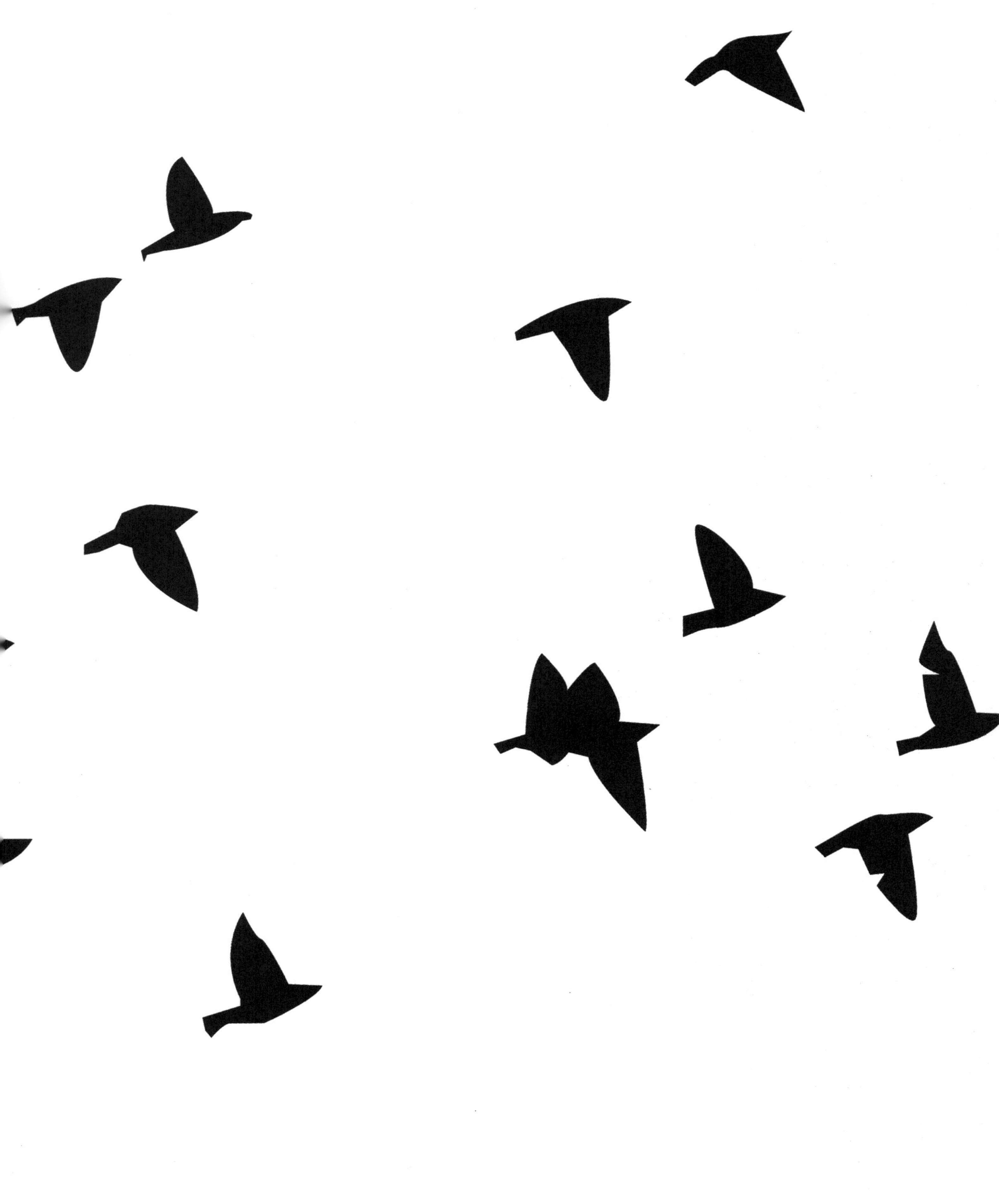

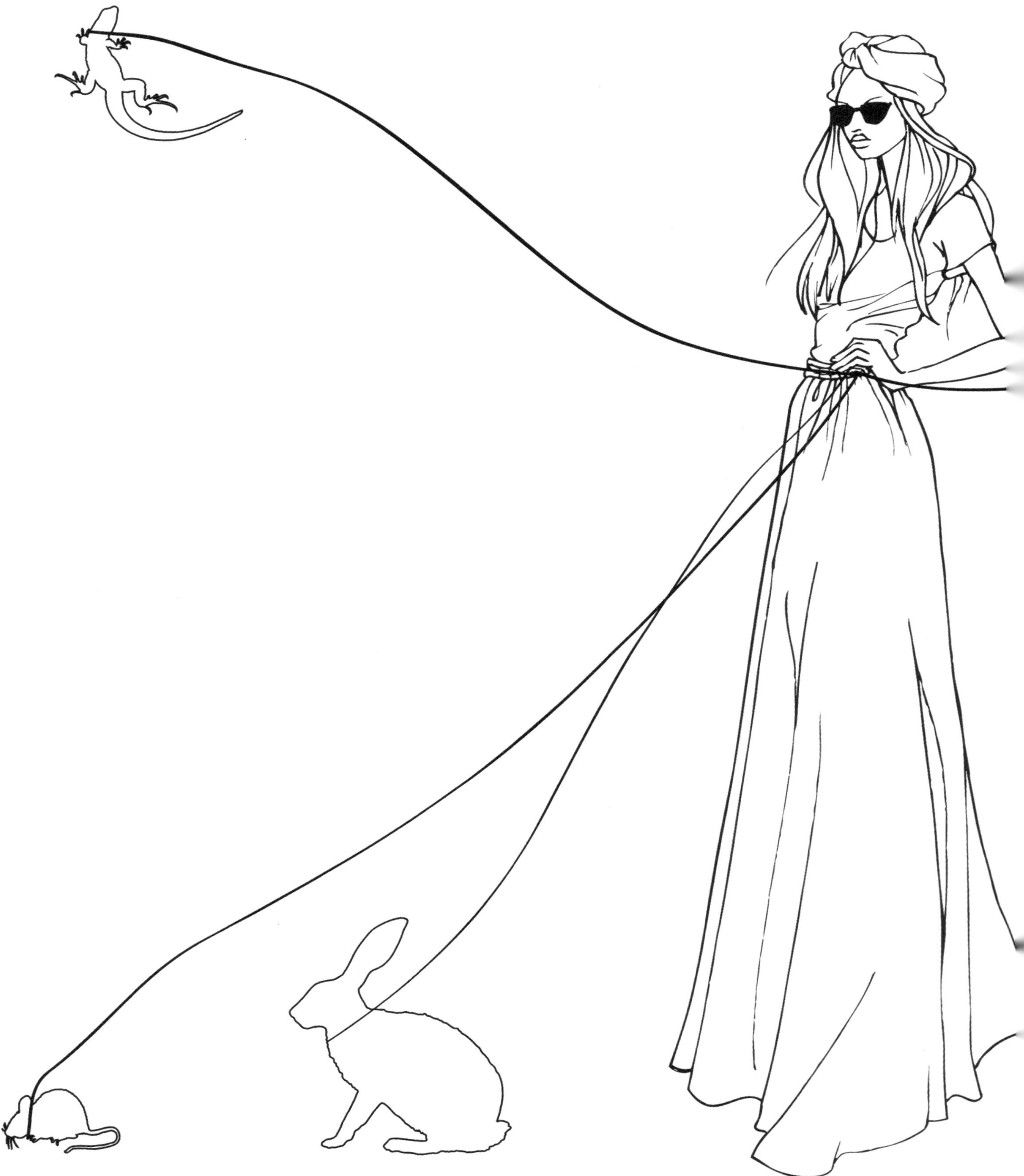

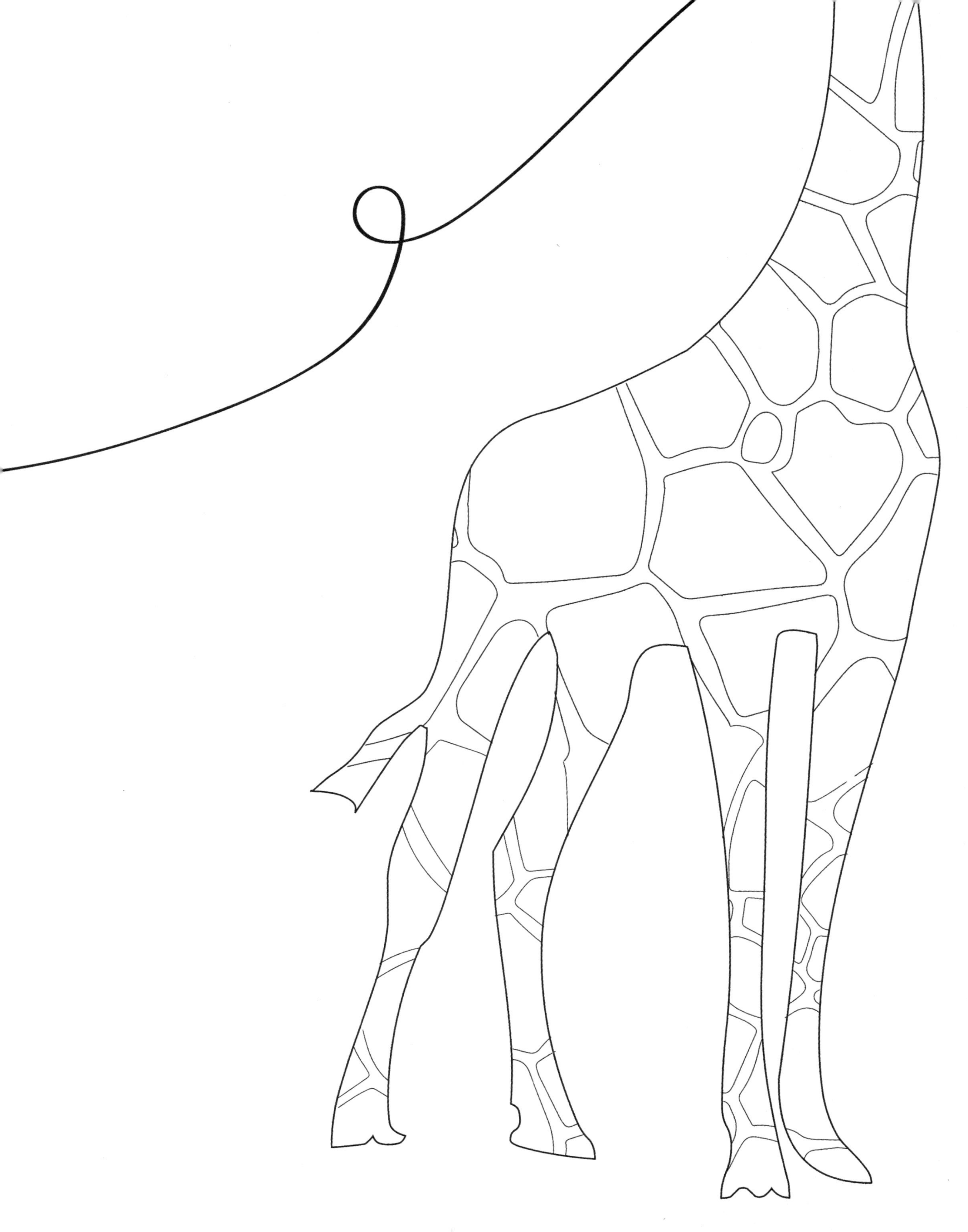

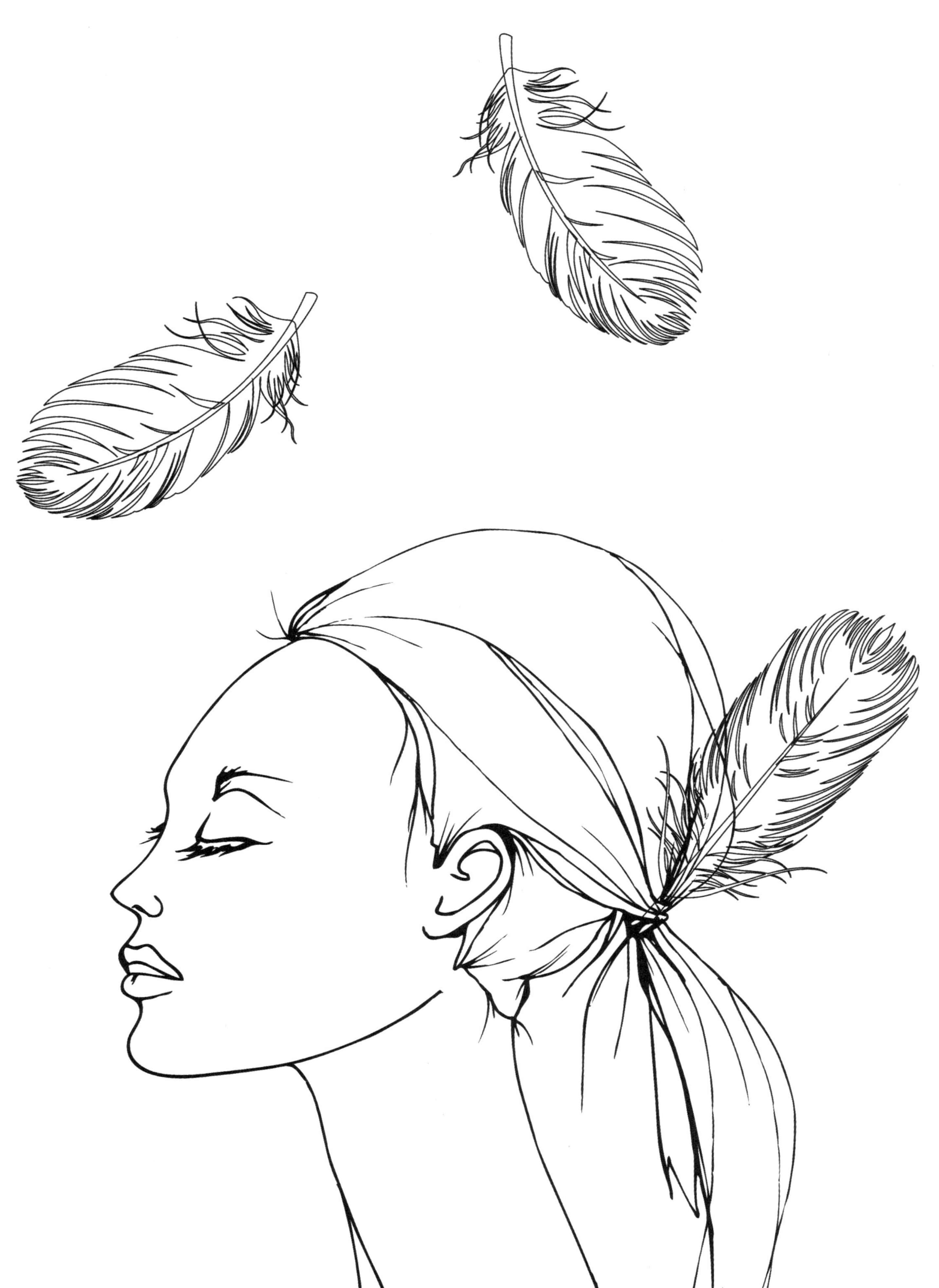

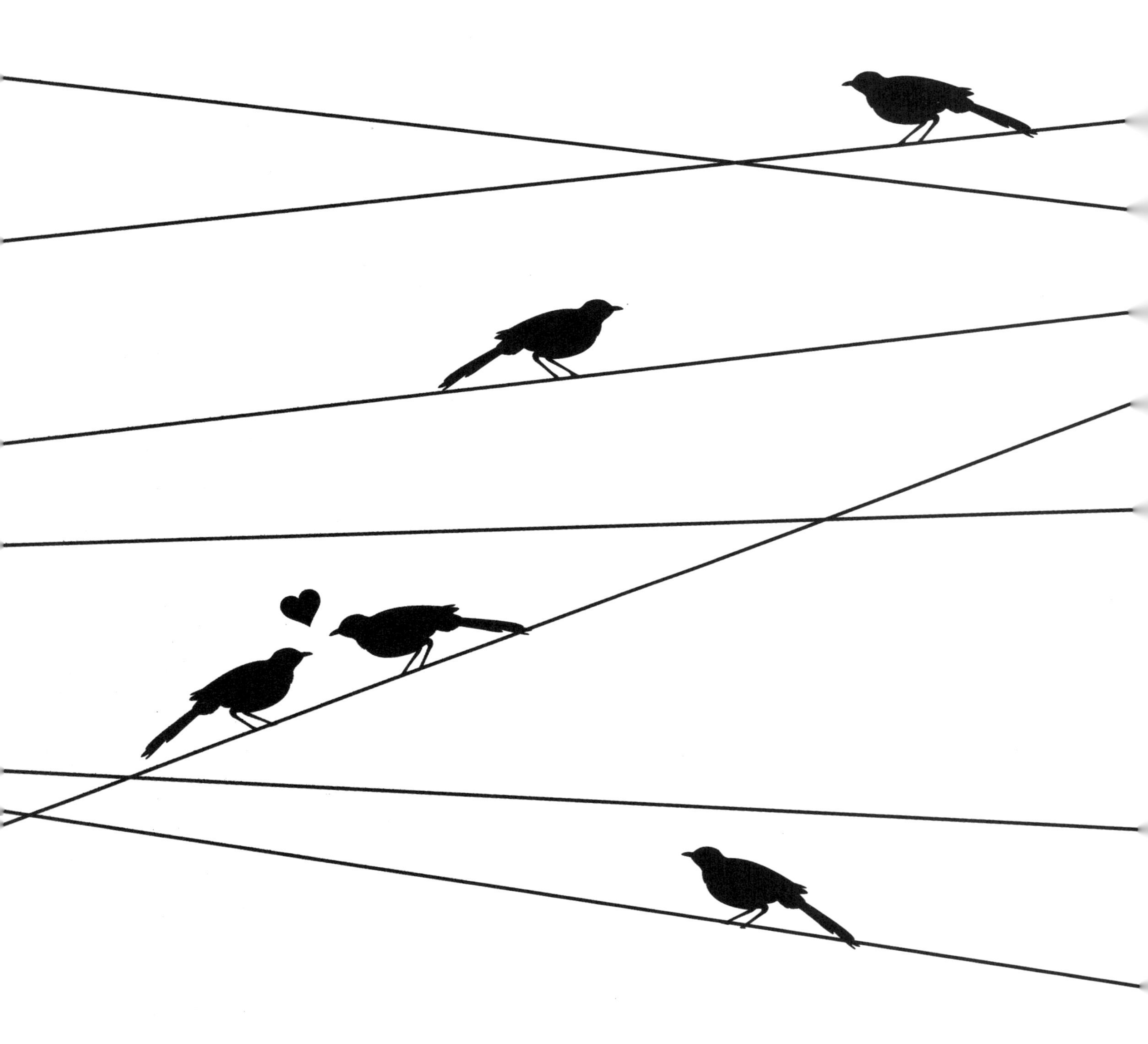

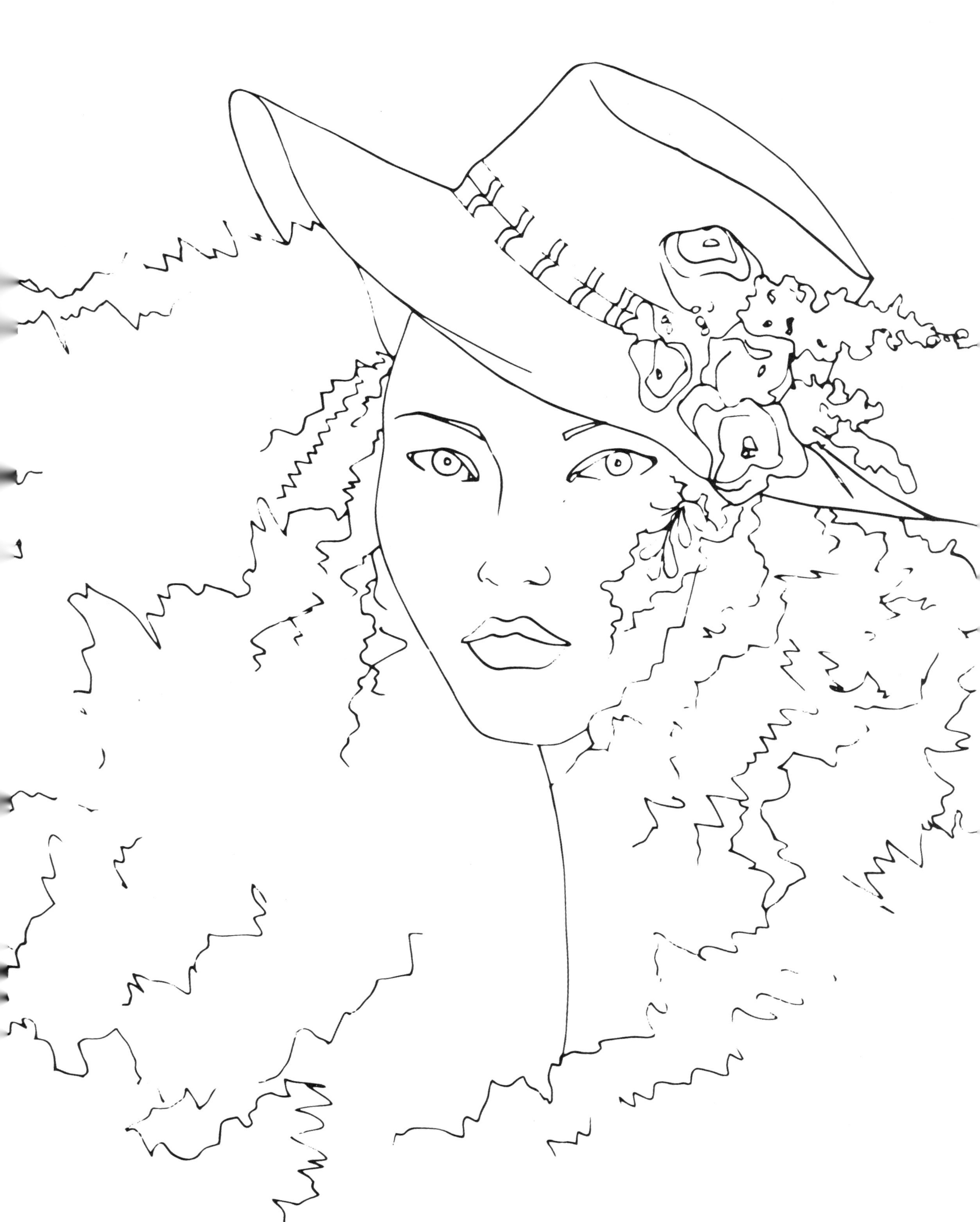

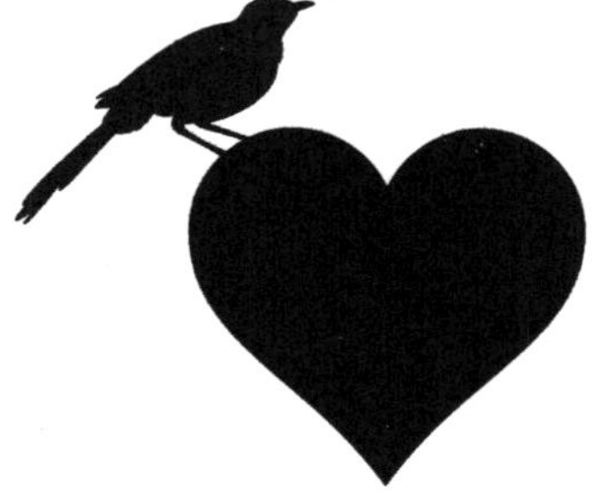

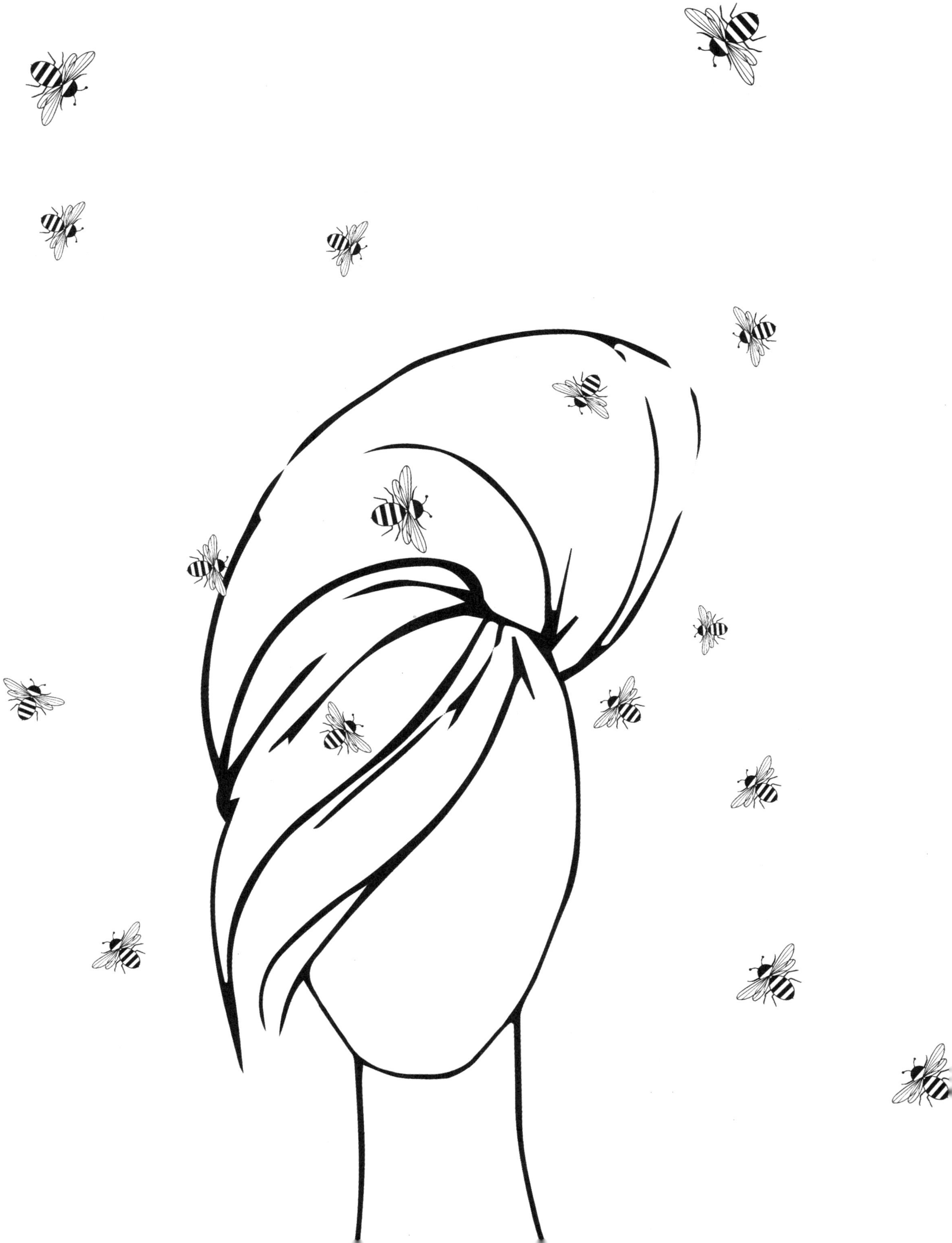

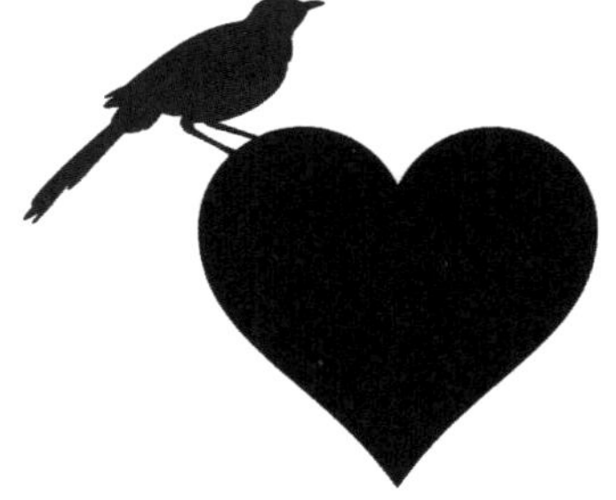

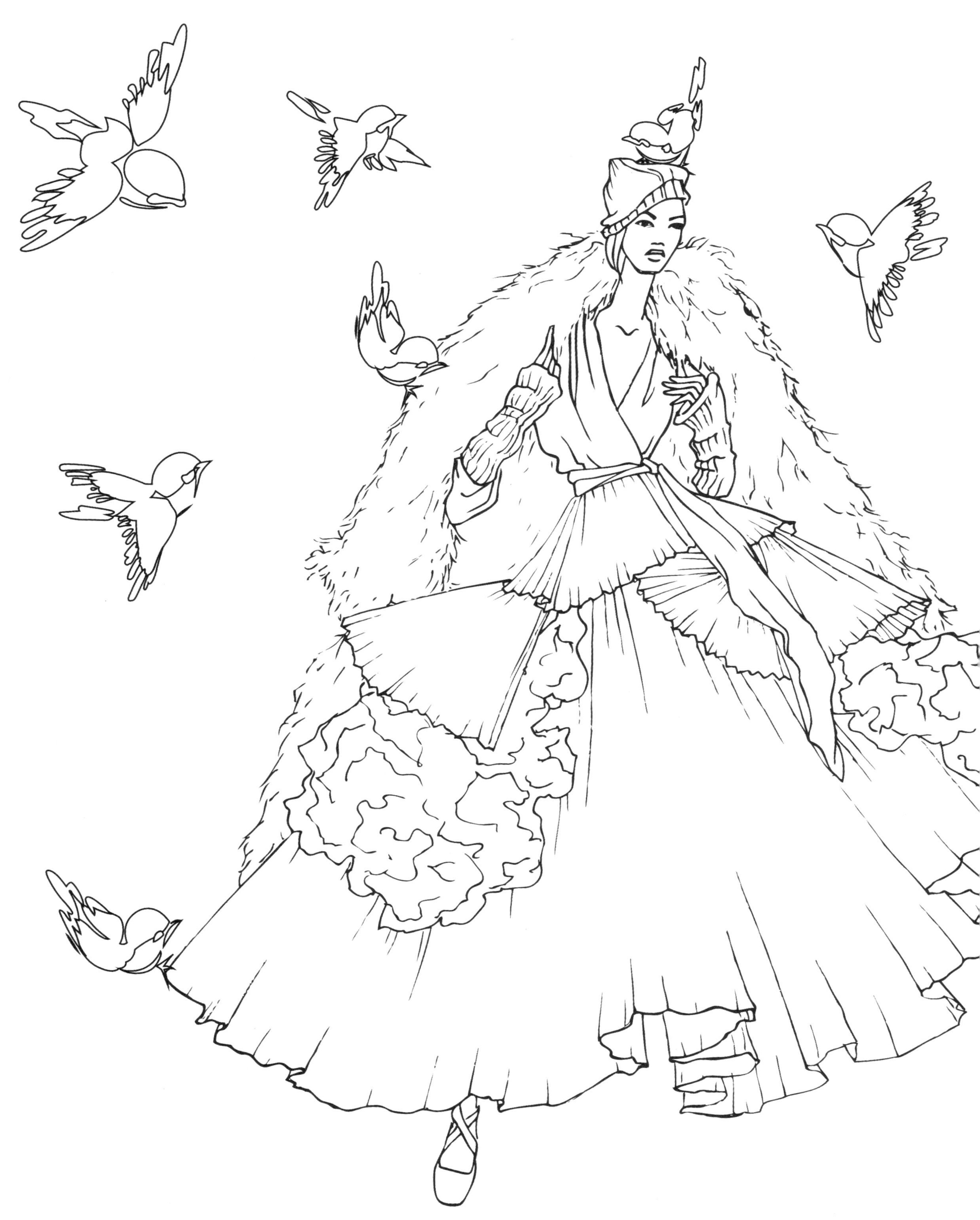

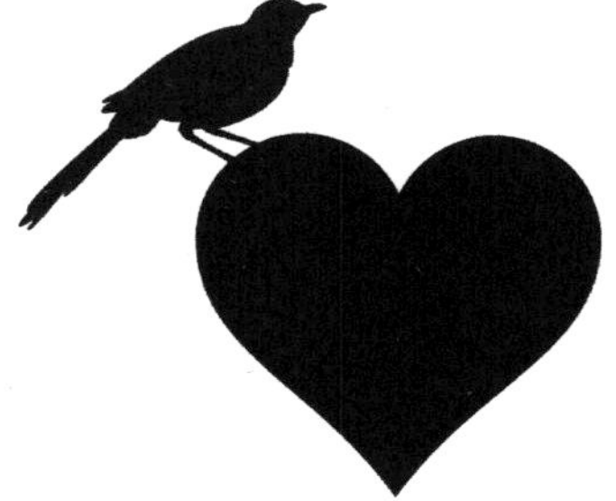

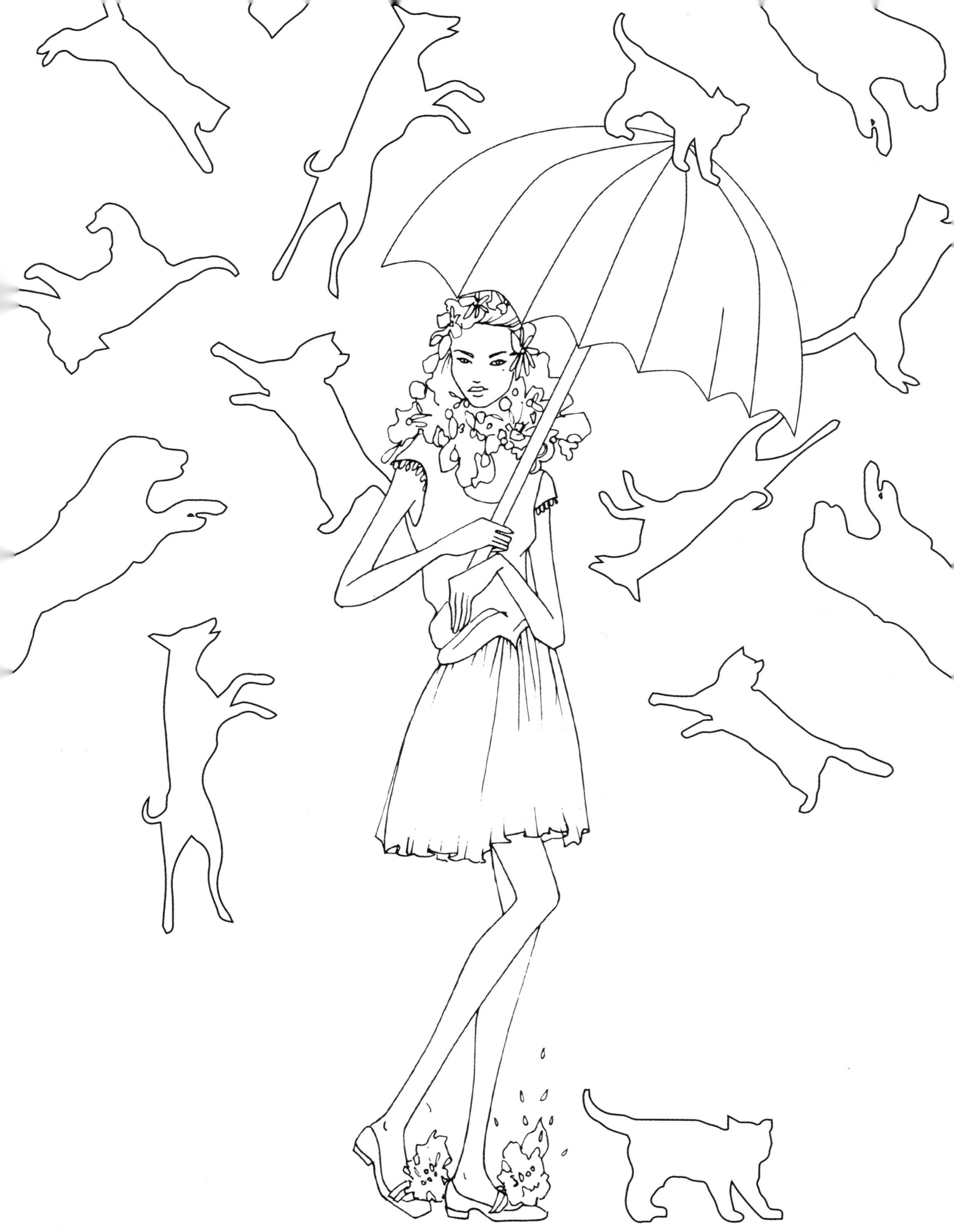

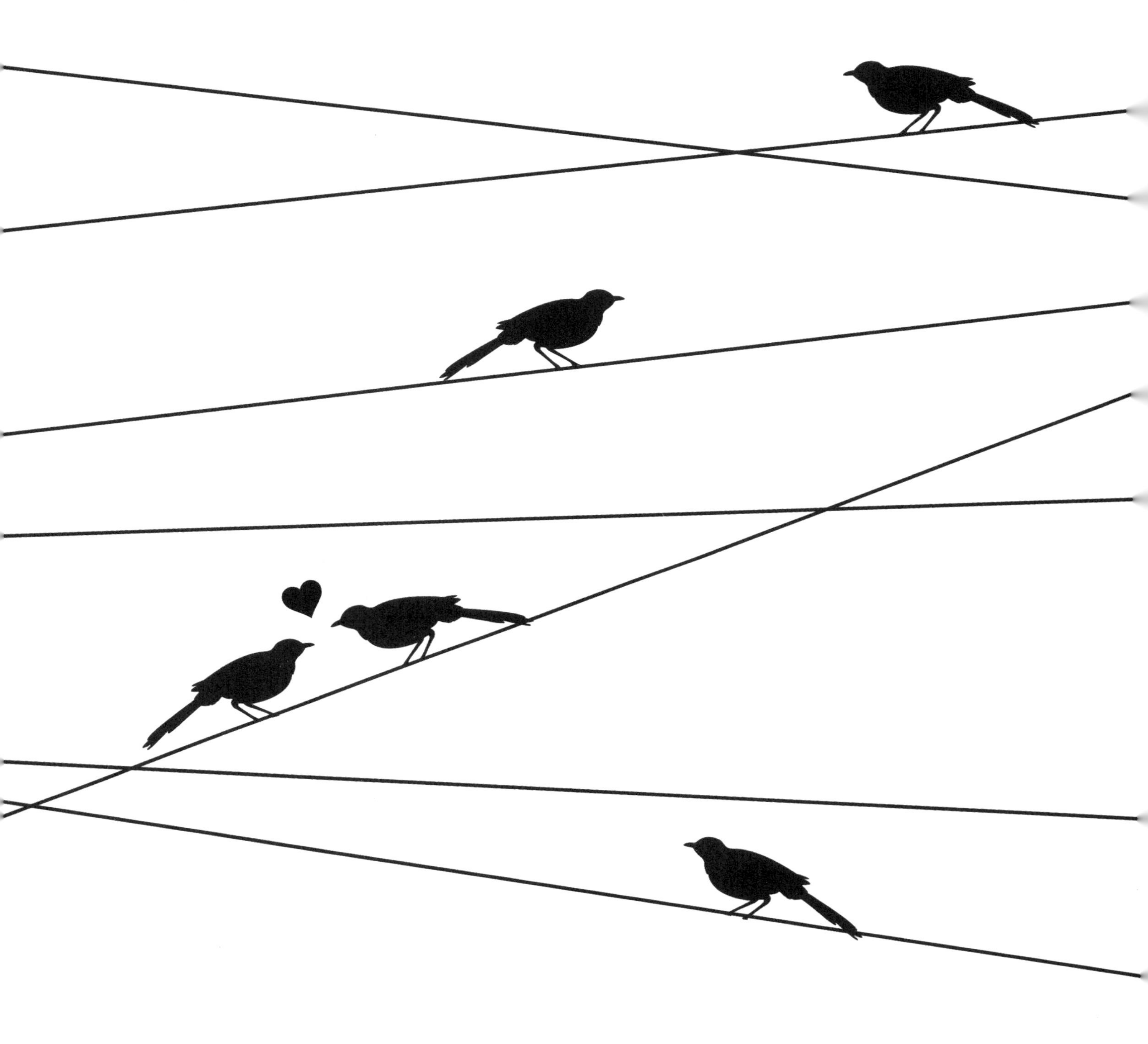

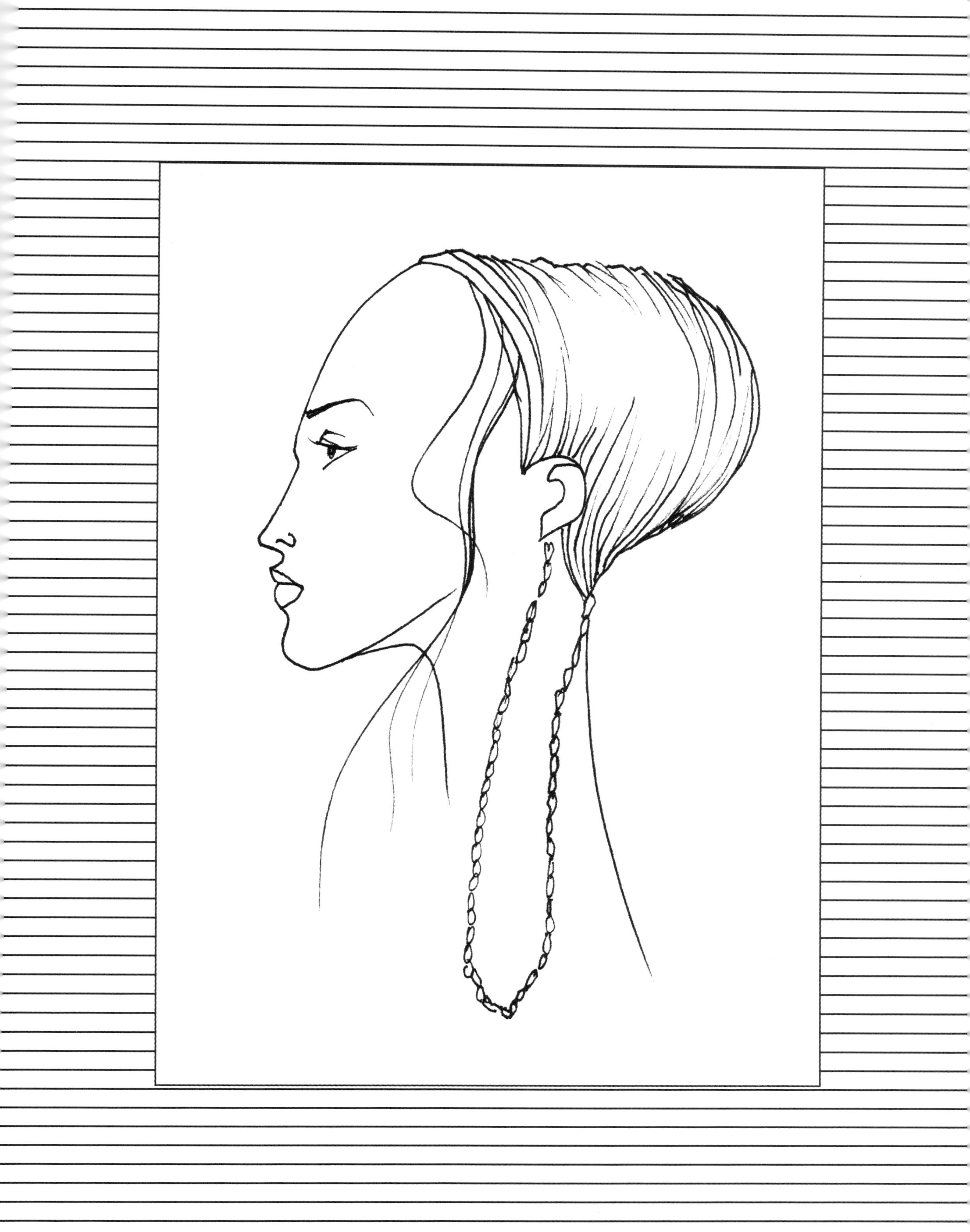

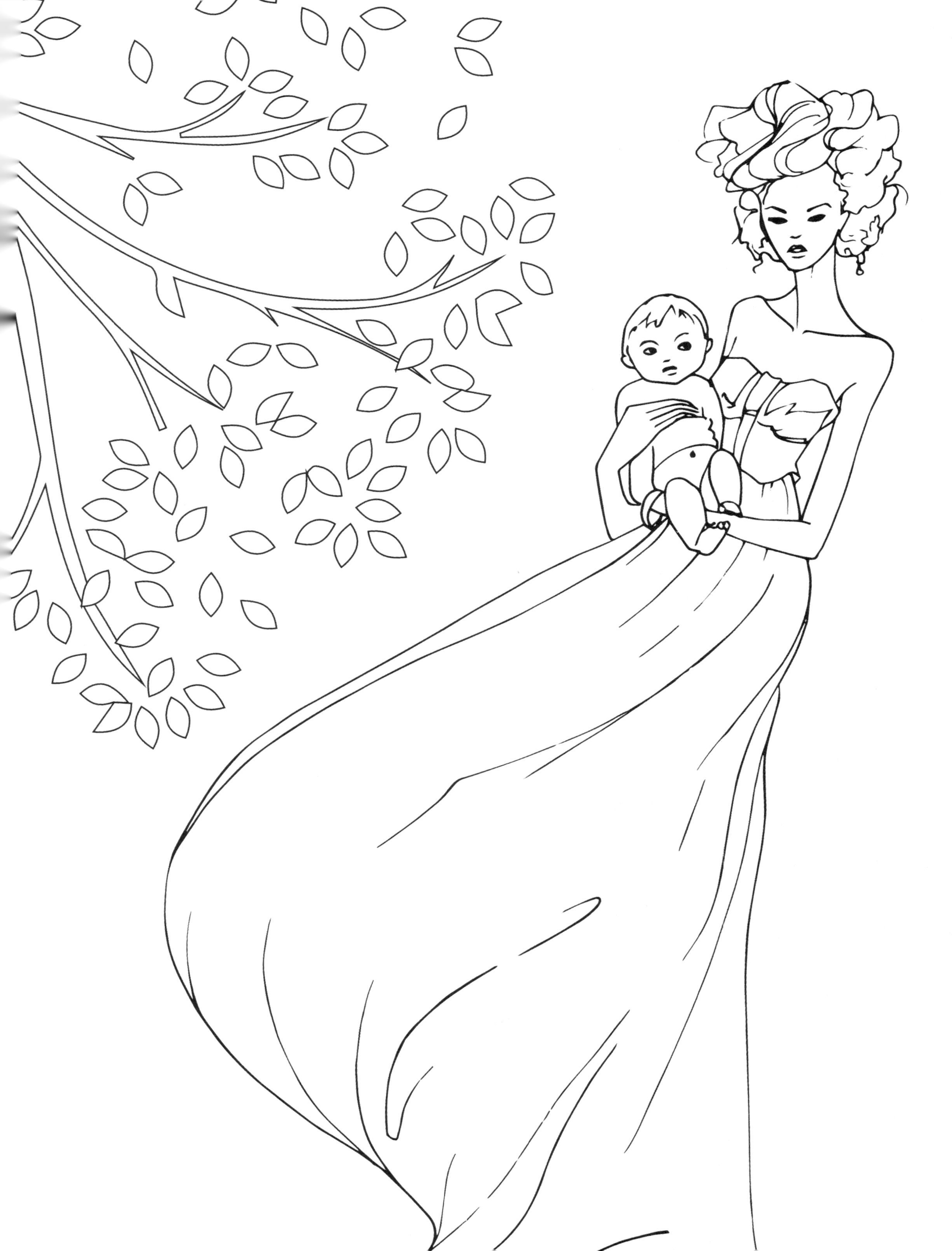

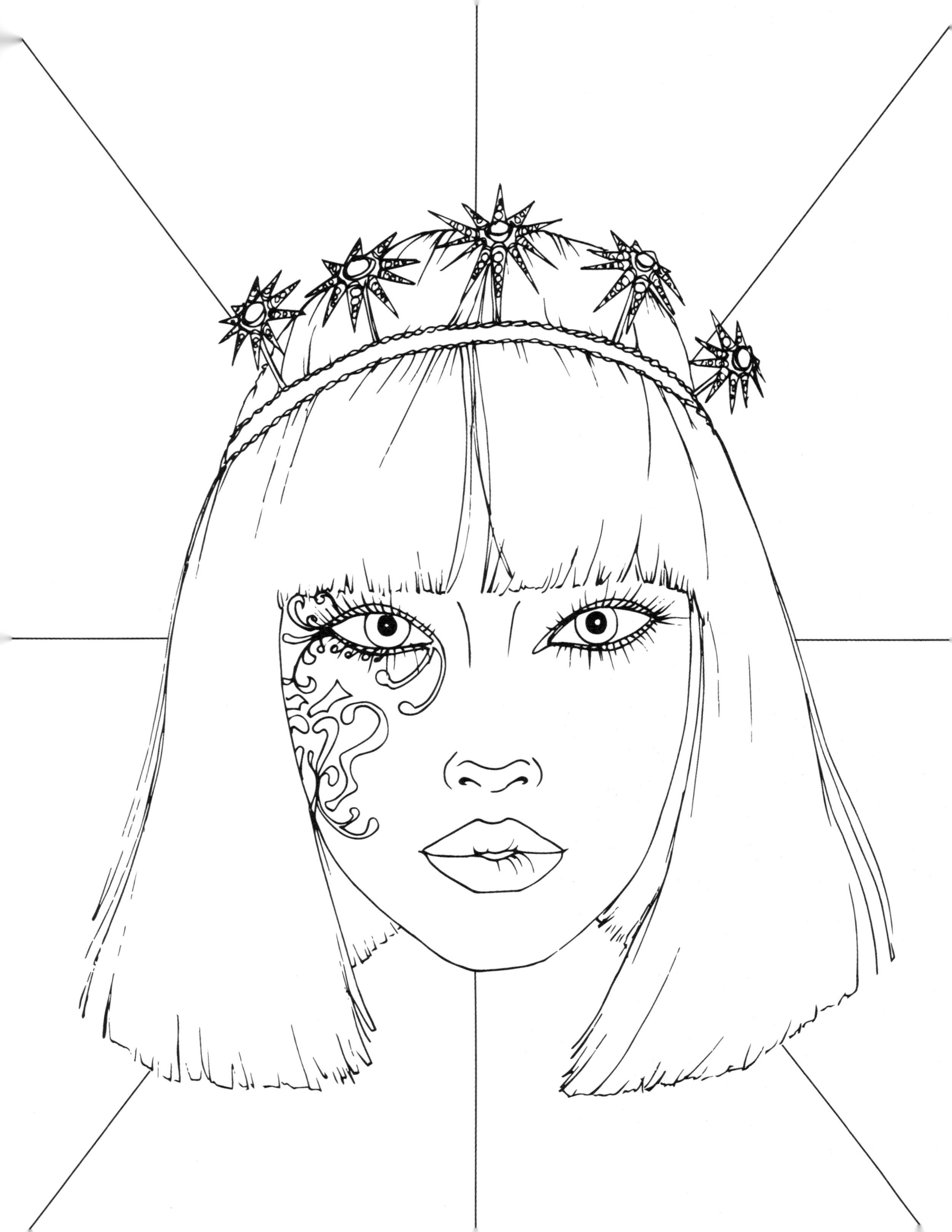

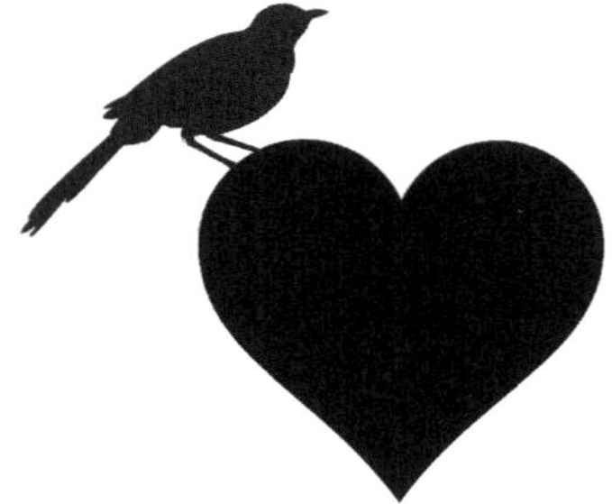

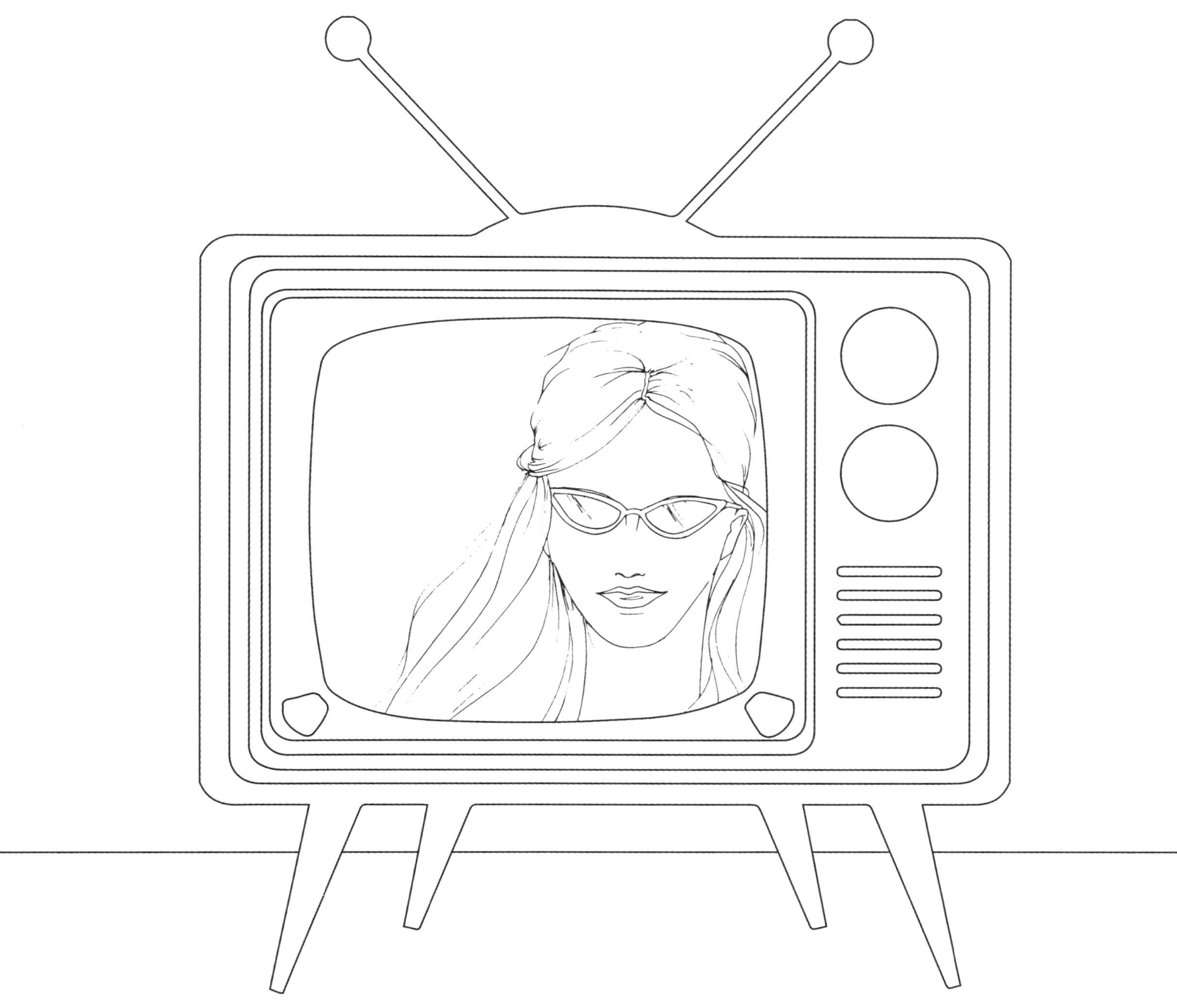

A DRAWING IS SIMPLY A LINE GOING FOR A WALK.

PAUL KLEE

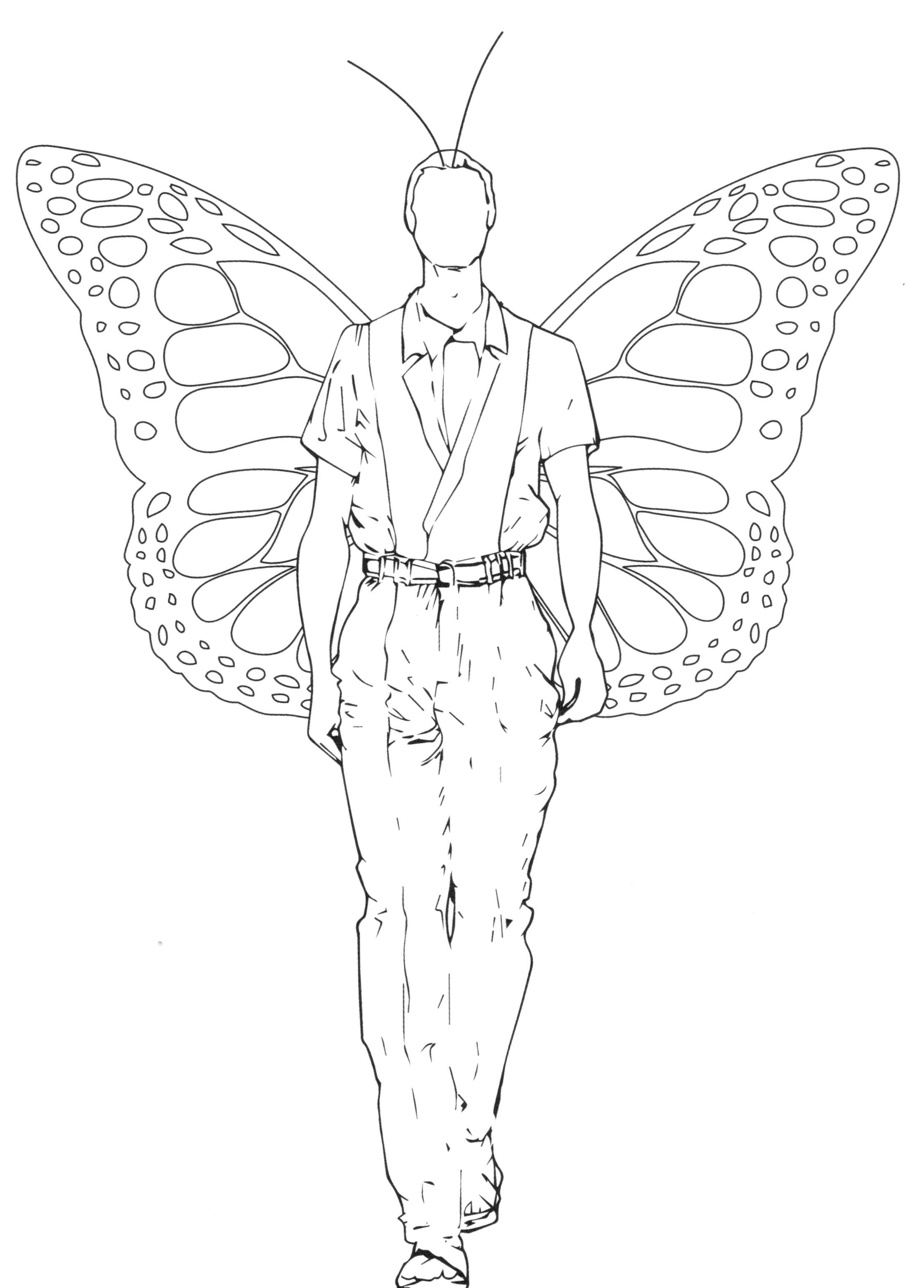

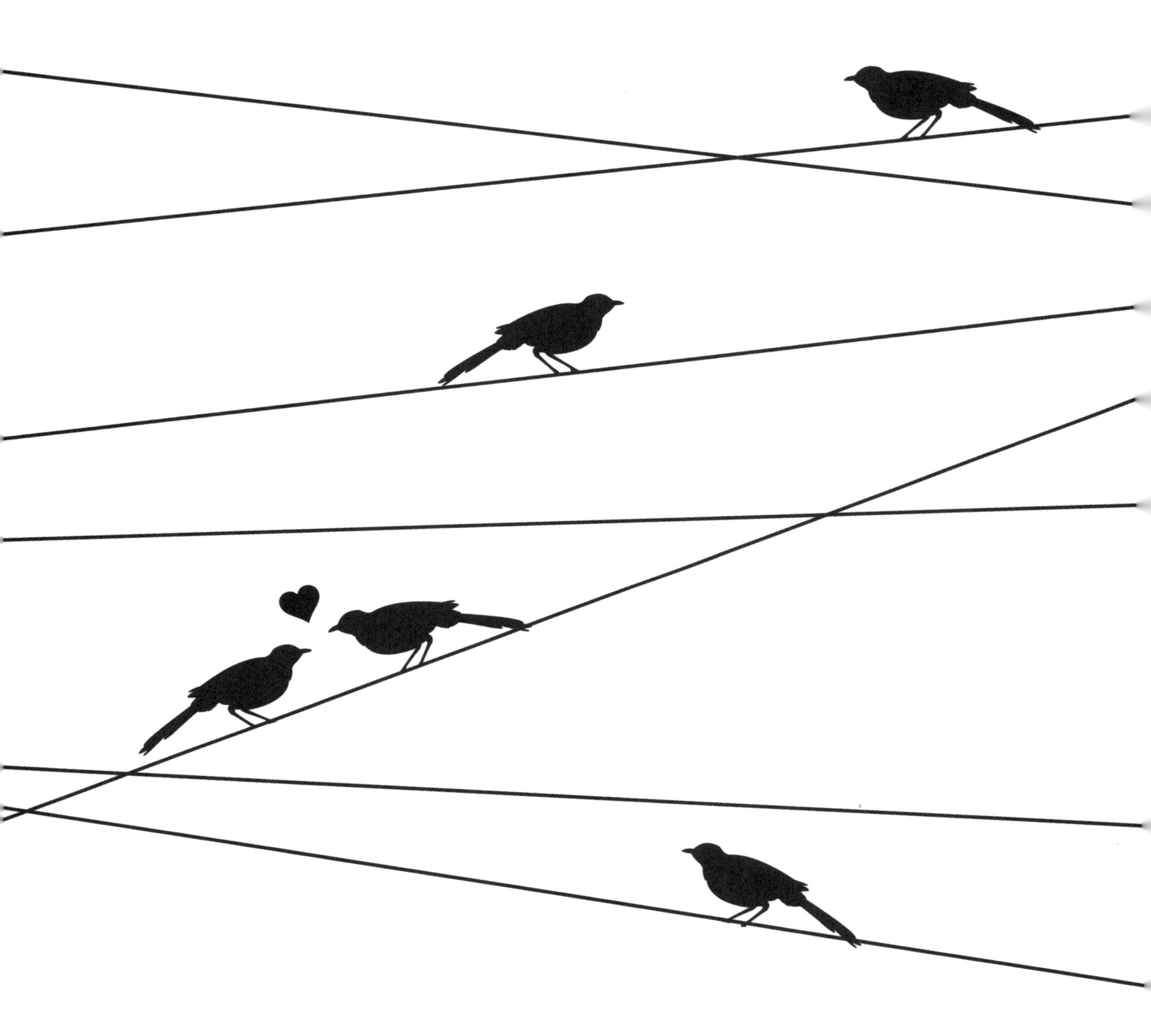

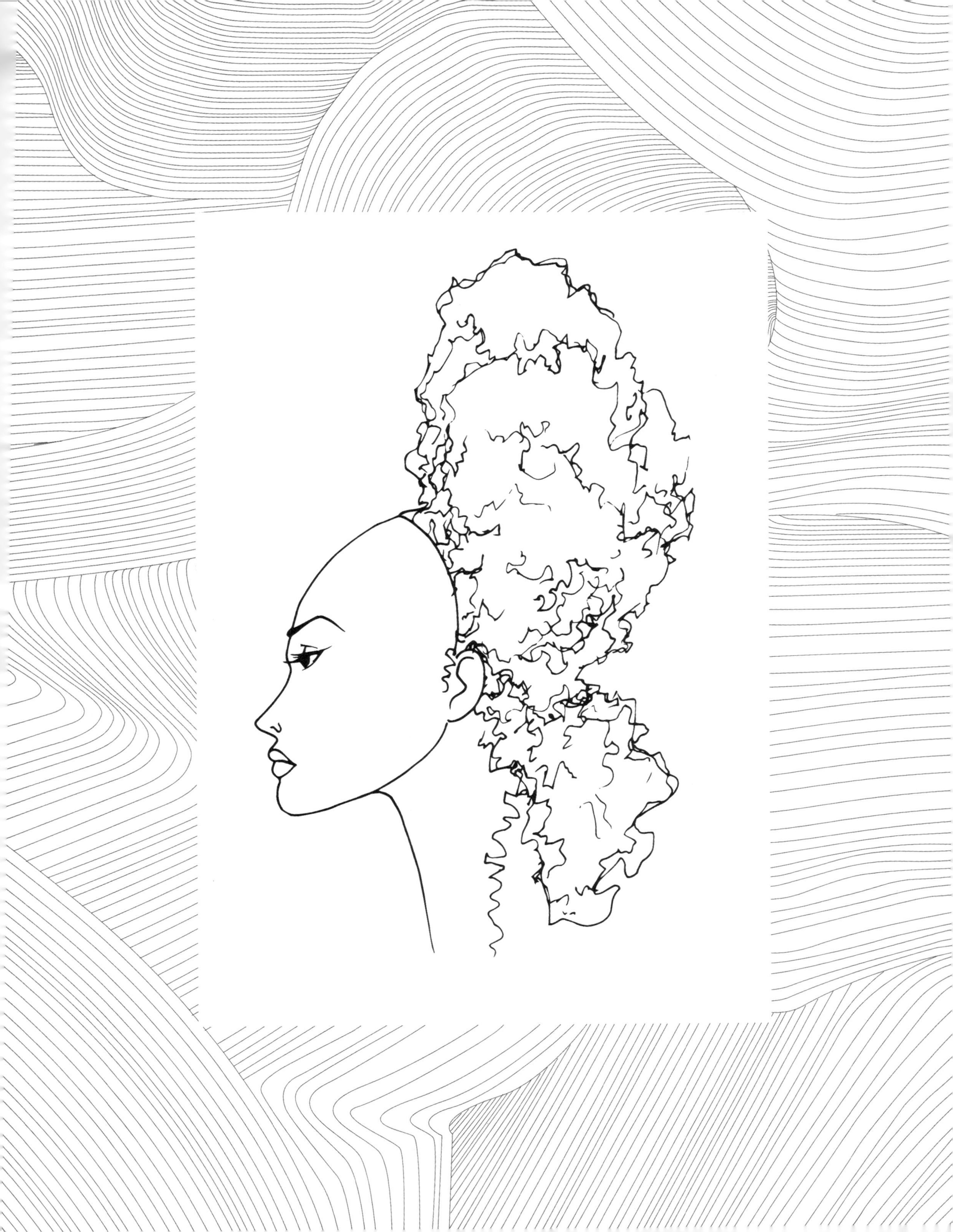

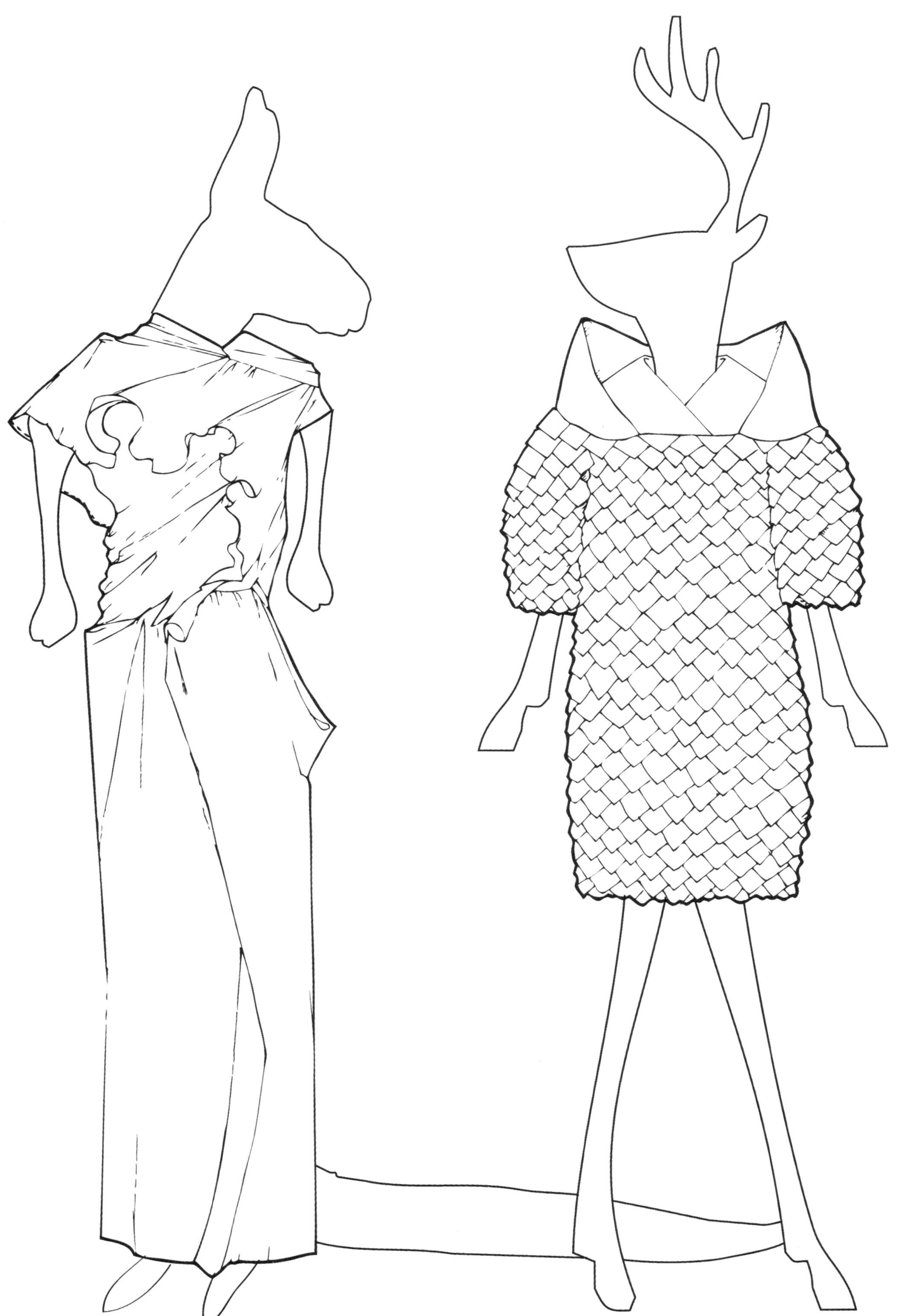

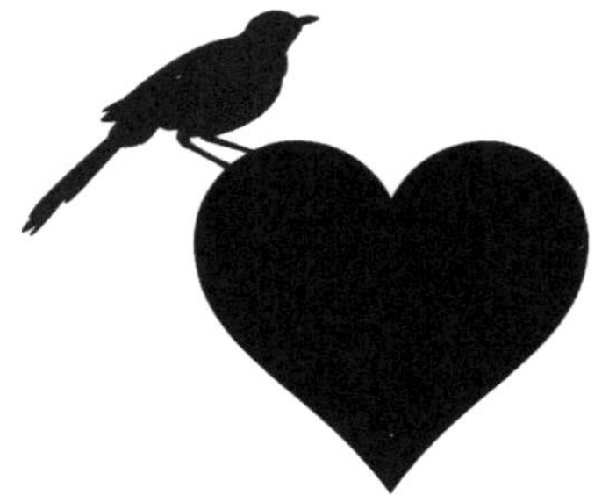

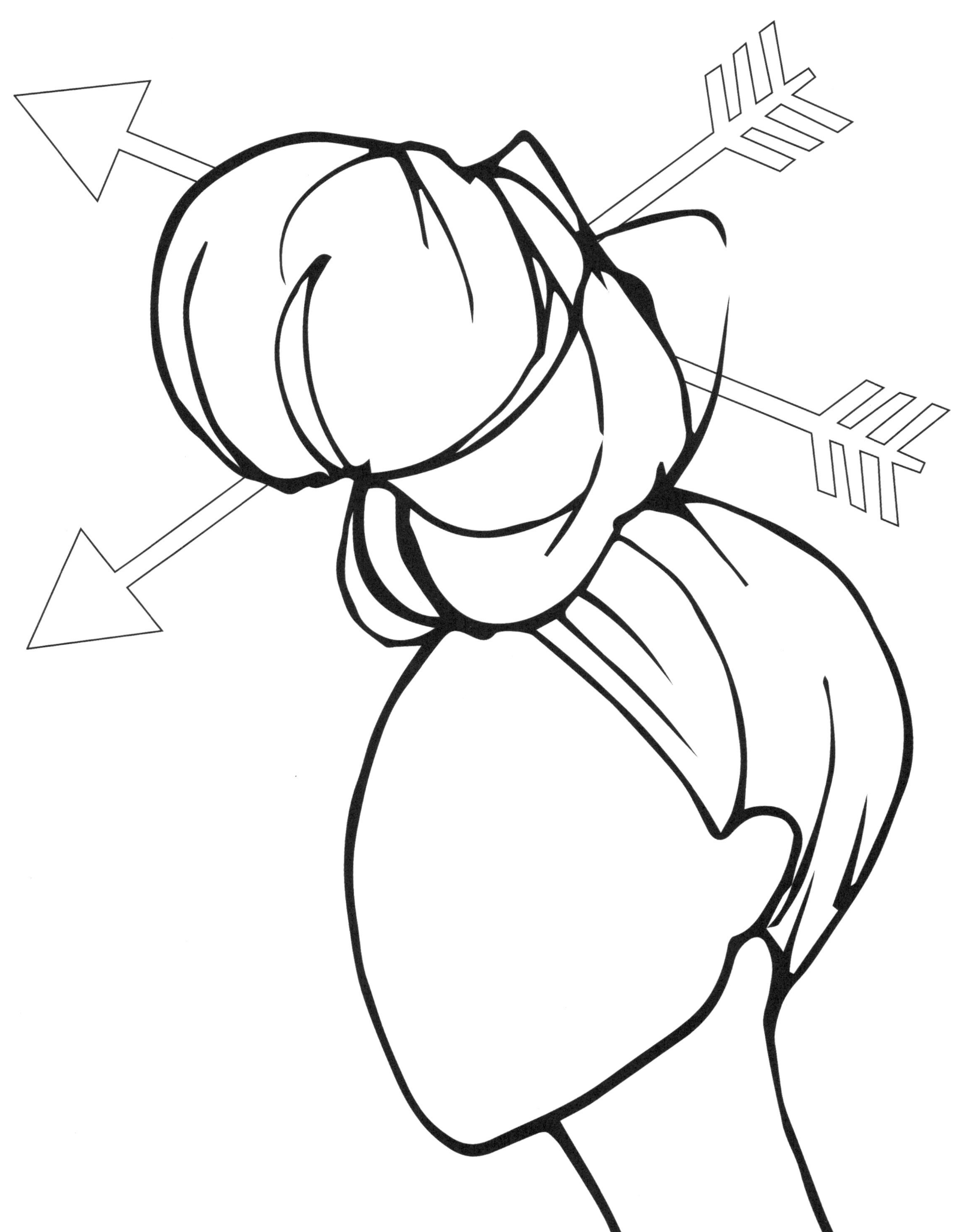

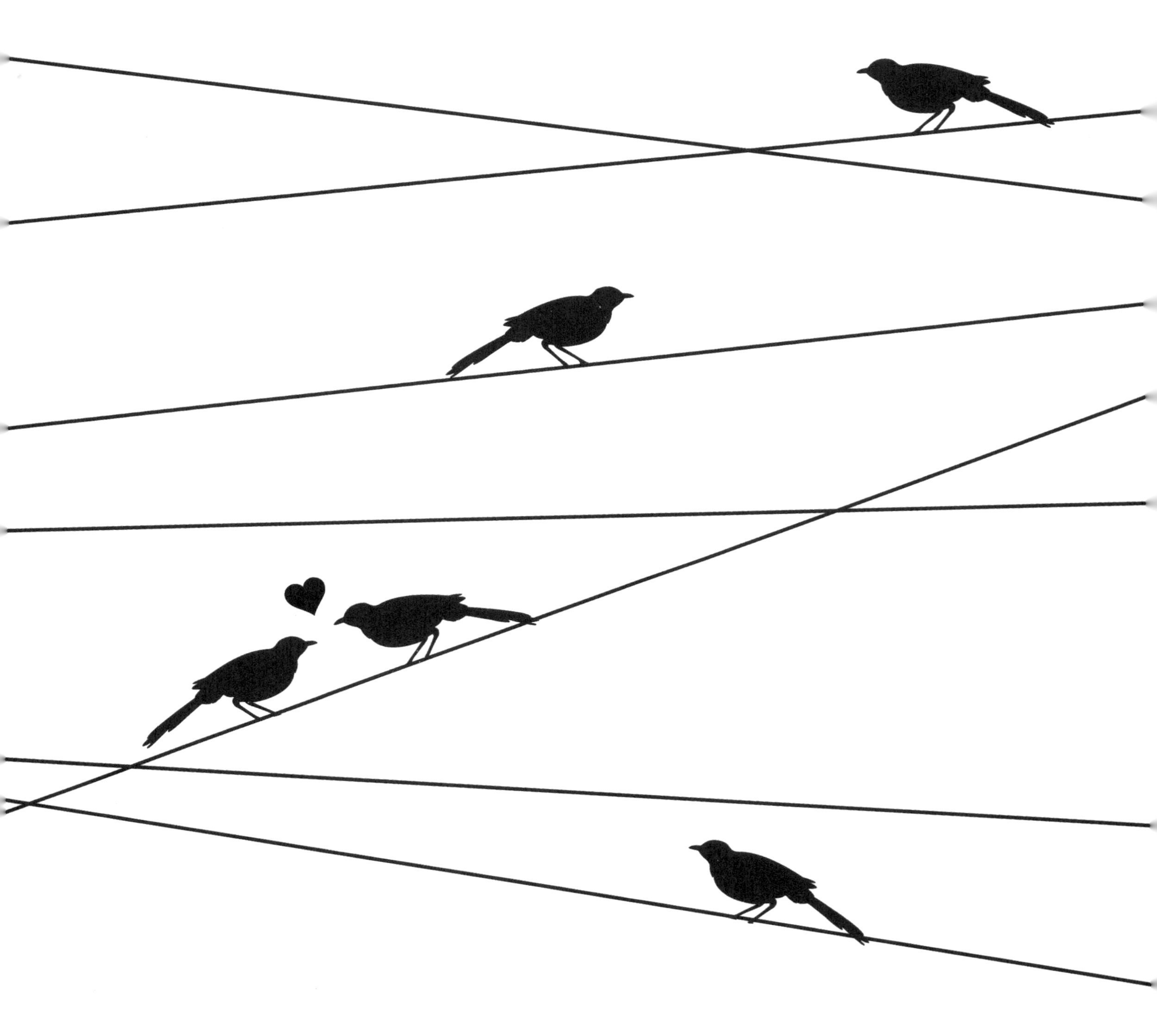

ANDROGYNOUS
BROCADE
CATWALK
DENIM
ELEGANCE
FRINGE
GINGHAM
HAUTE COUTURE
ICON
JODHPUR
KNICKERS
LEATHER
MODERN
NEUTRAL
ORGANZA
PREPPY
QUALITY
REVERSIBLE
STYLE
TASTE
UTILITARIAN
VOGUE
WEAVE
XOXO
YOKE
ZEITGEIST

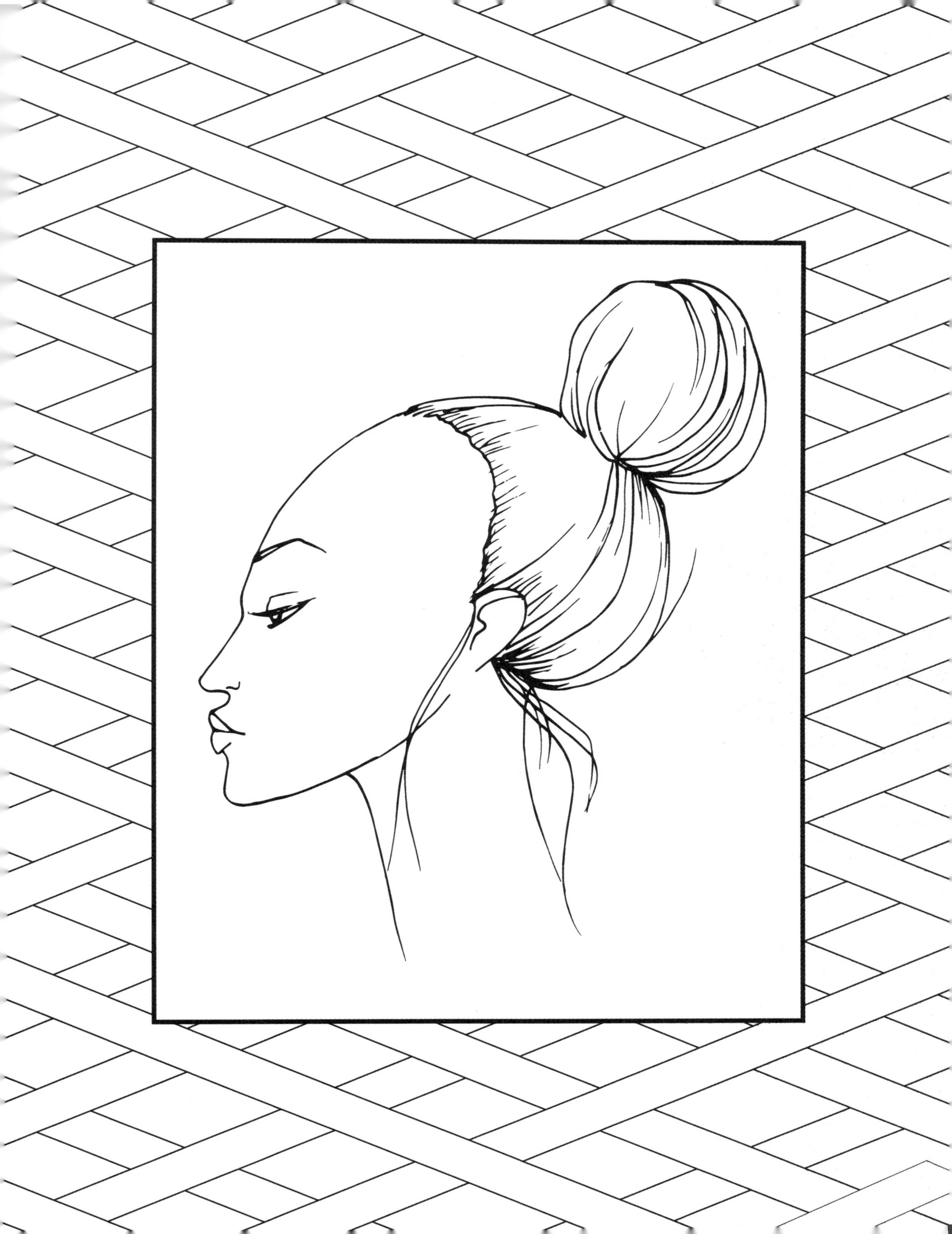

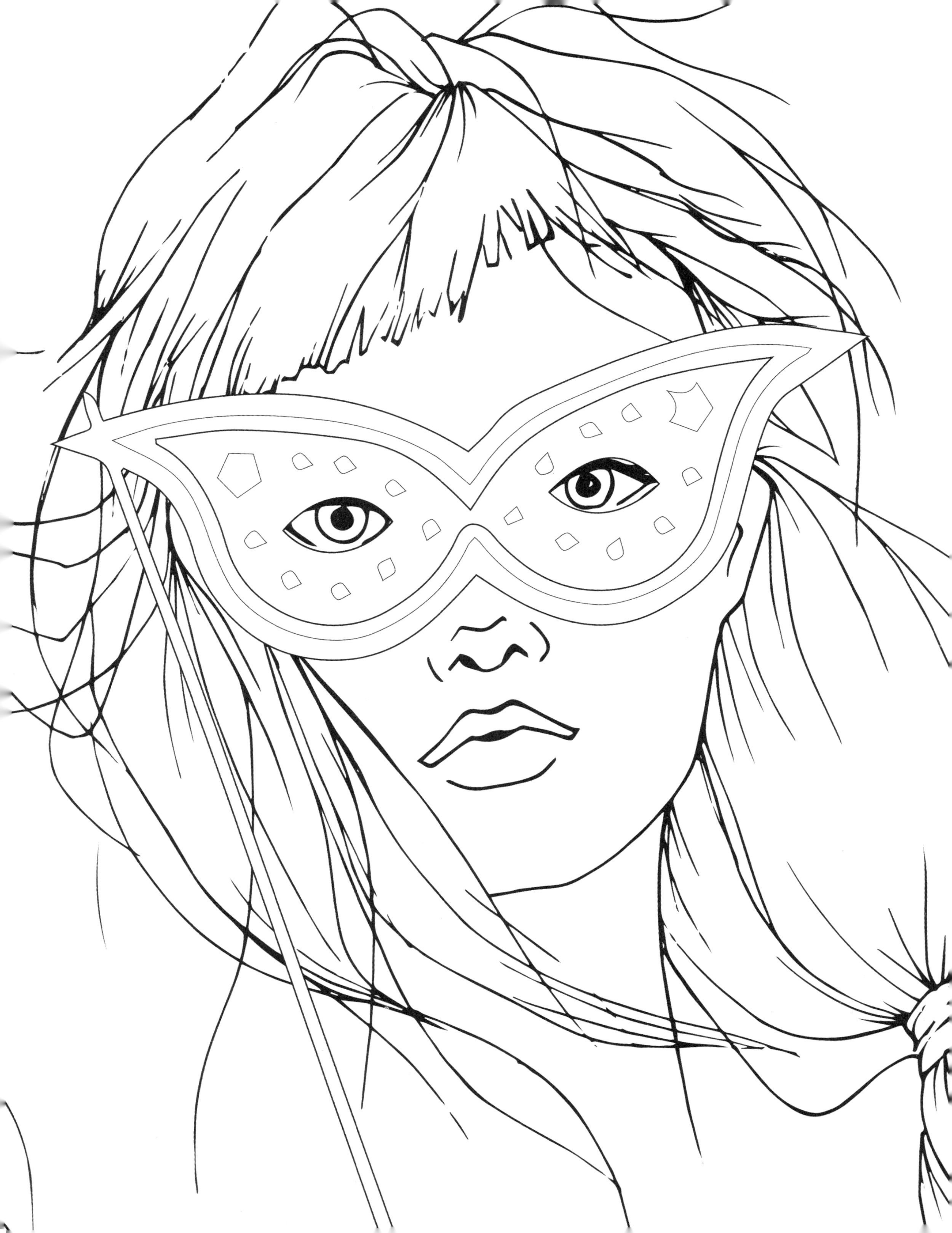

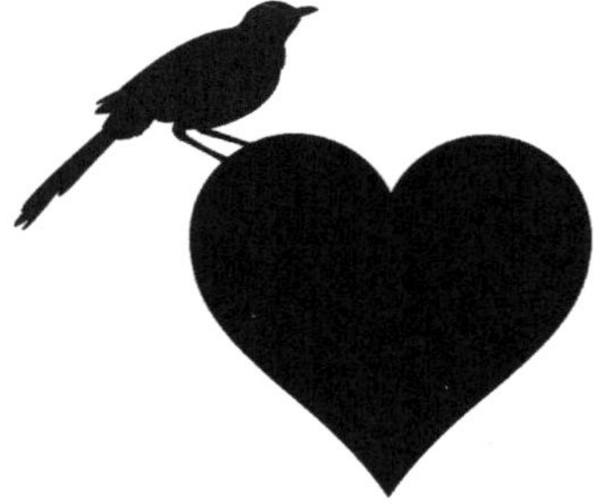

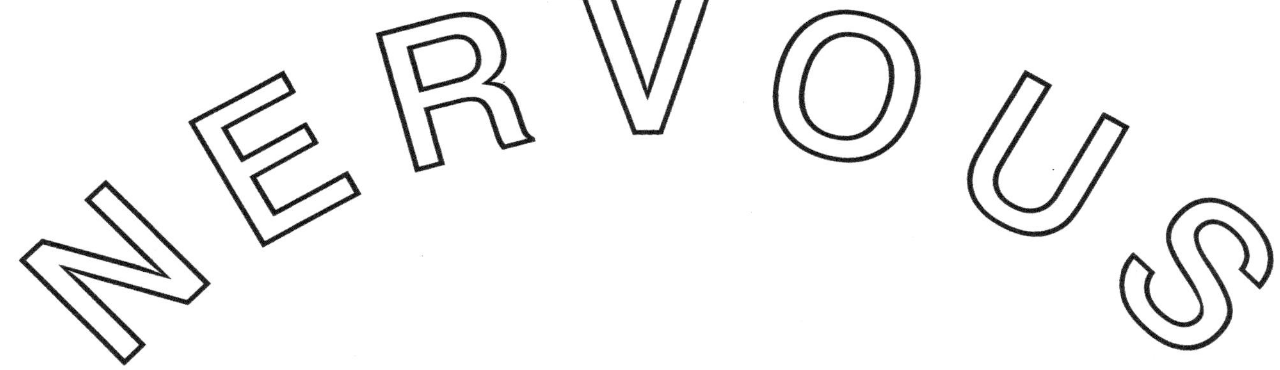

MODERN &
NERVOUS

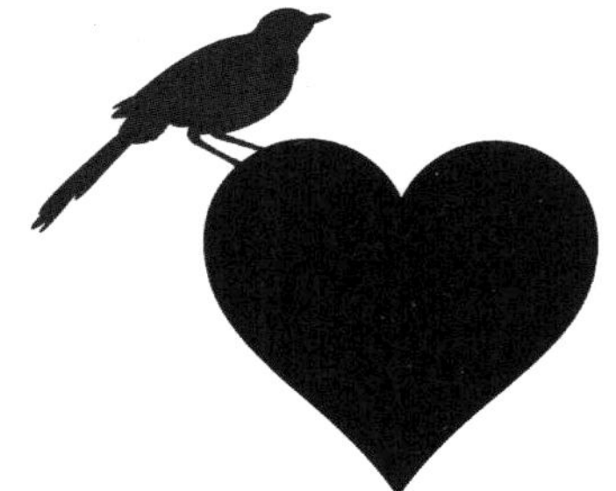

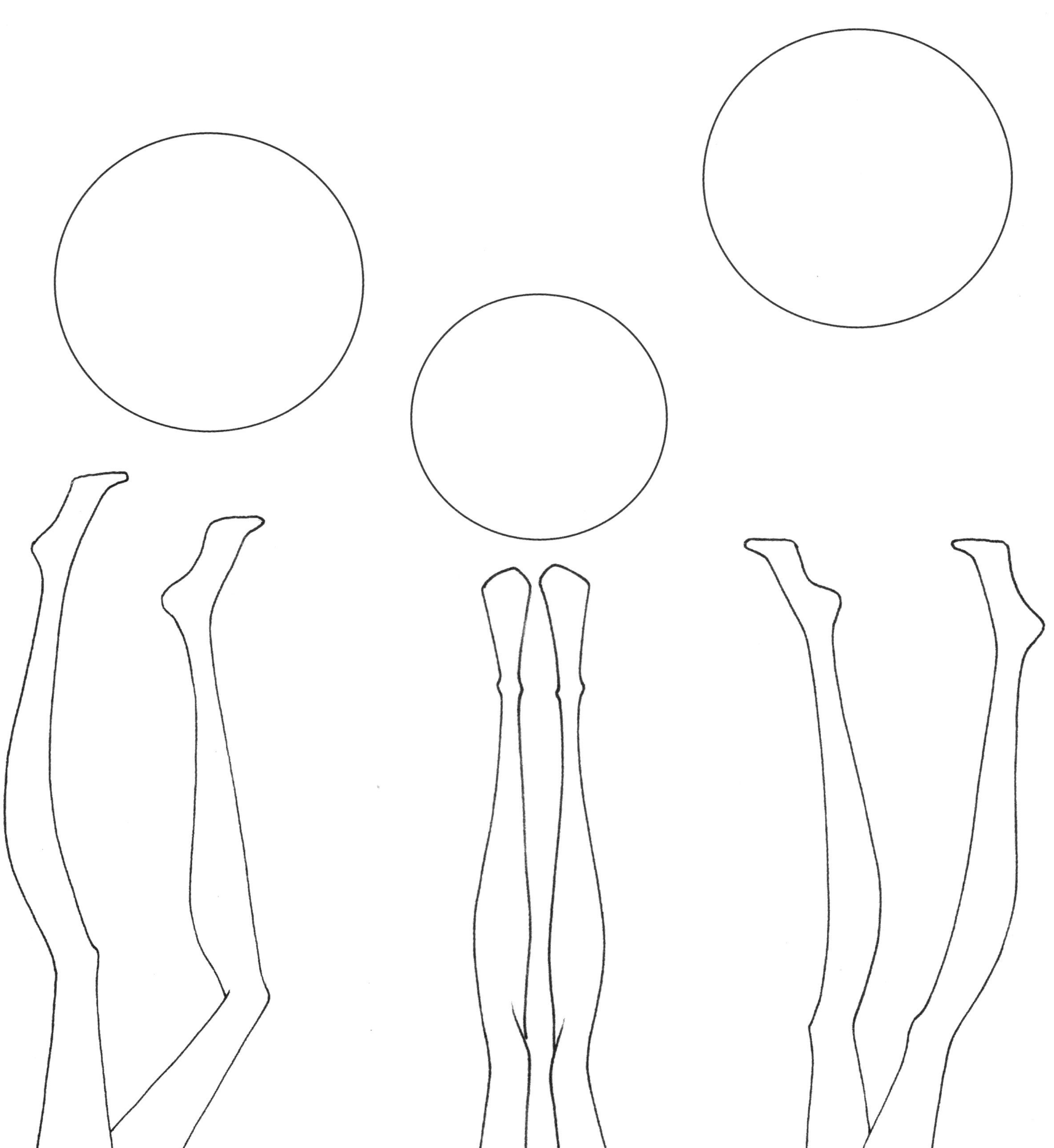

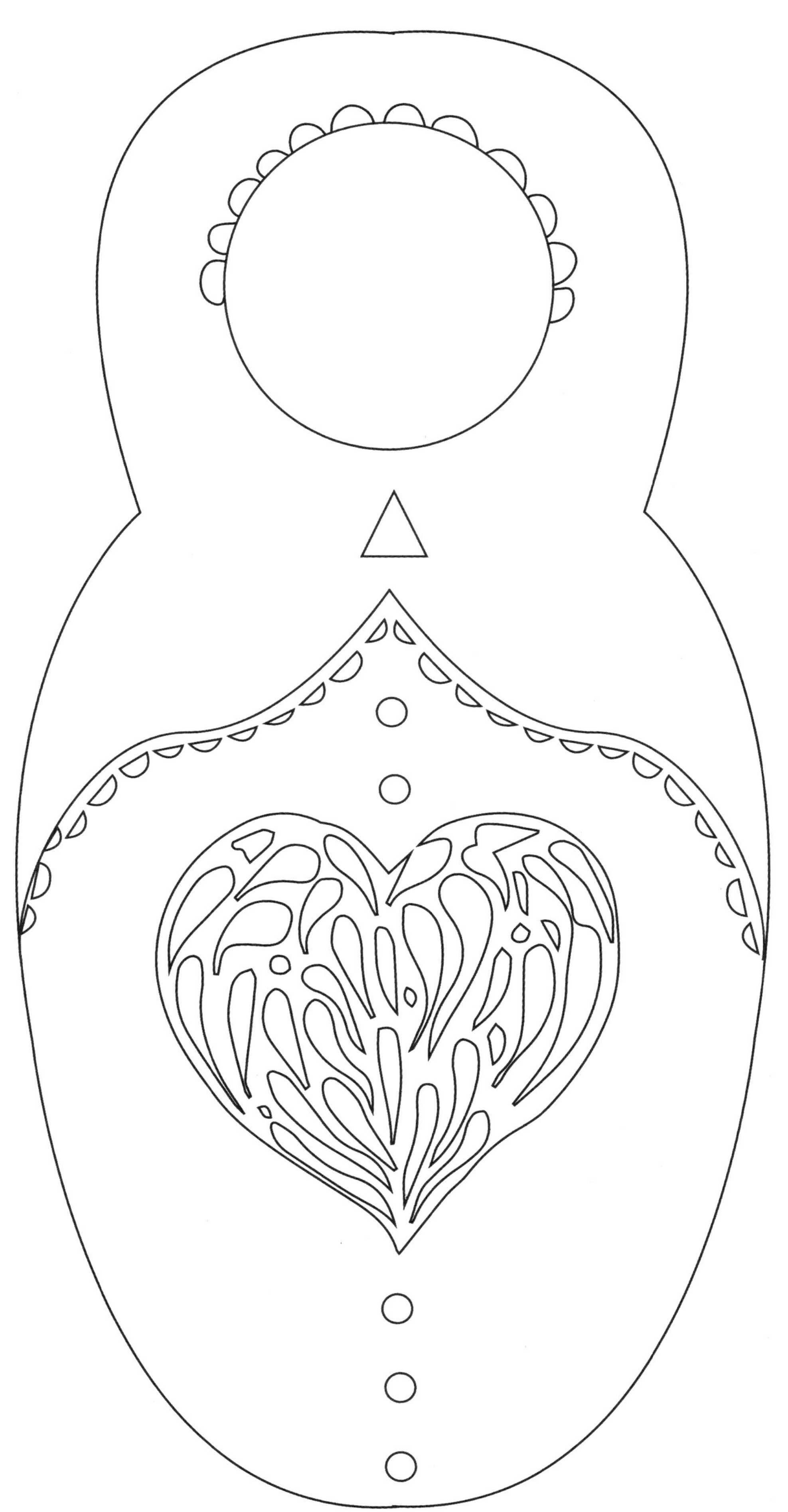

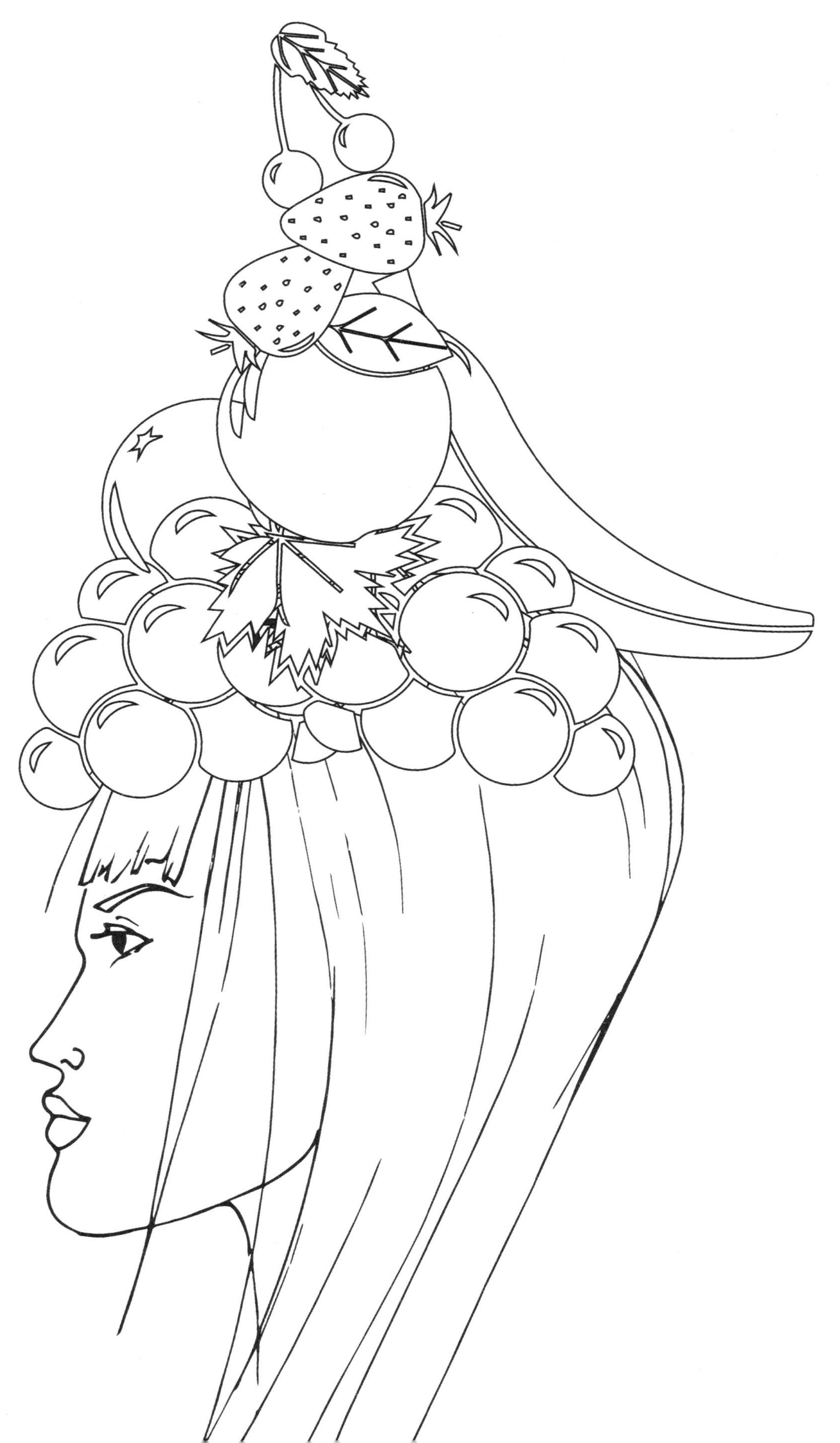

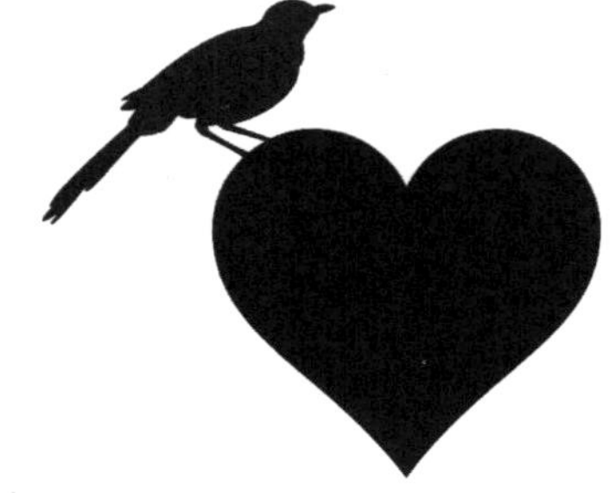

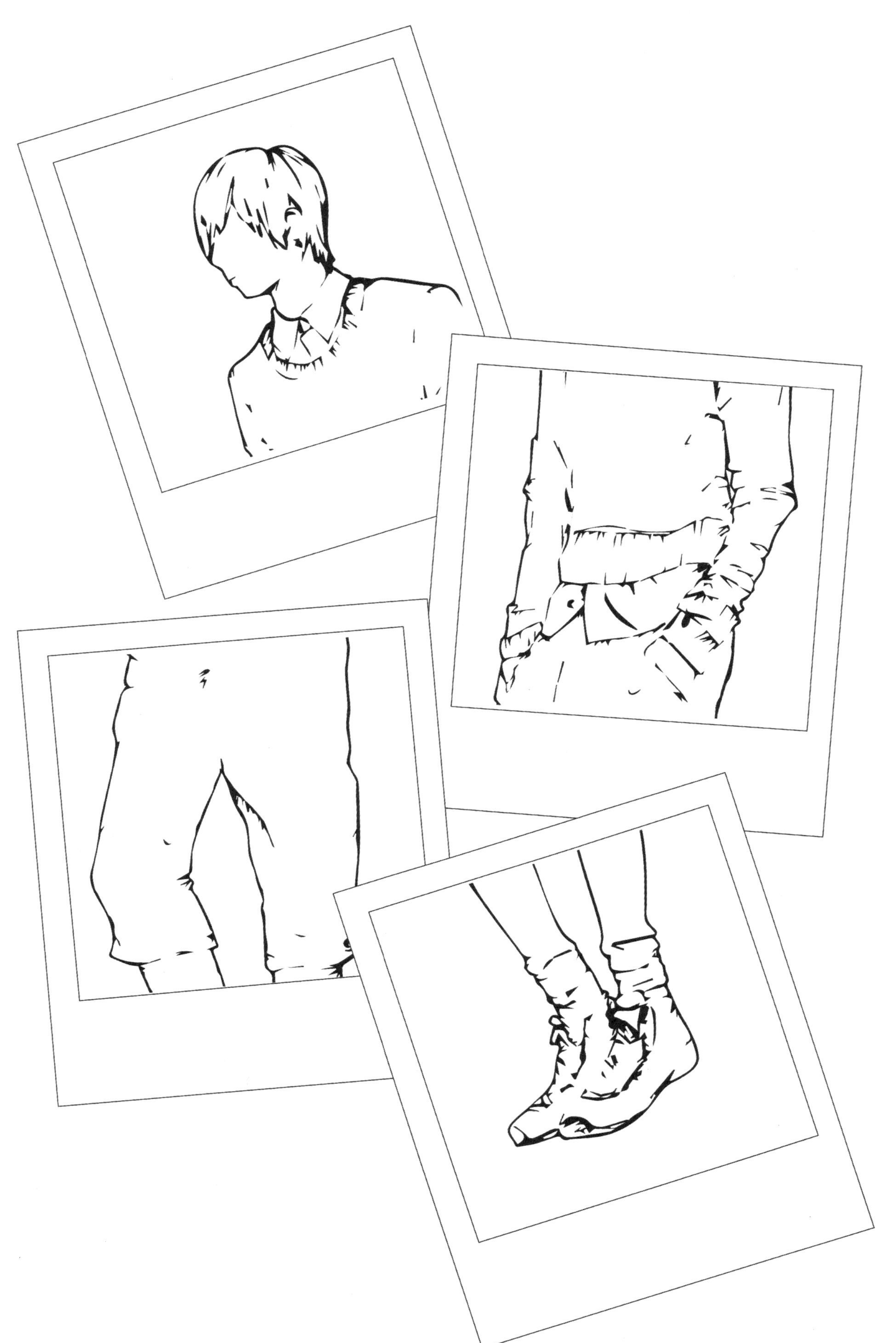

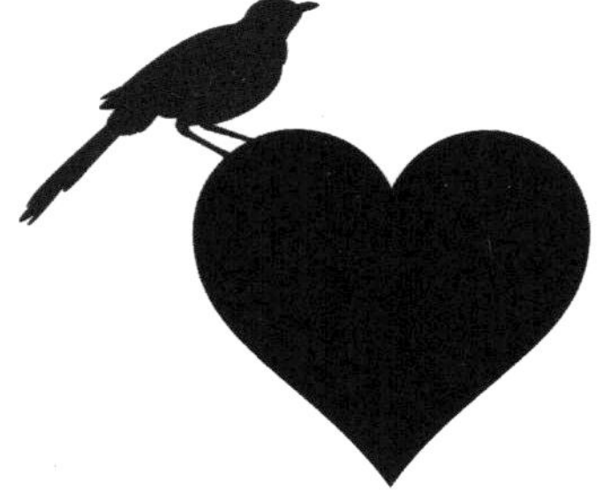

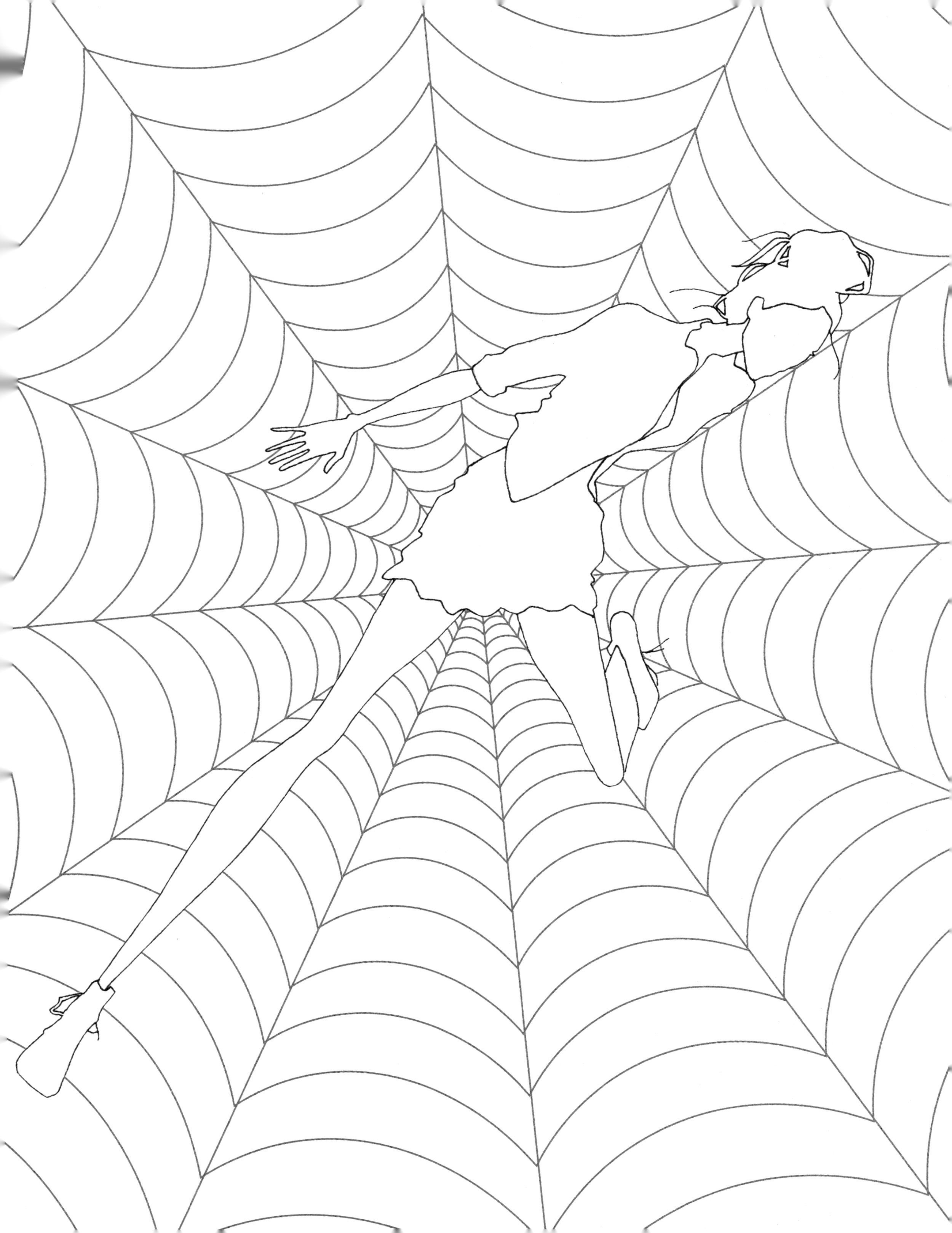

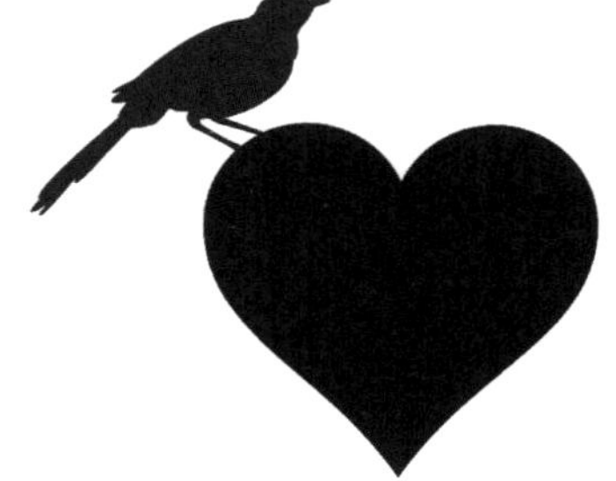

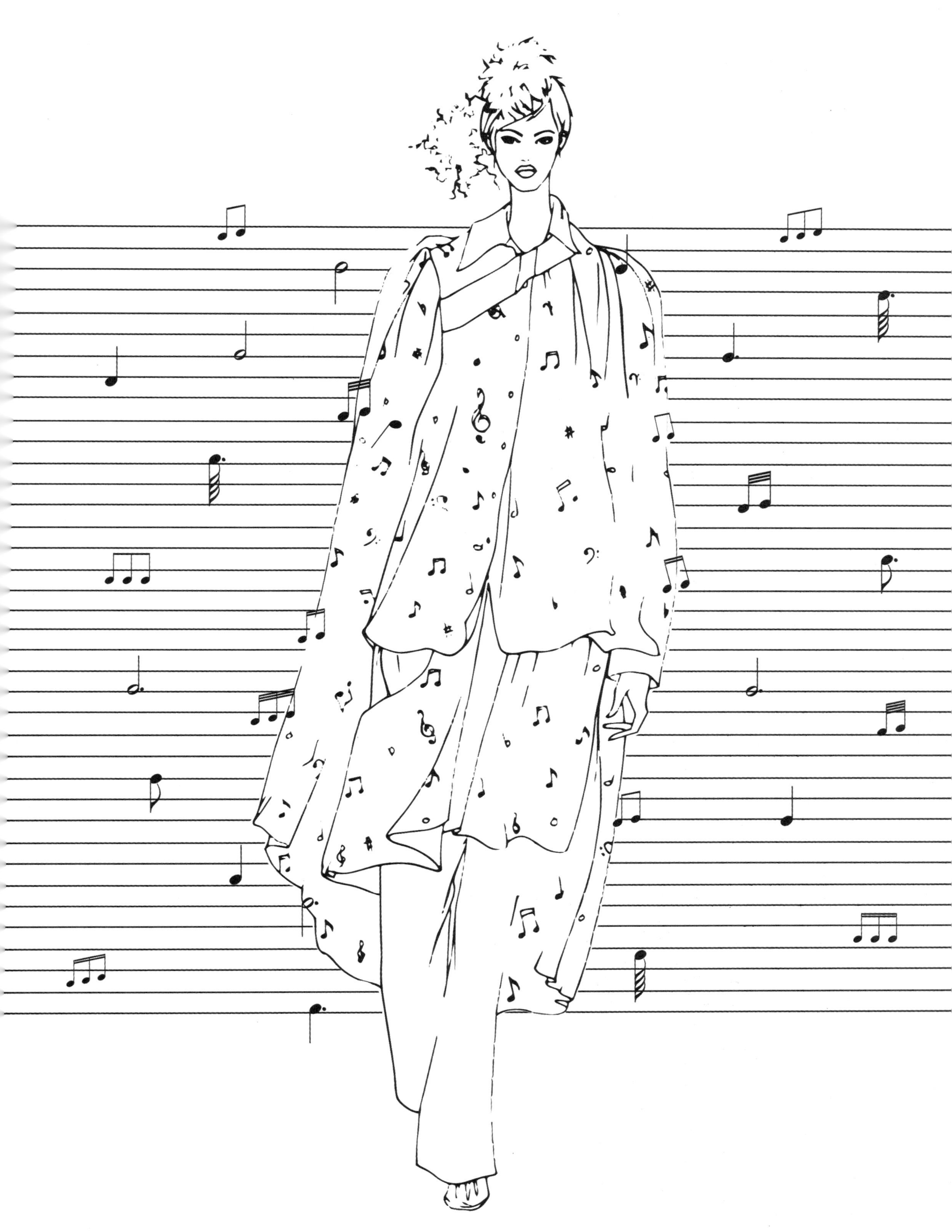

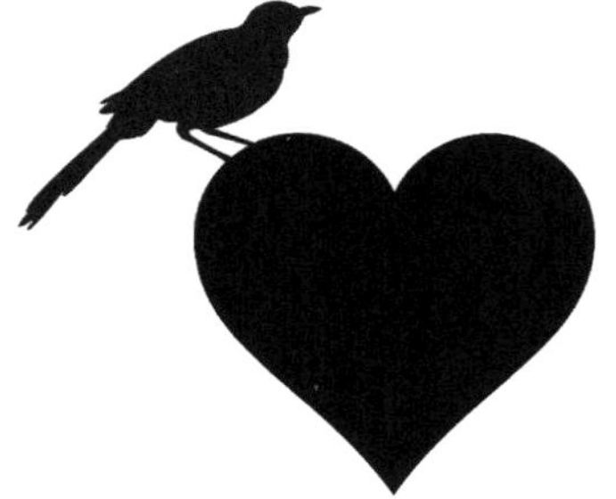

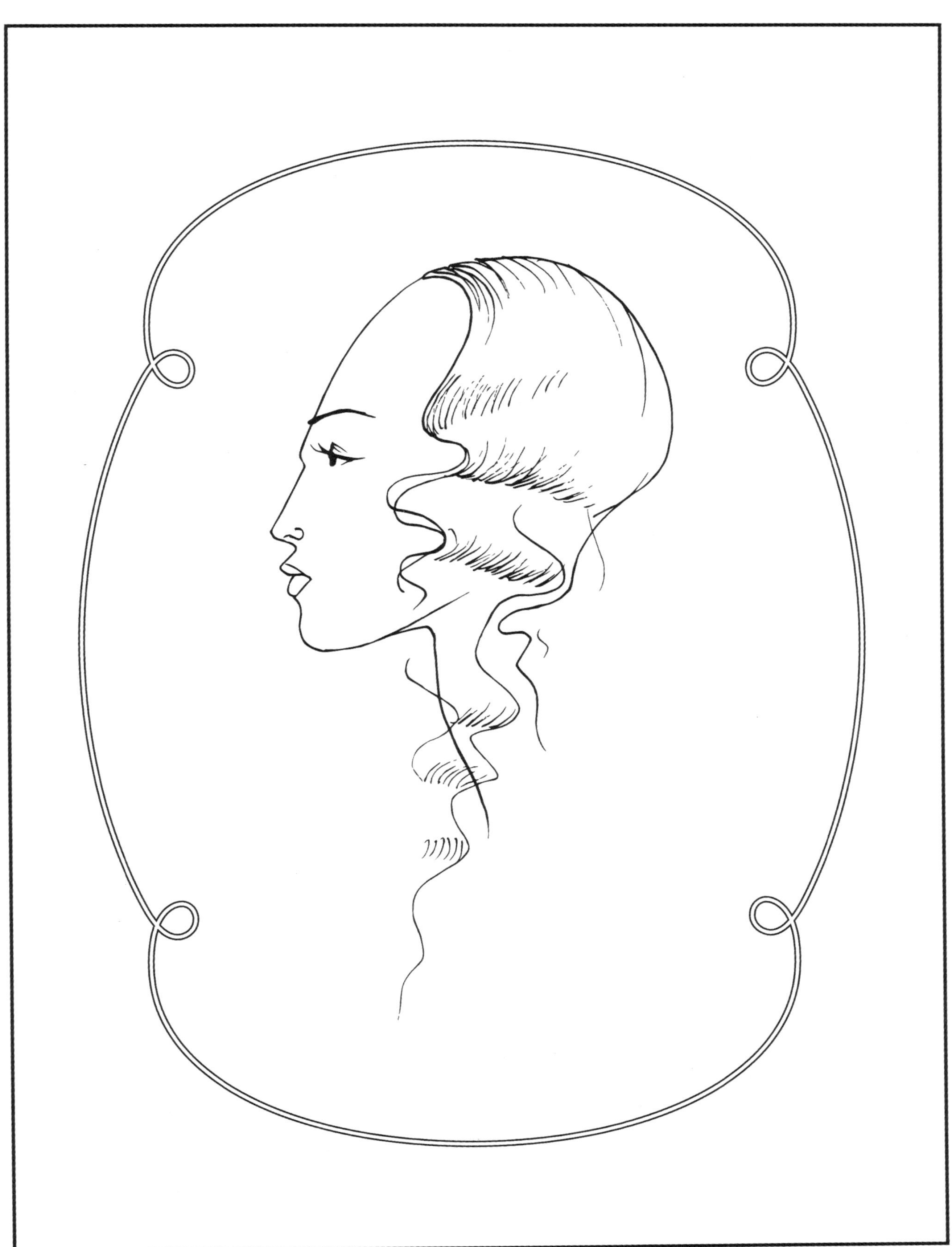

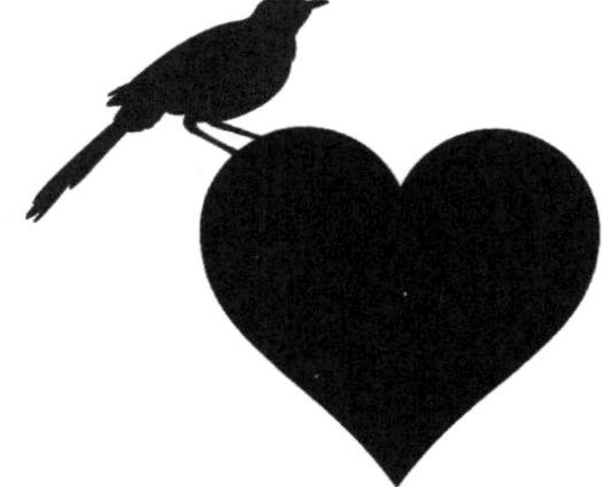

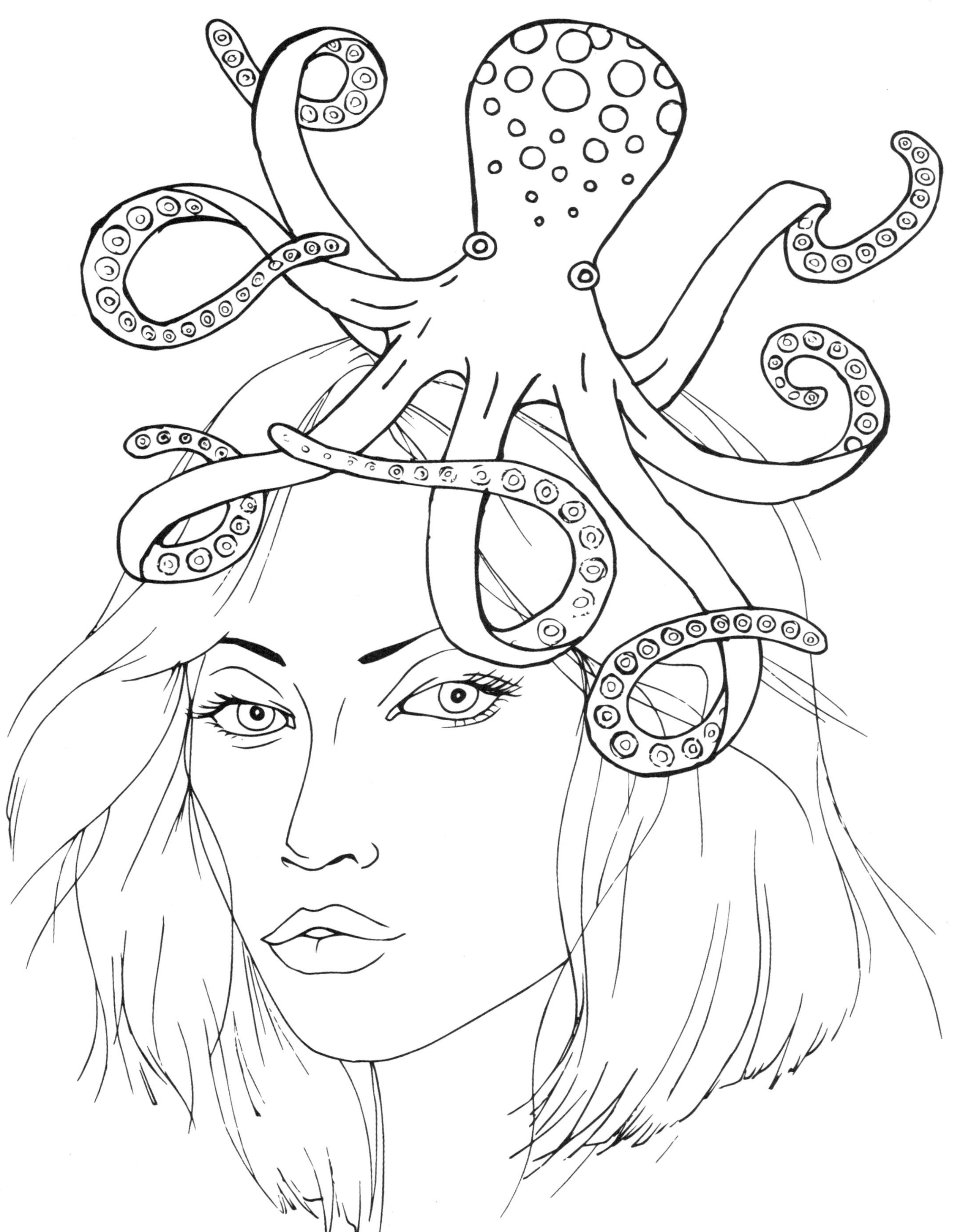

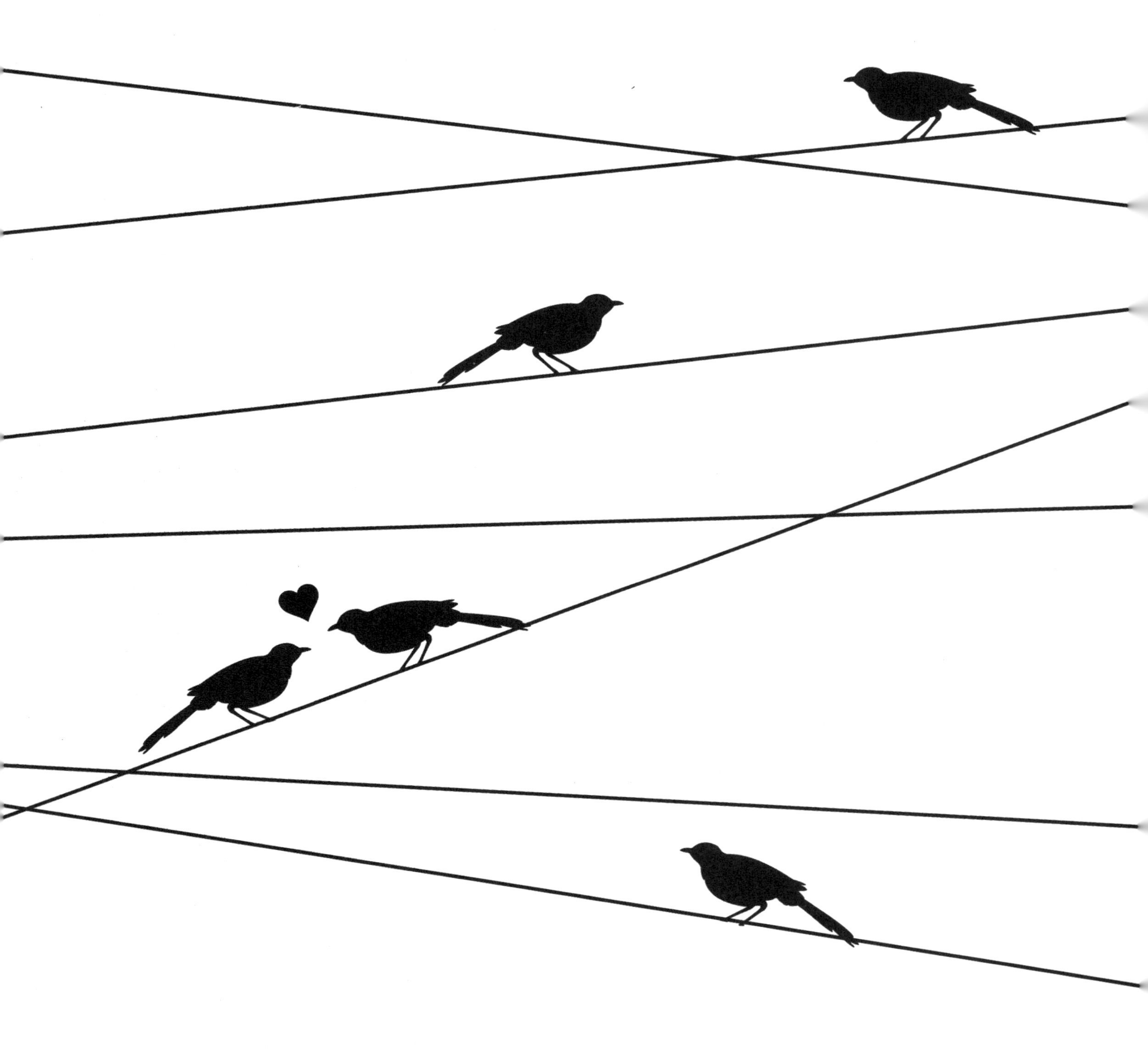

Drawing makes you
see things
clearer,
and clearer
and clearer
still,
until your eyes ache.

- David Hockney

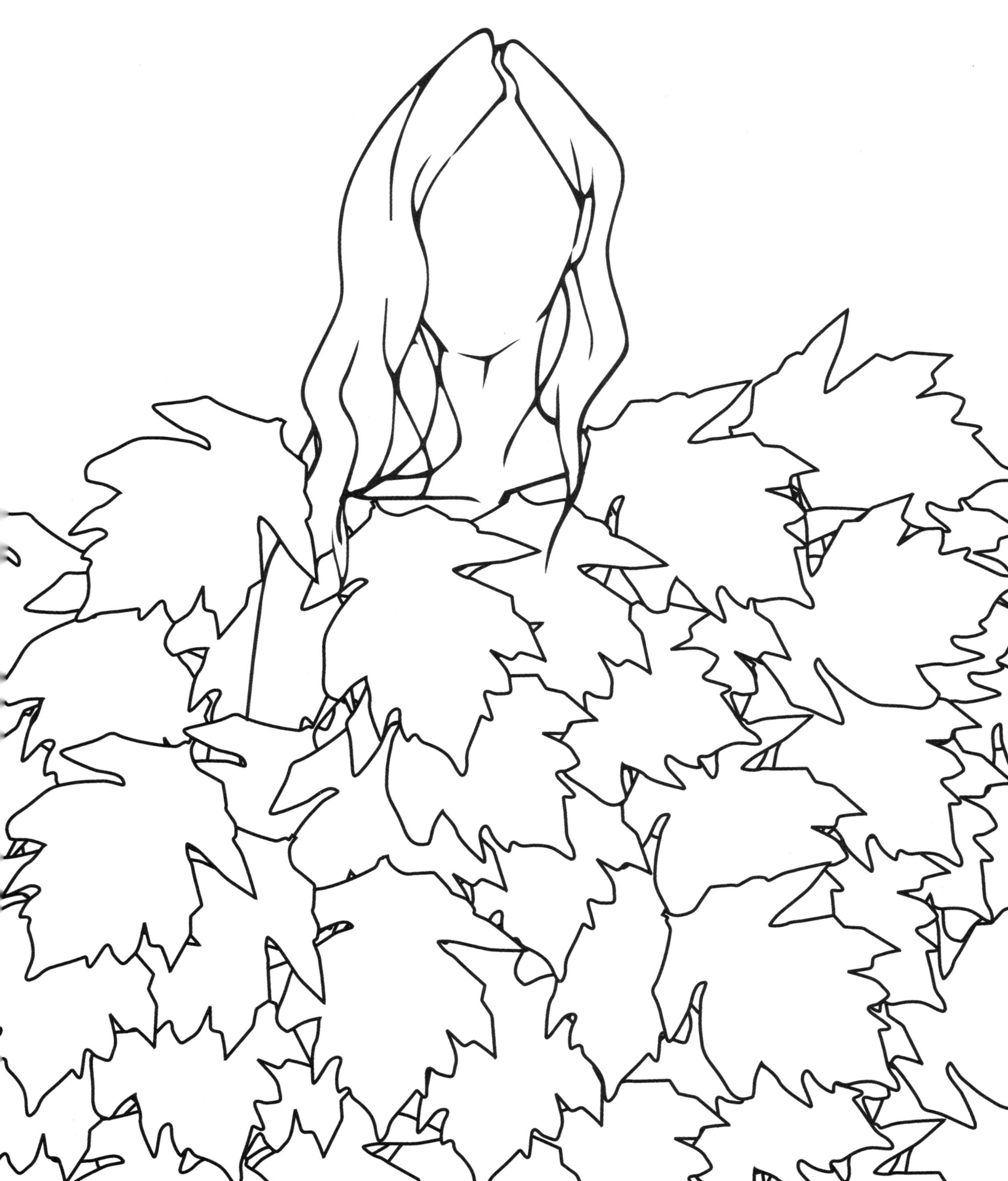

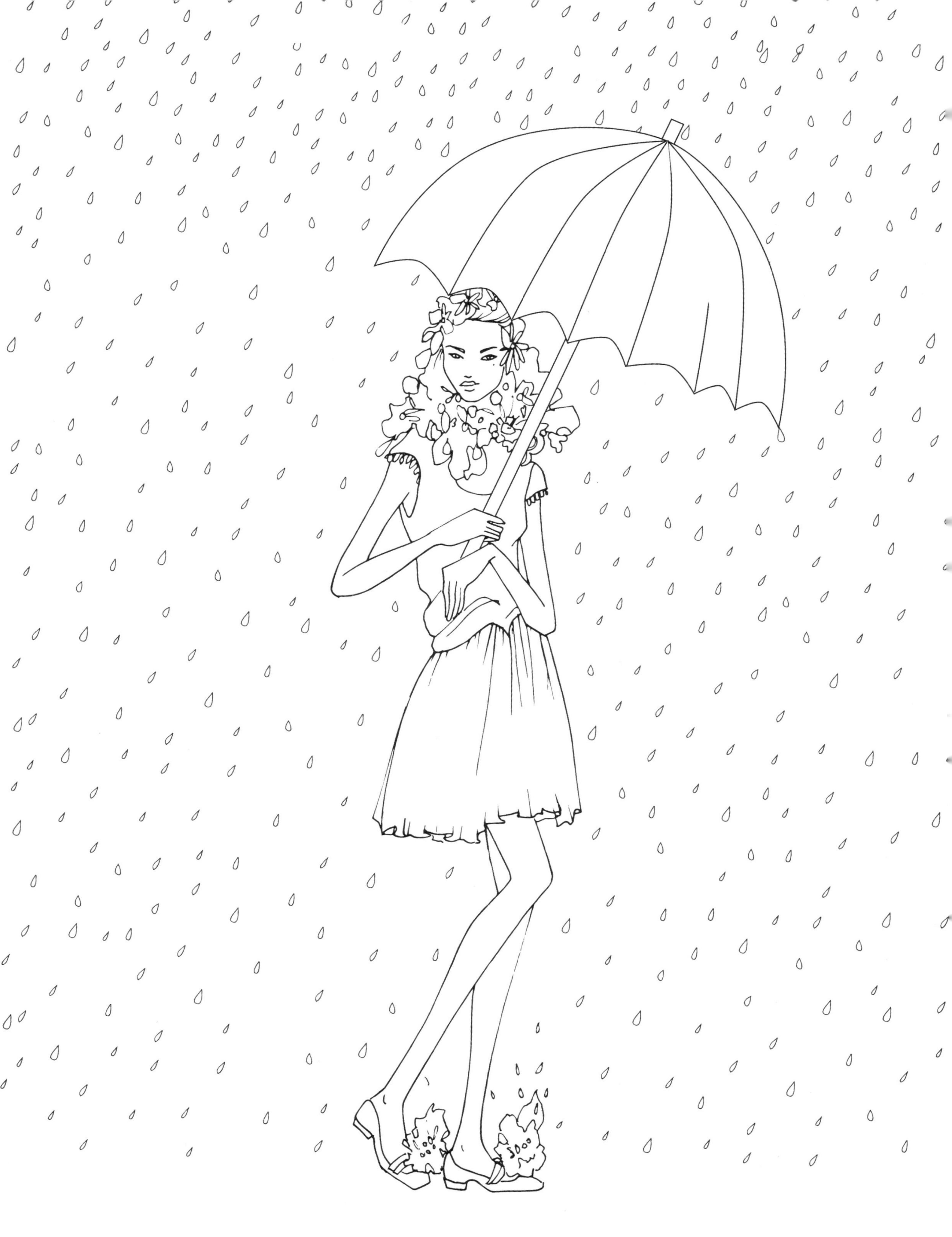

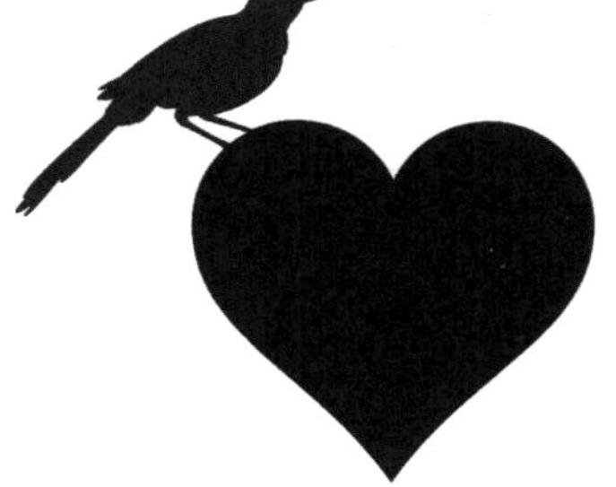

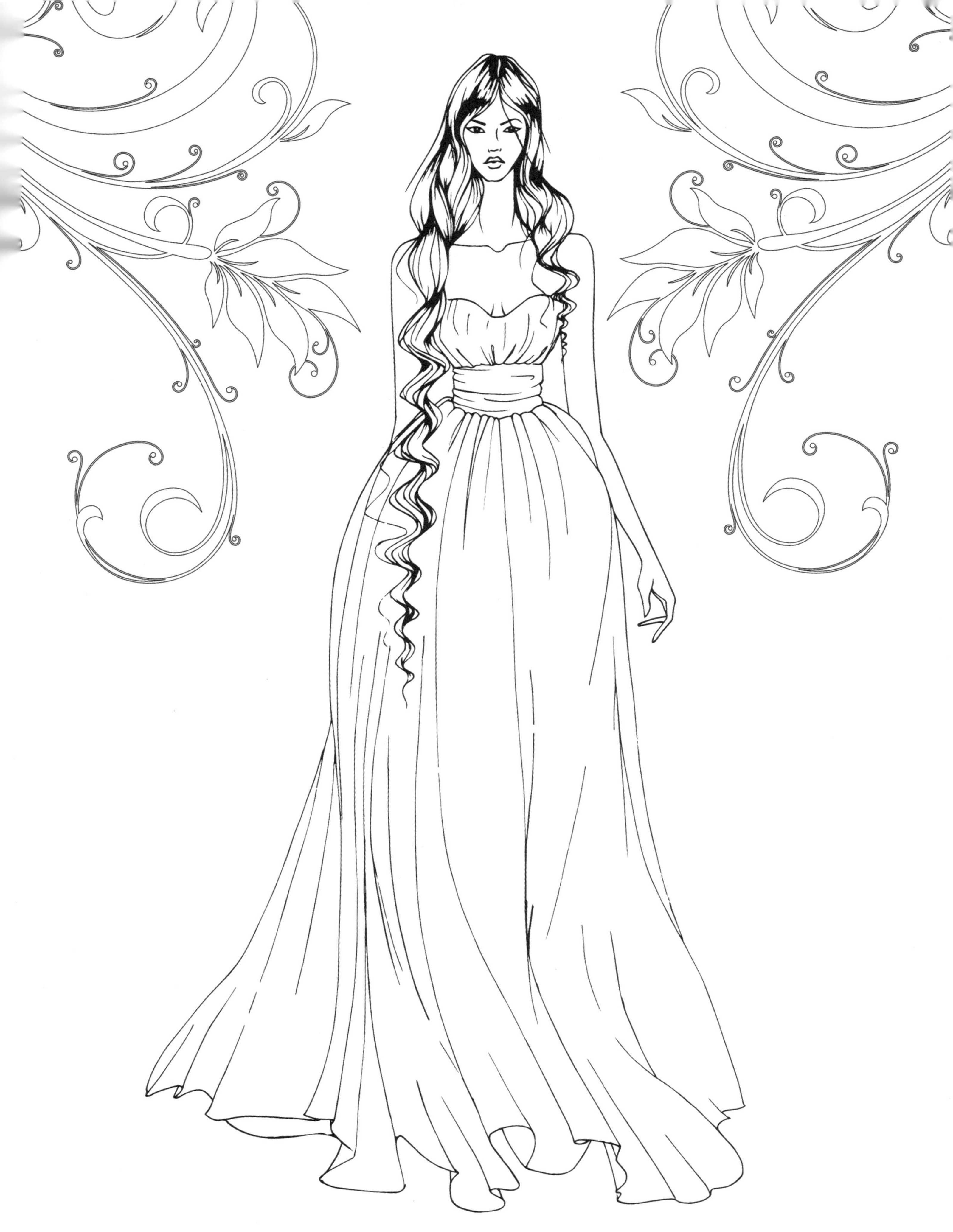

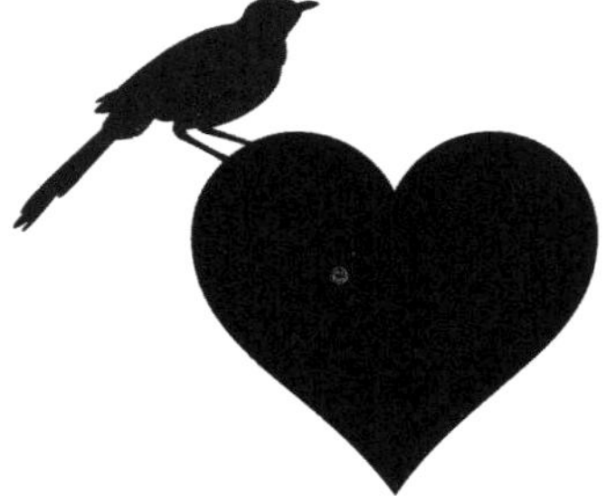

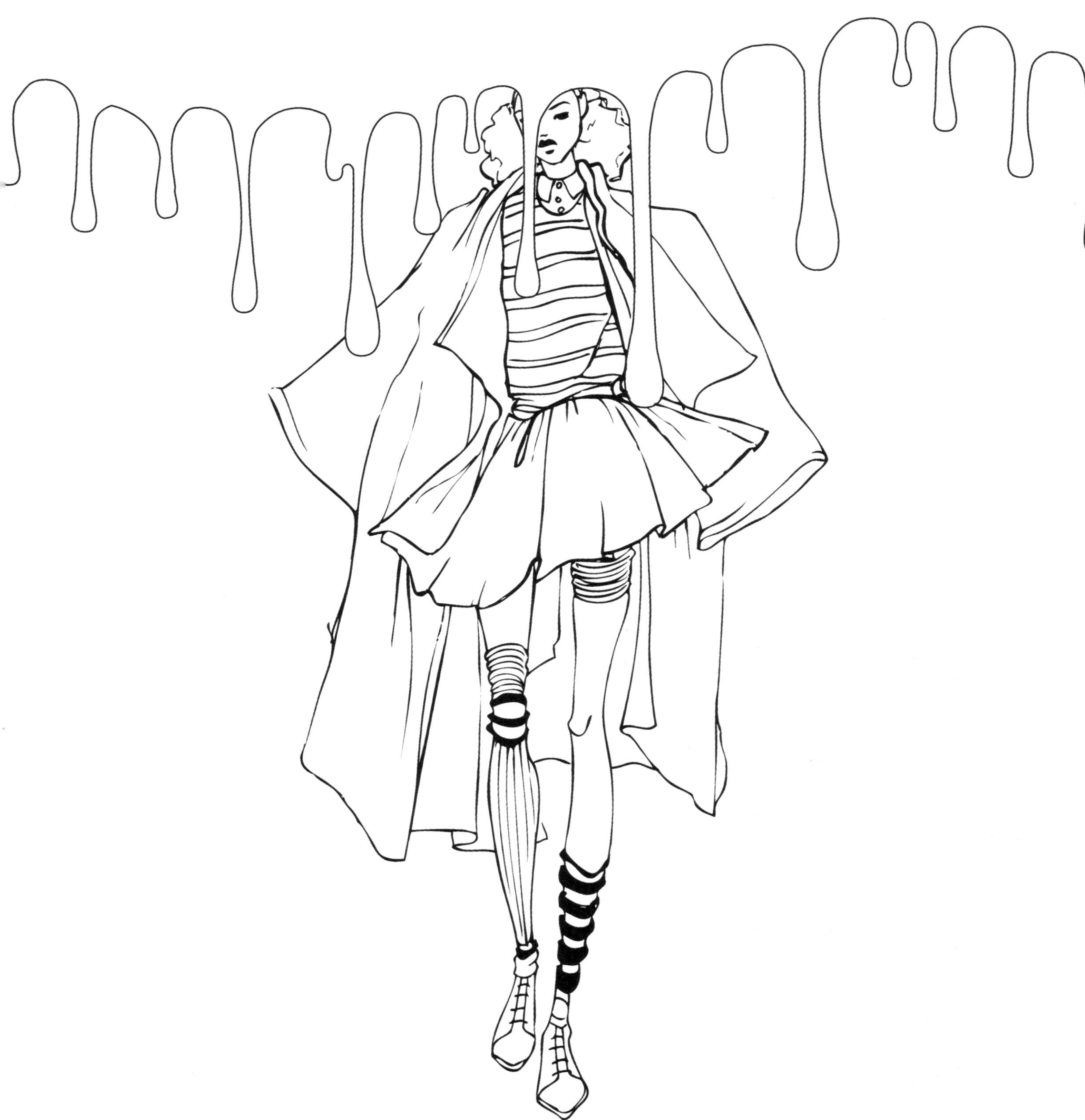

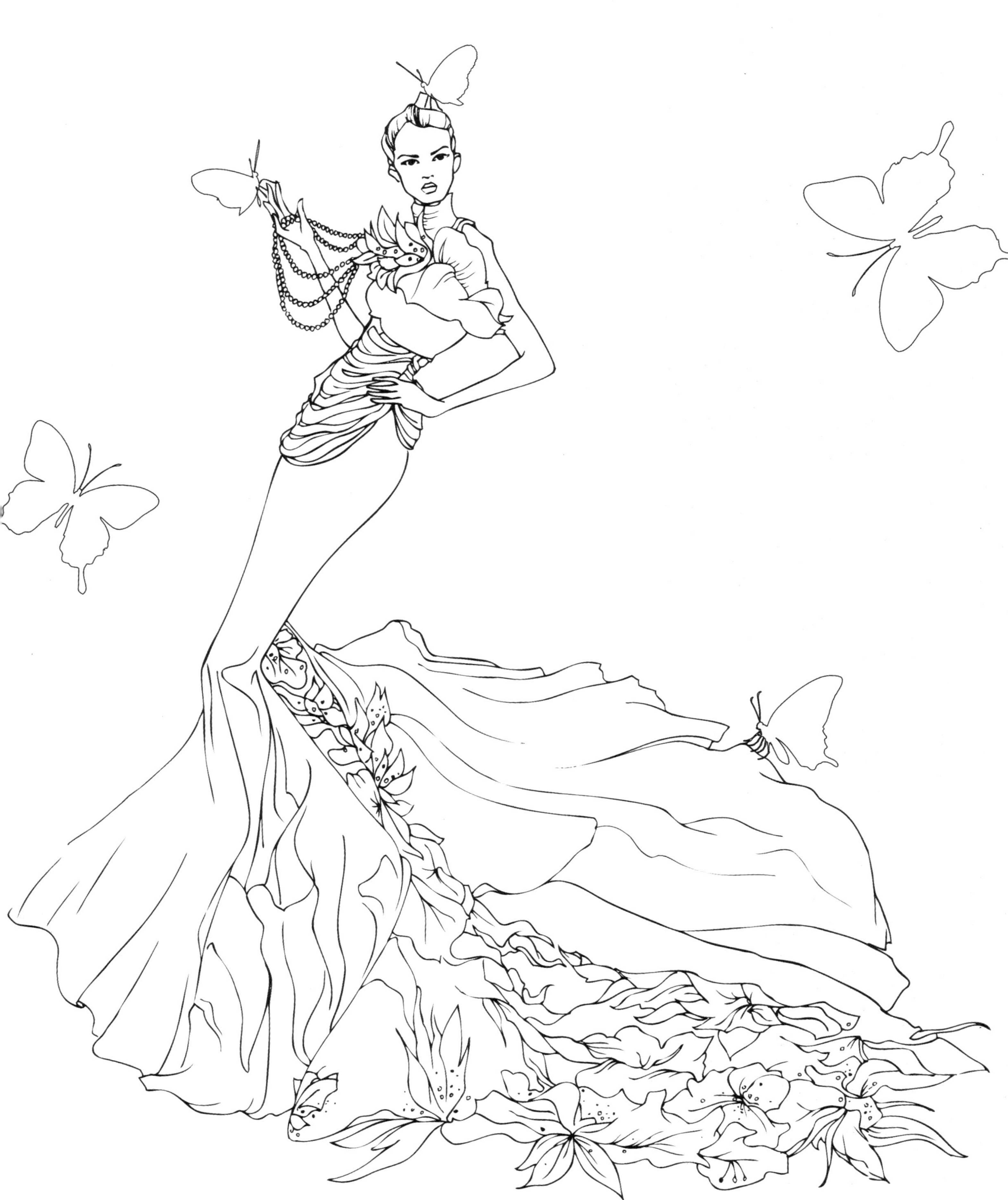

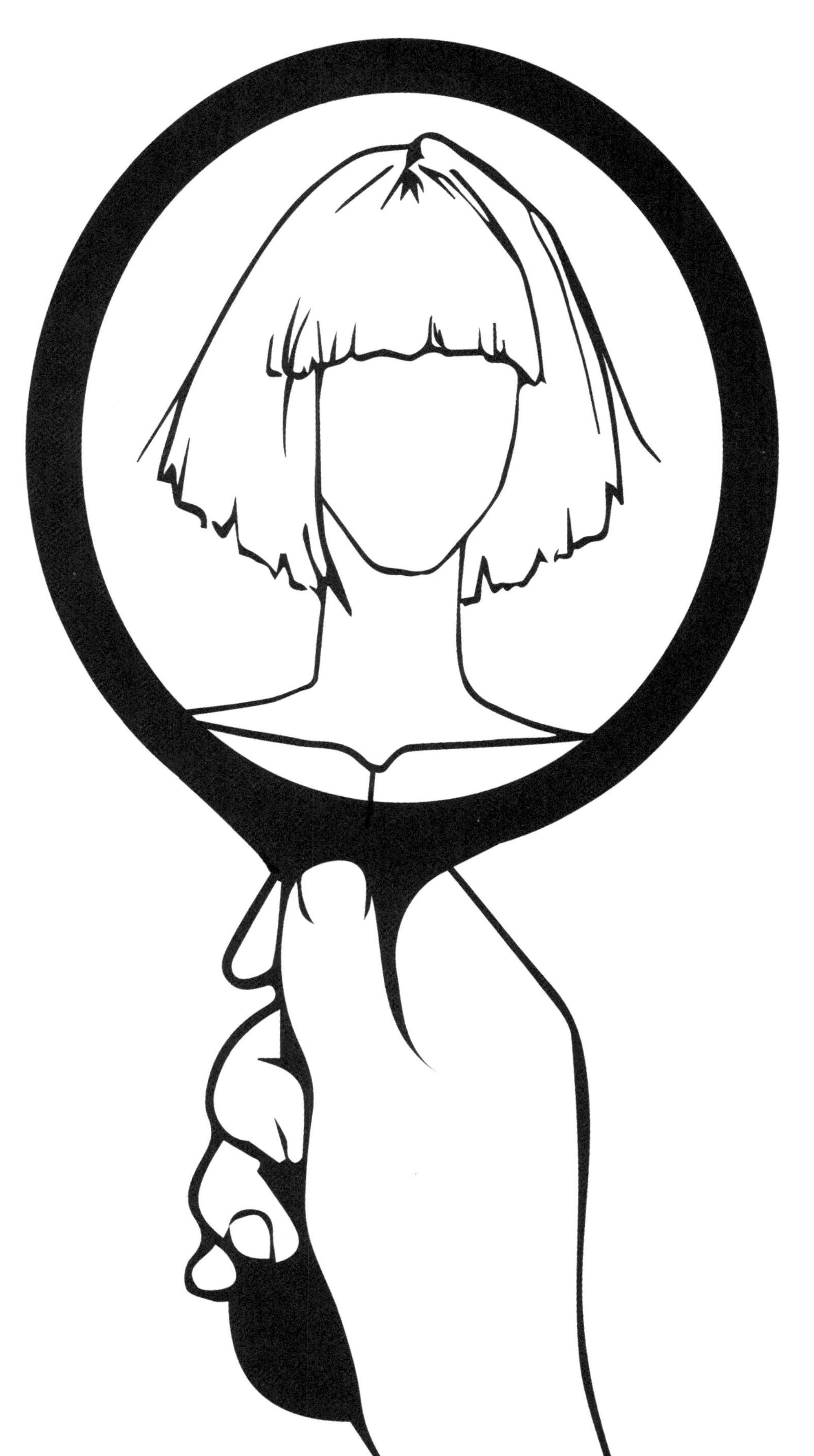

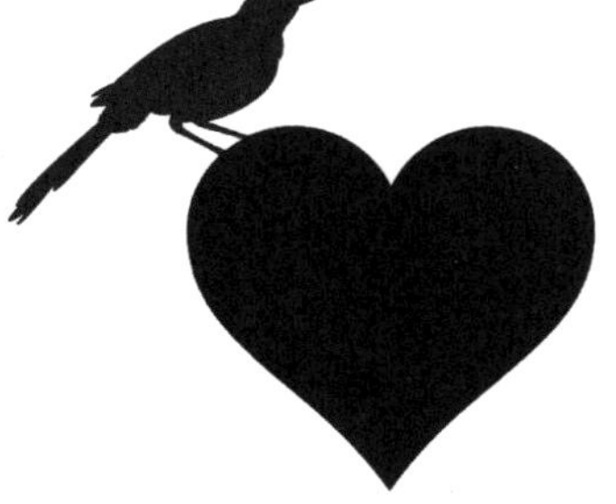

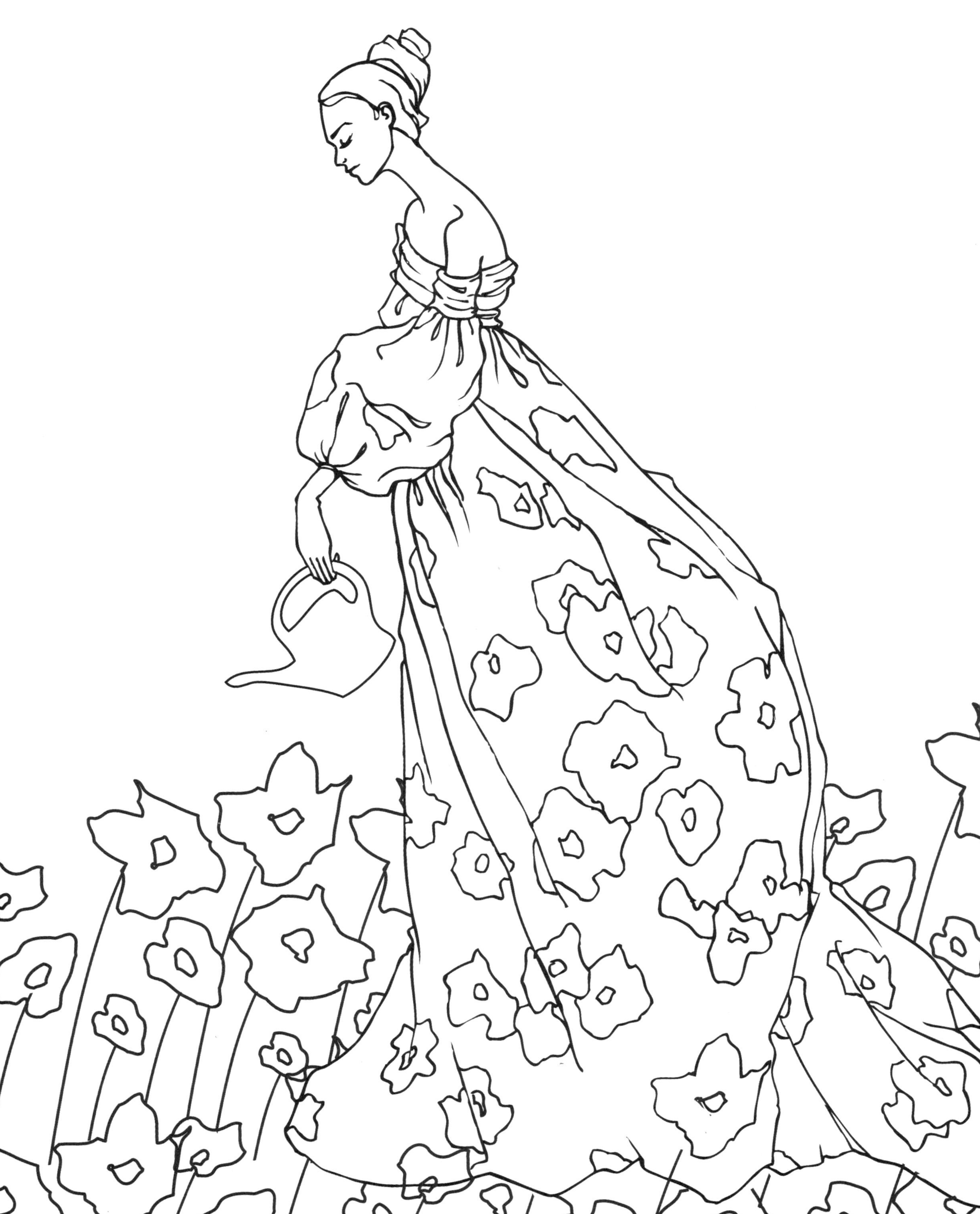

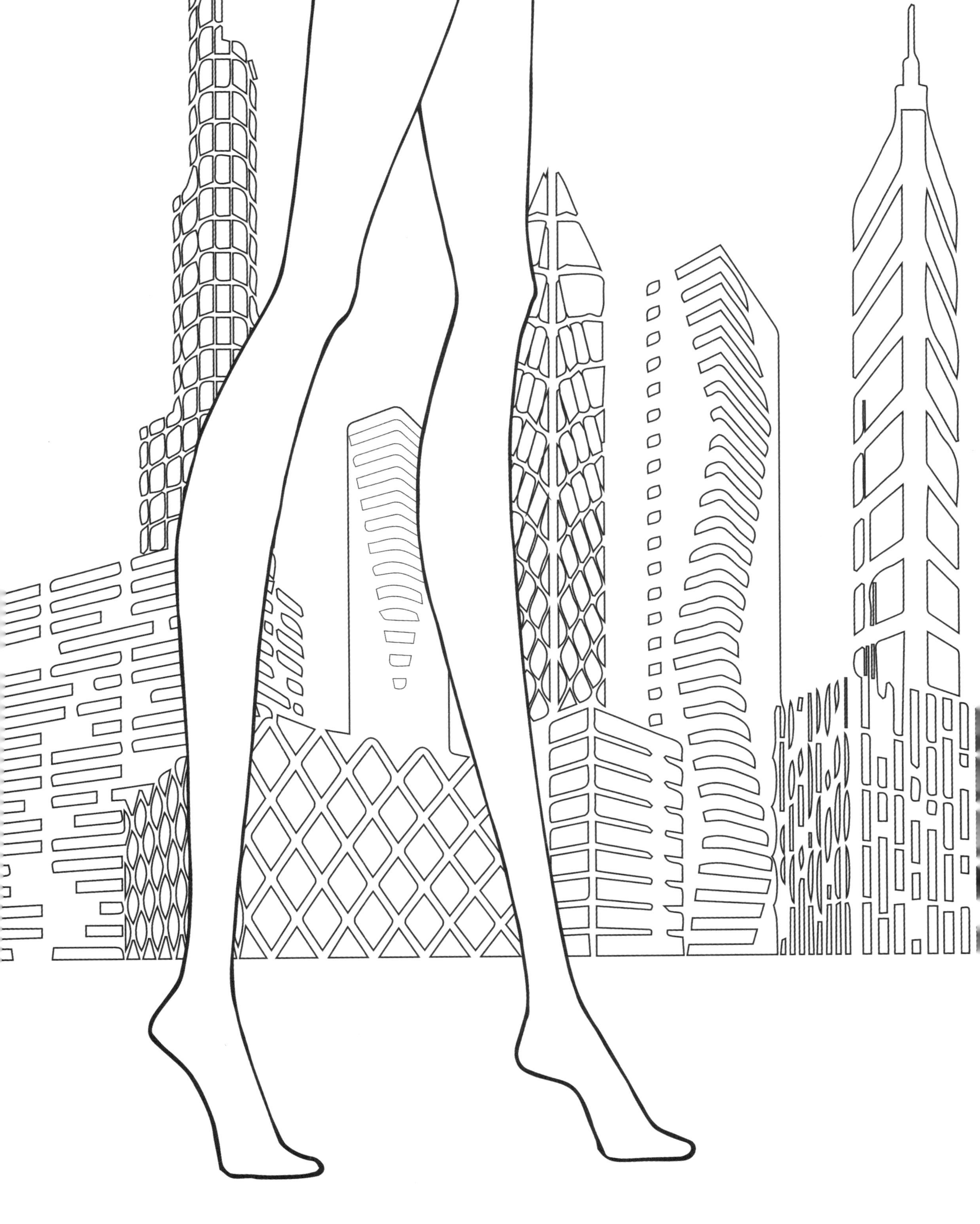

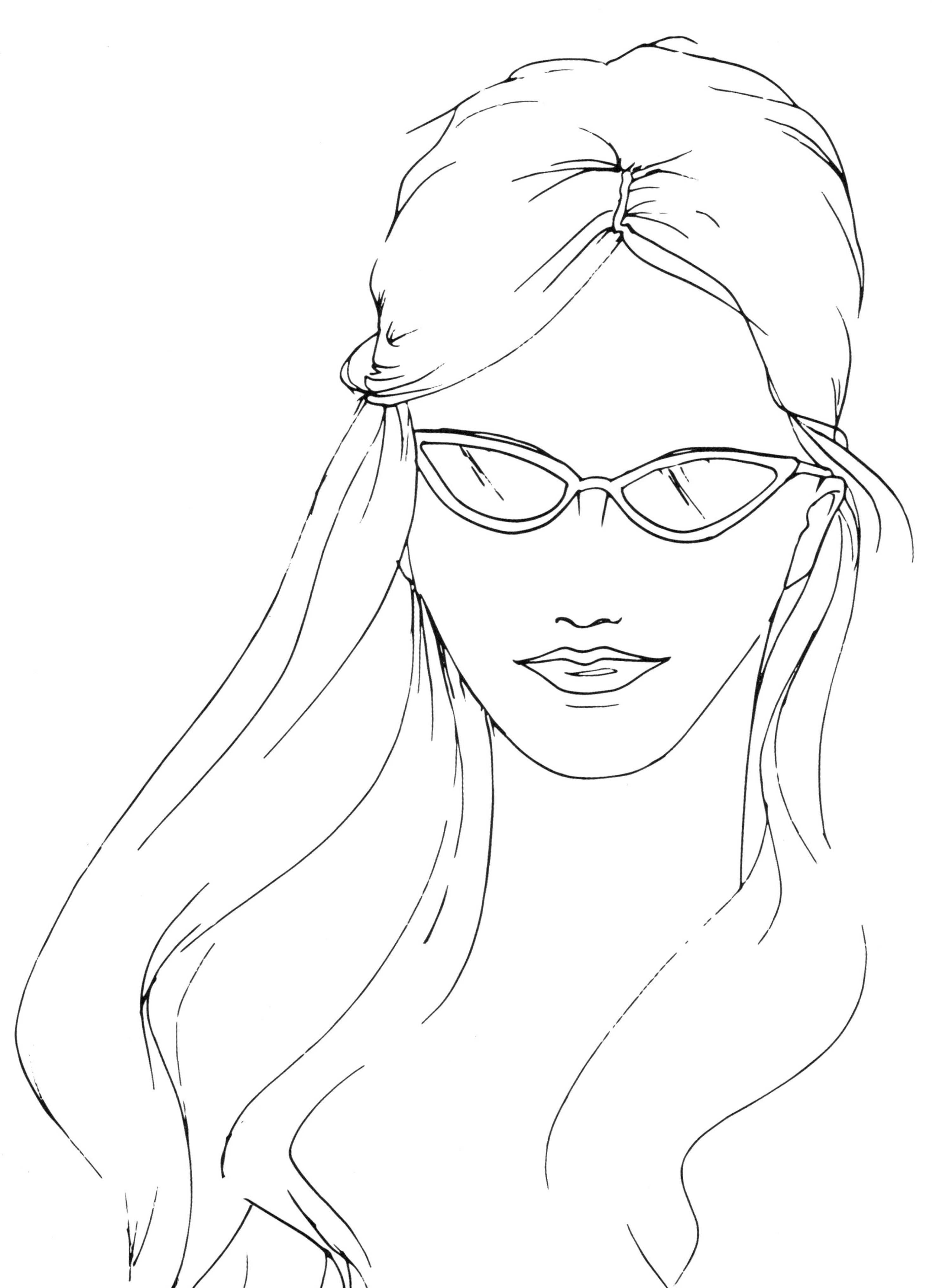

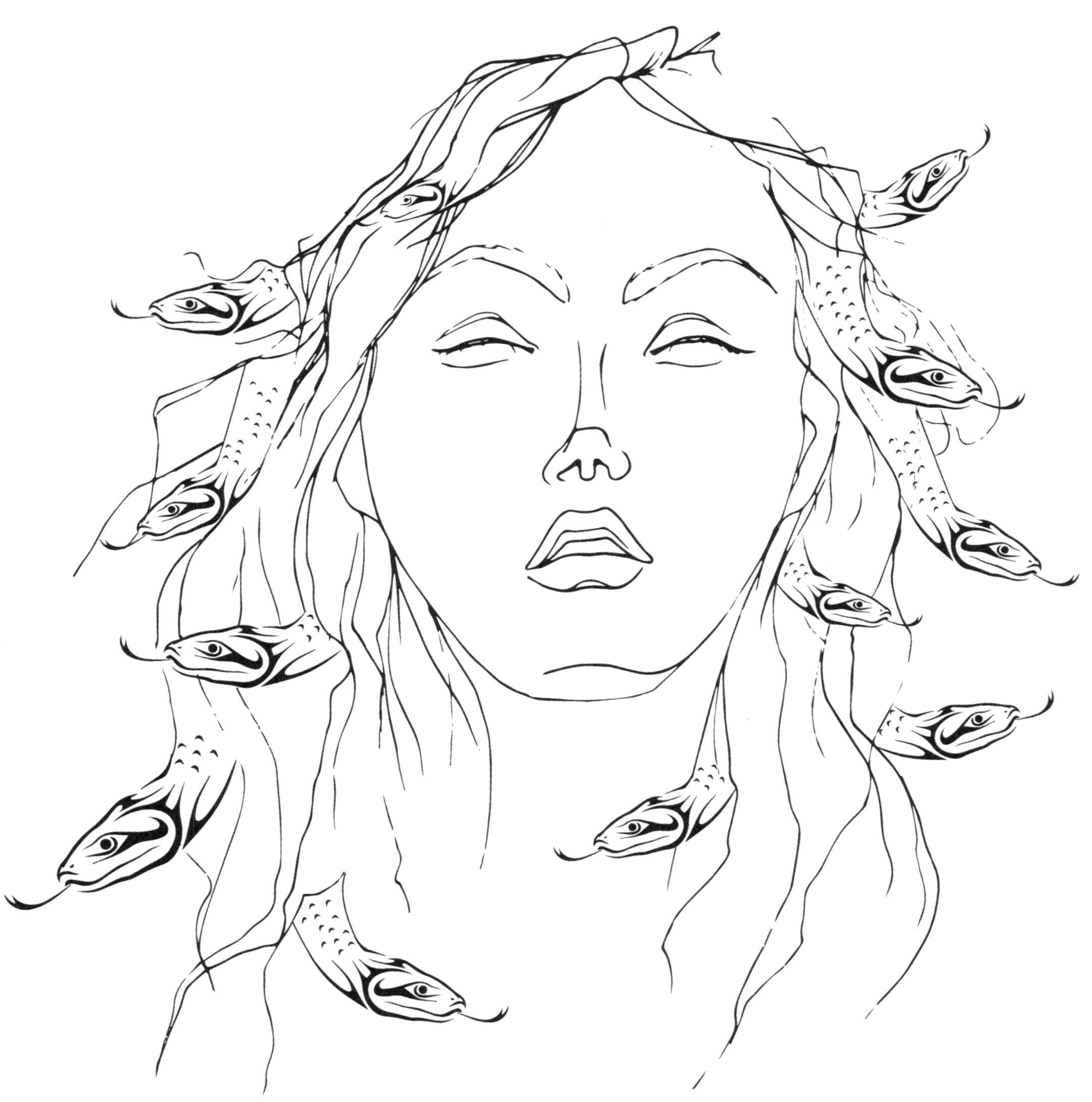

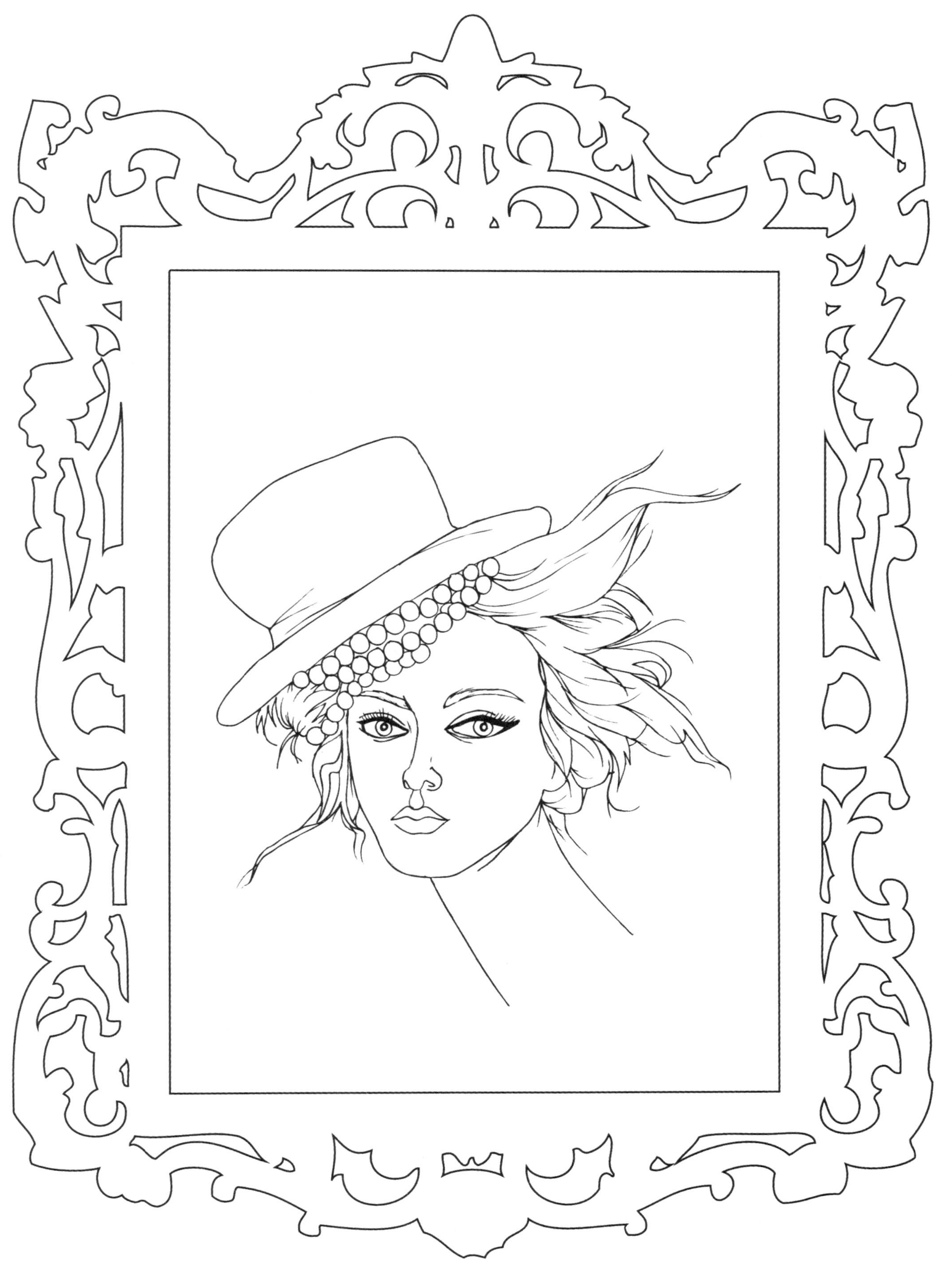

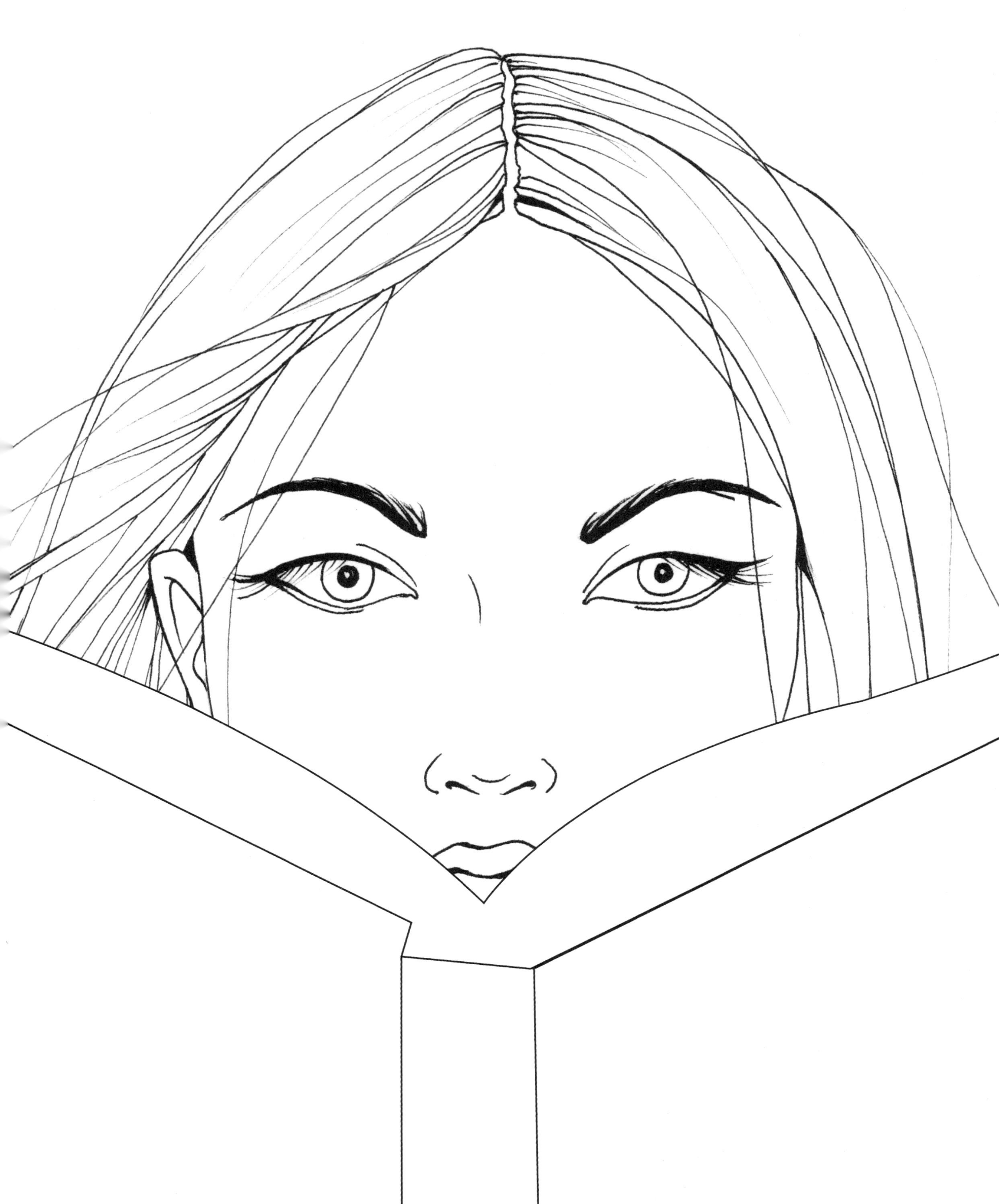

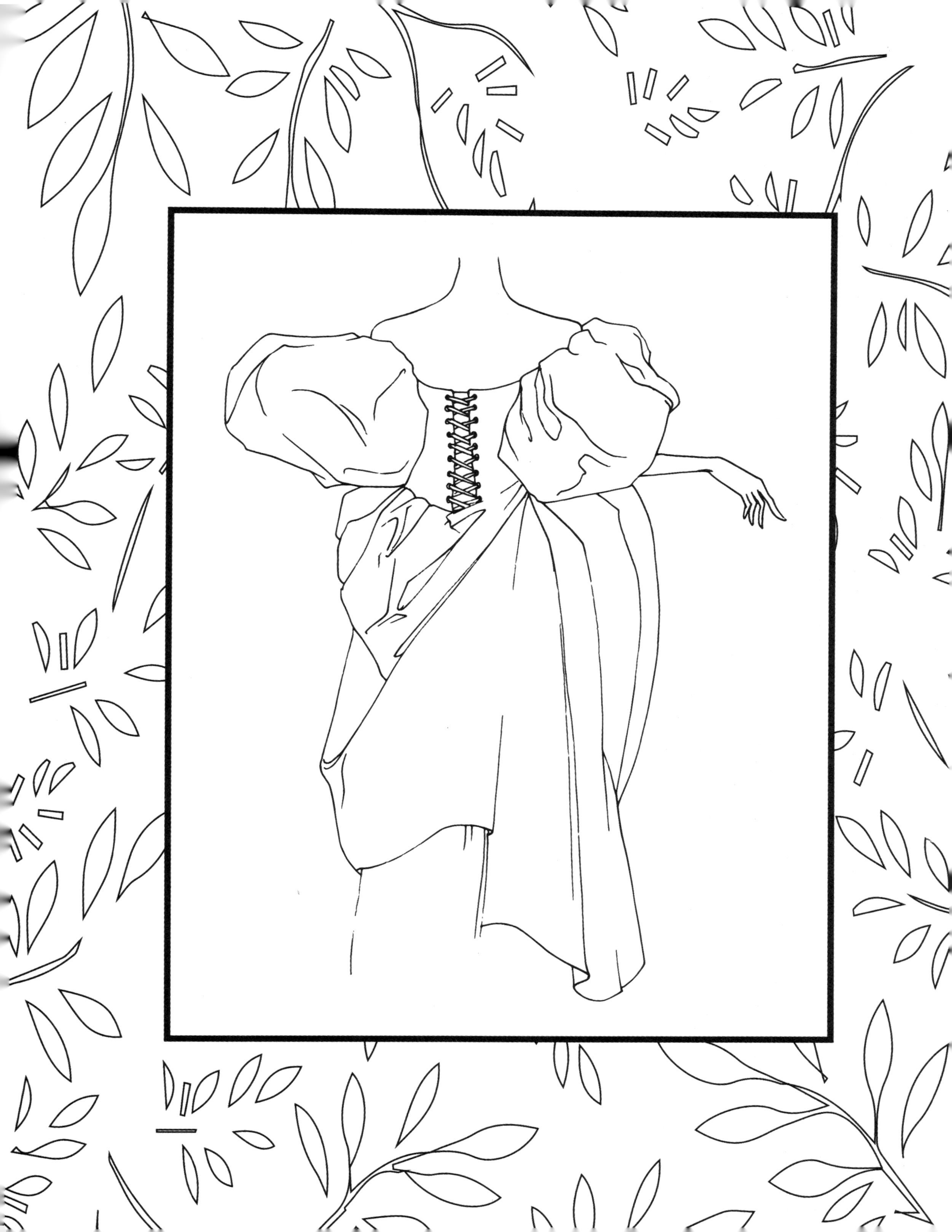

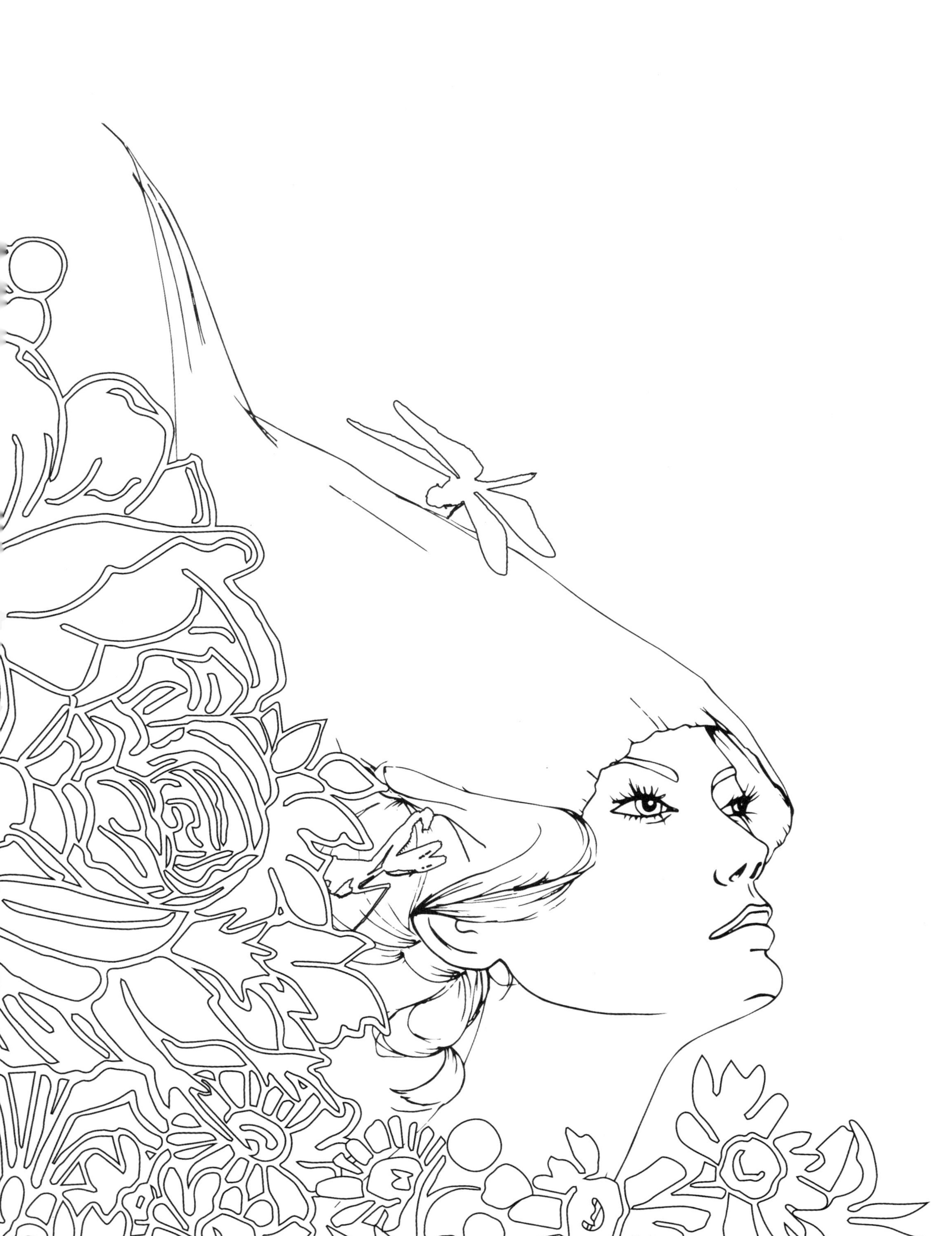

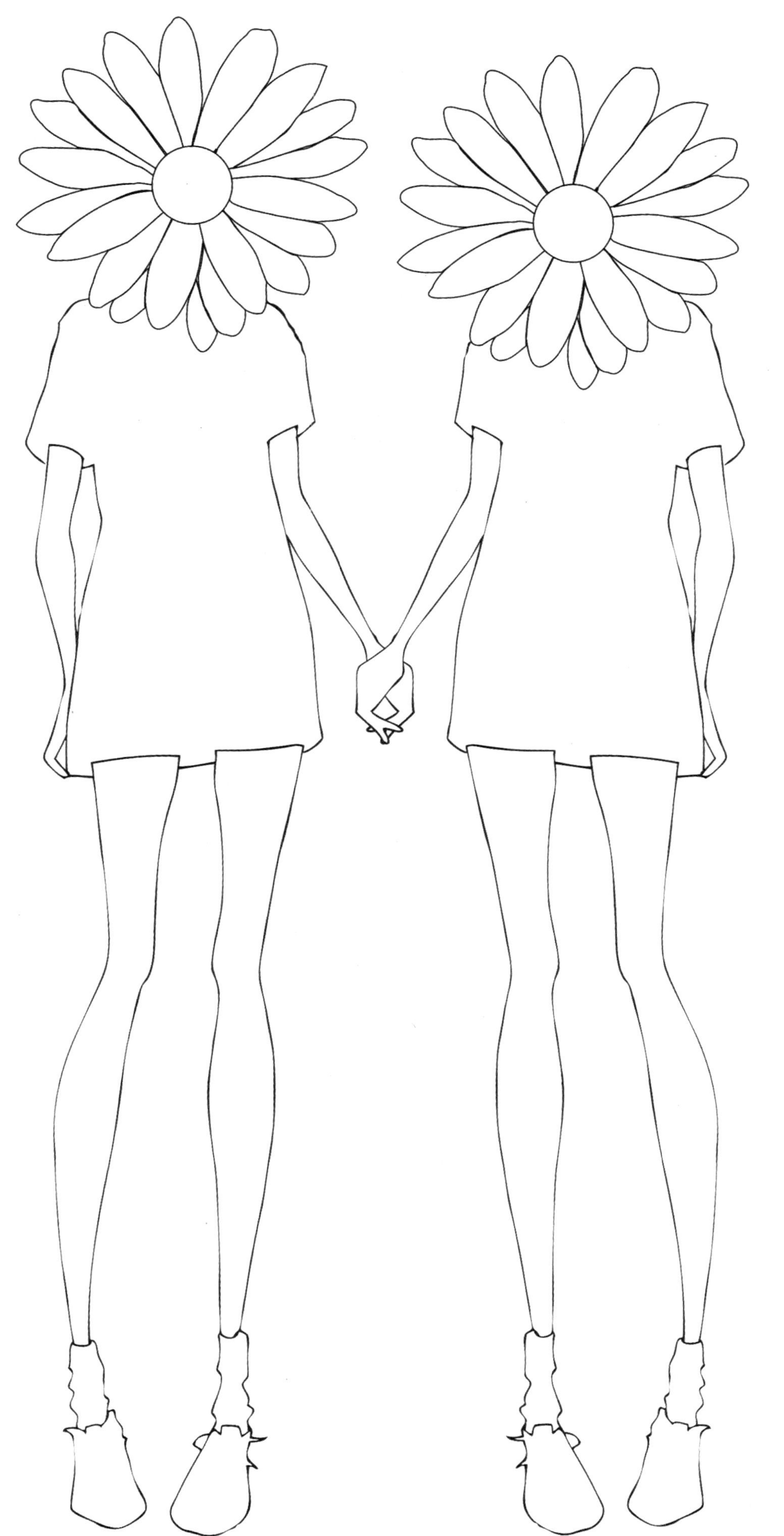

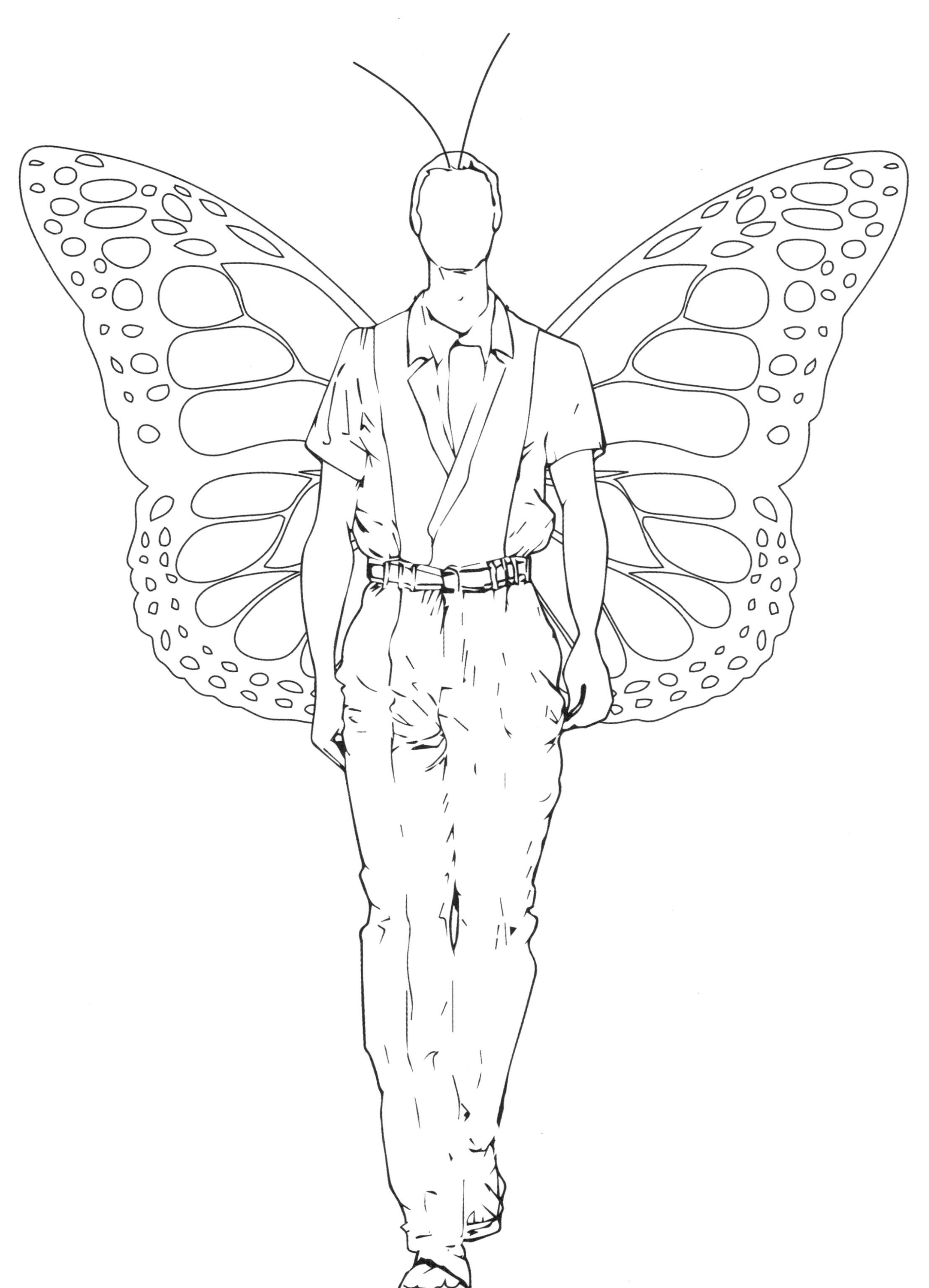

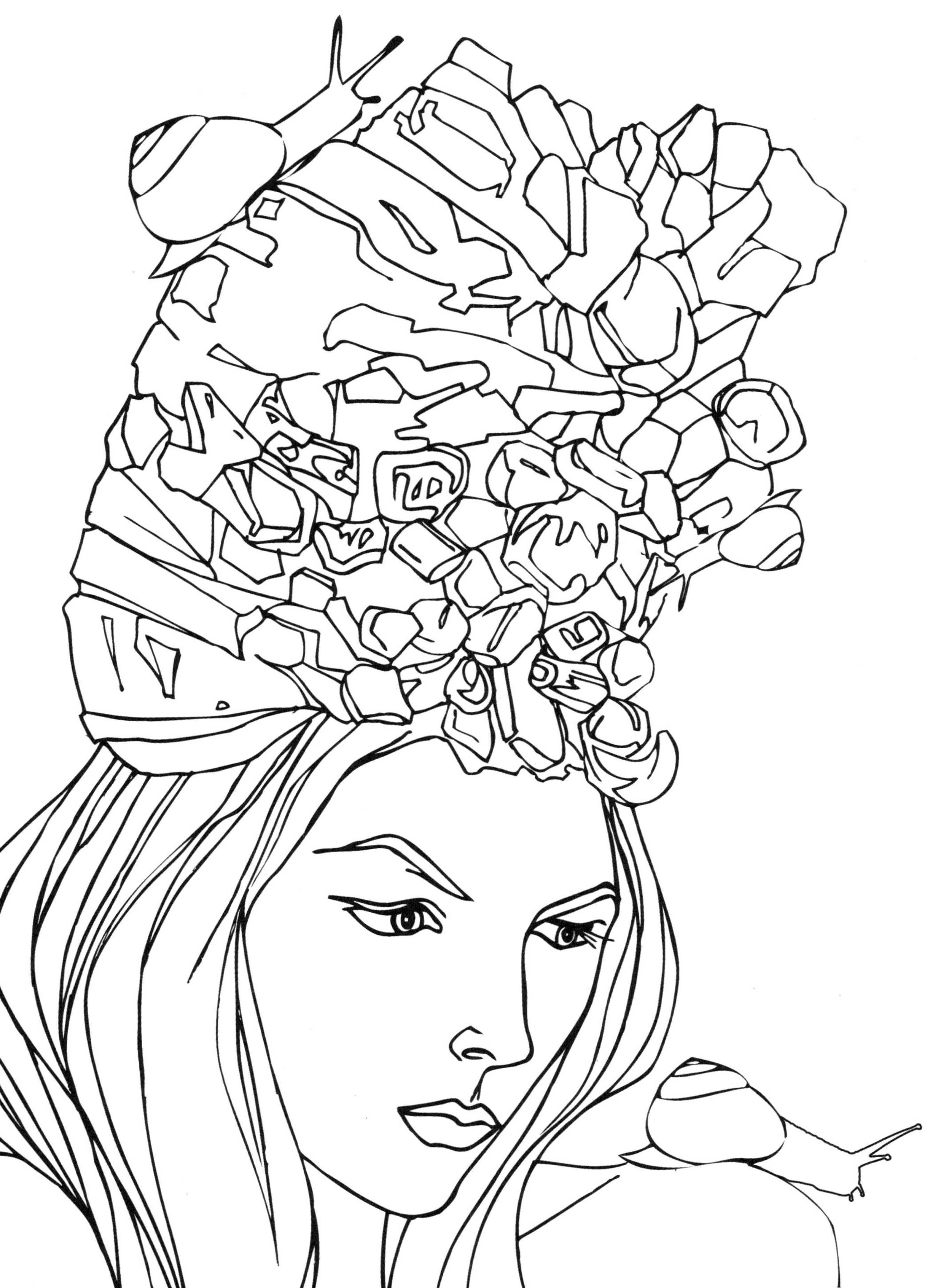

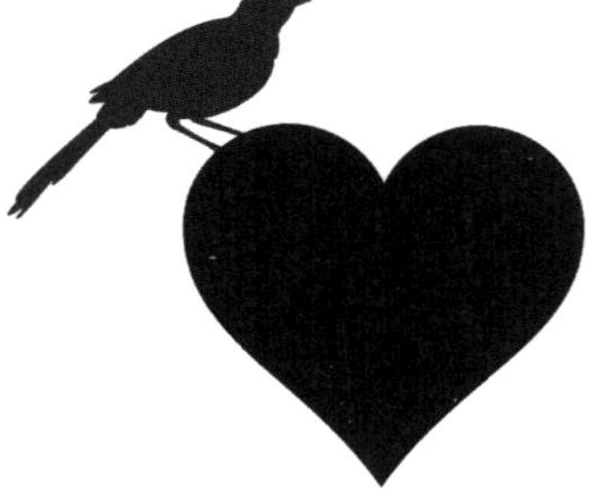

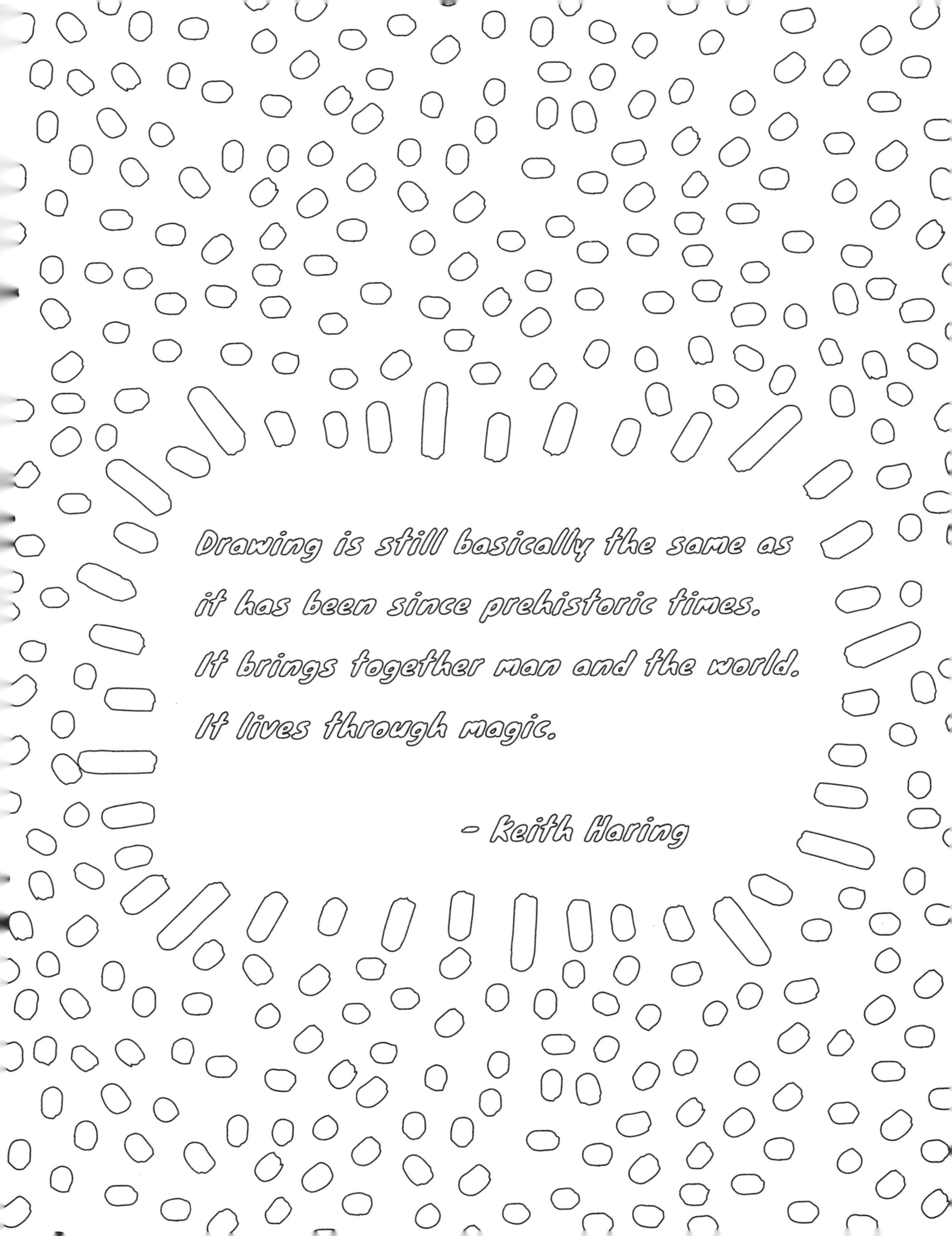

Drawing is still basically the same as
it has been since prehistoric times.
It brings together man and the world.
It lives through magic.

- Keith Haring

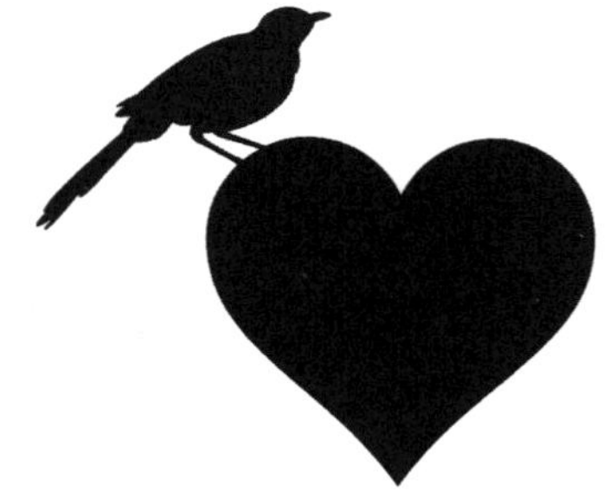

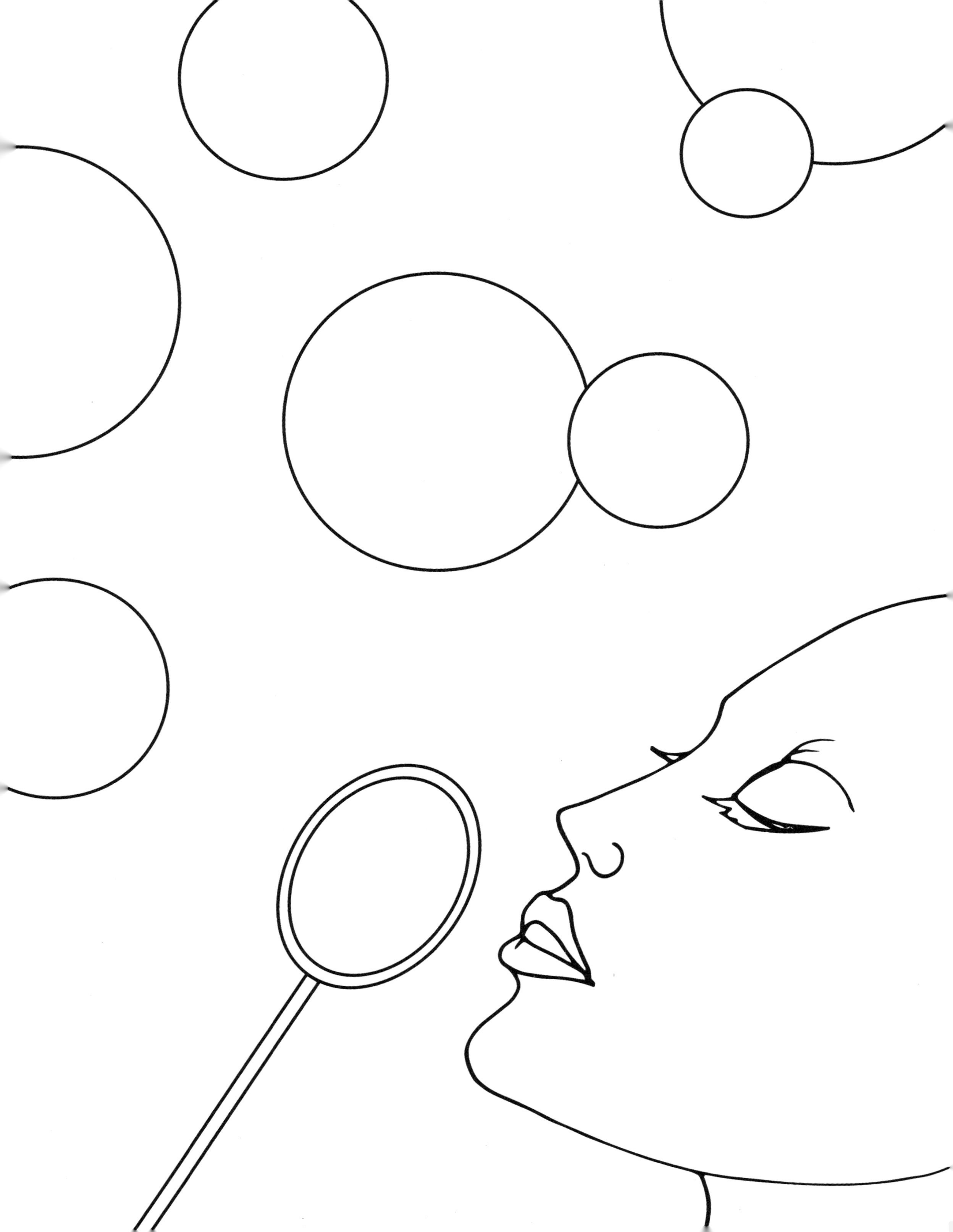

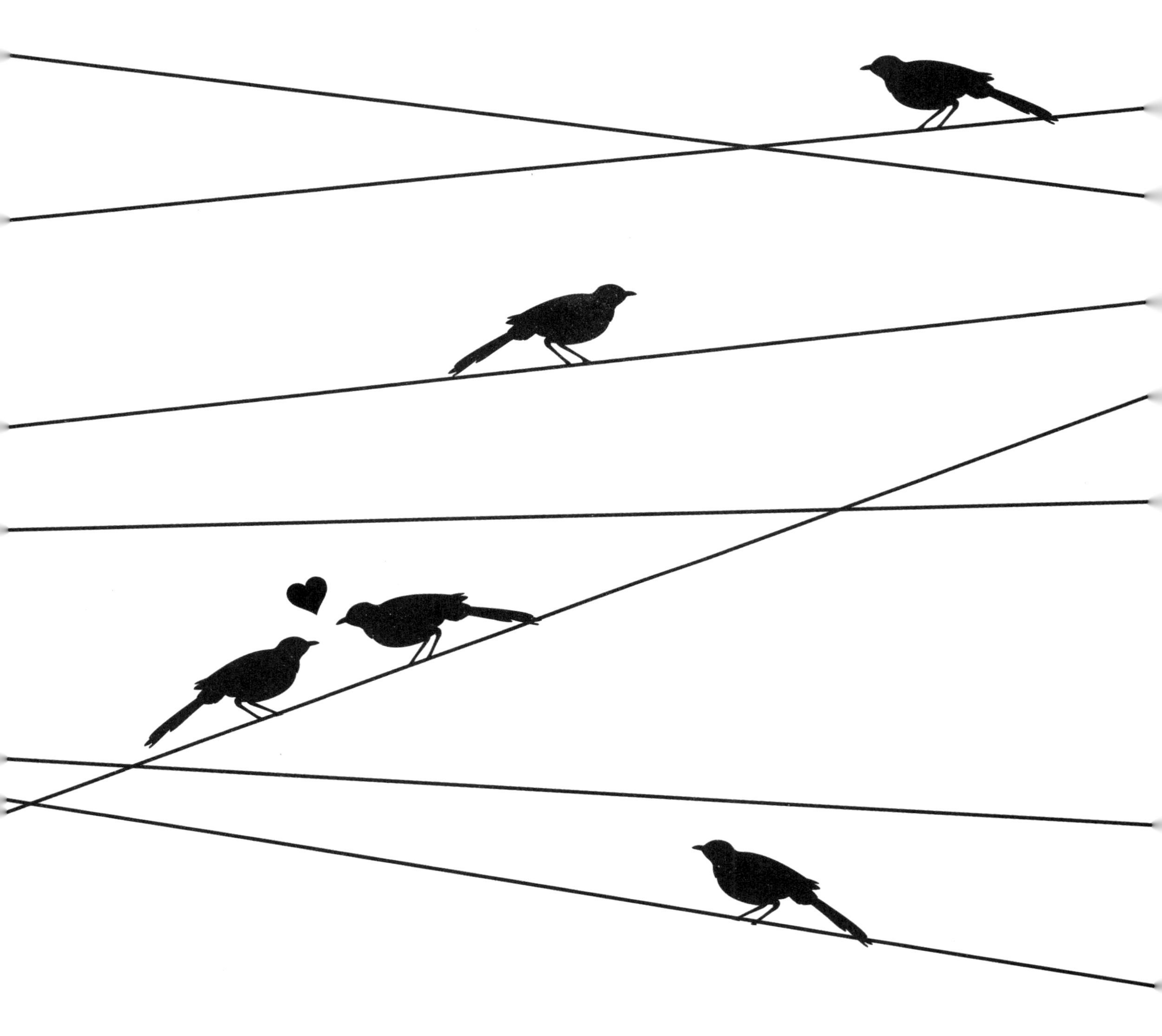

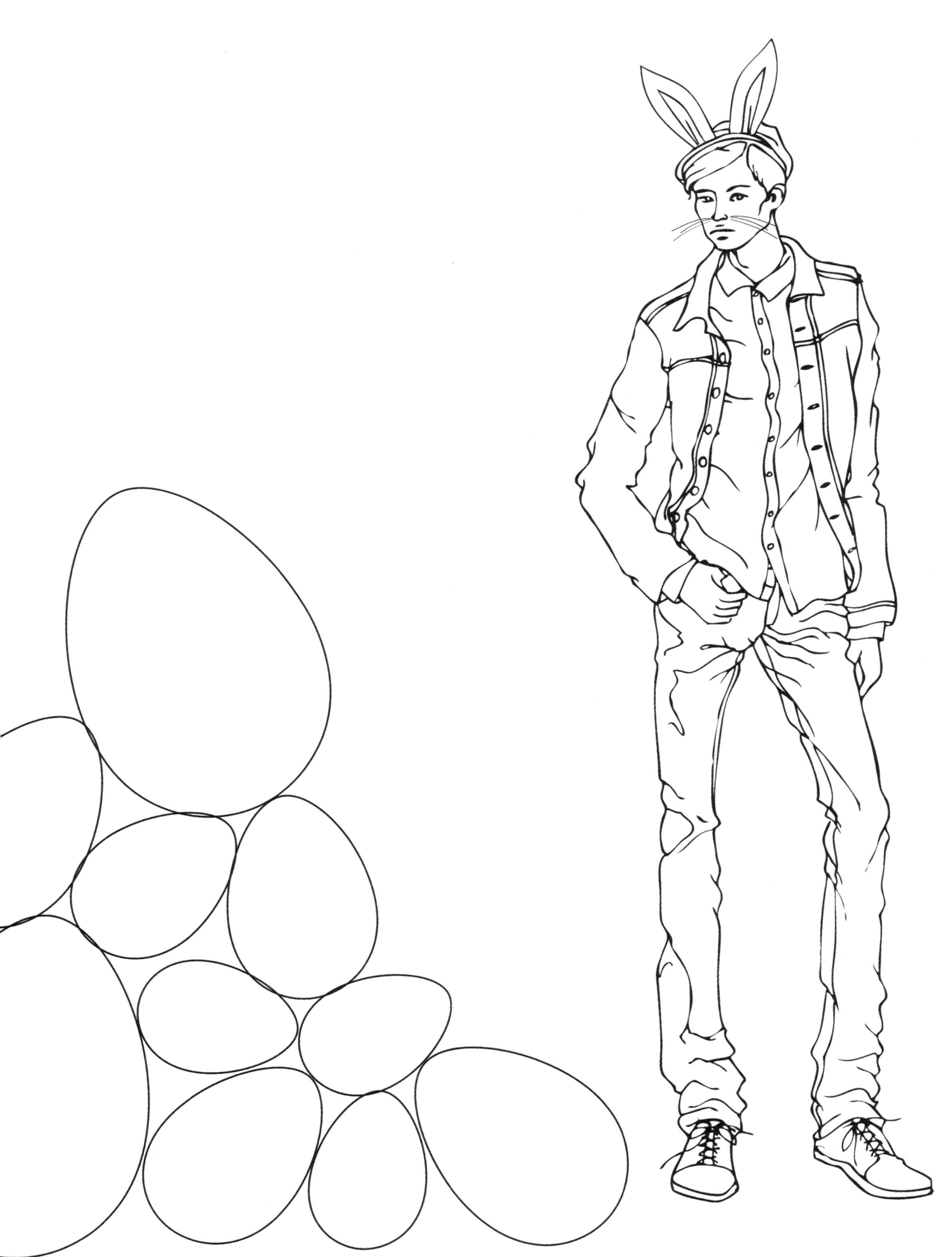

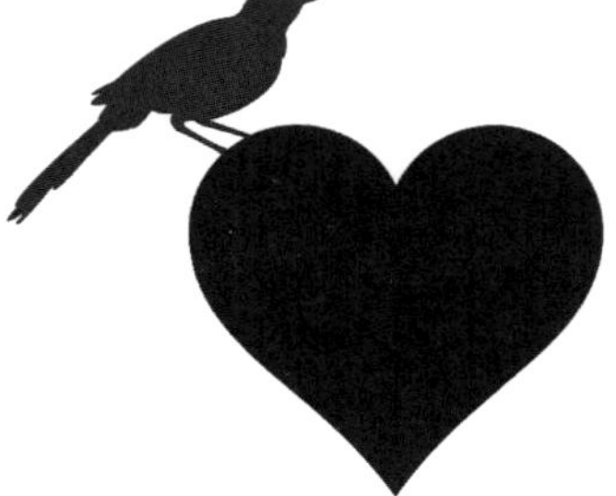

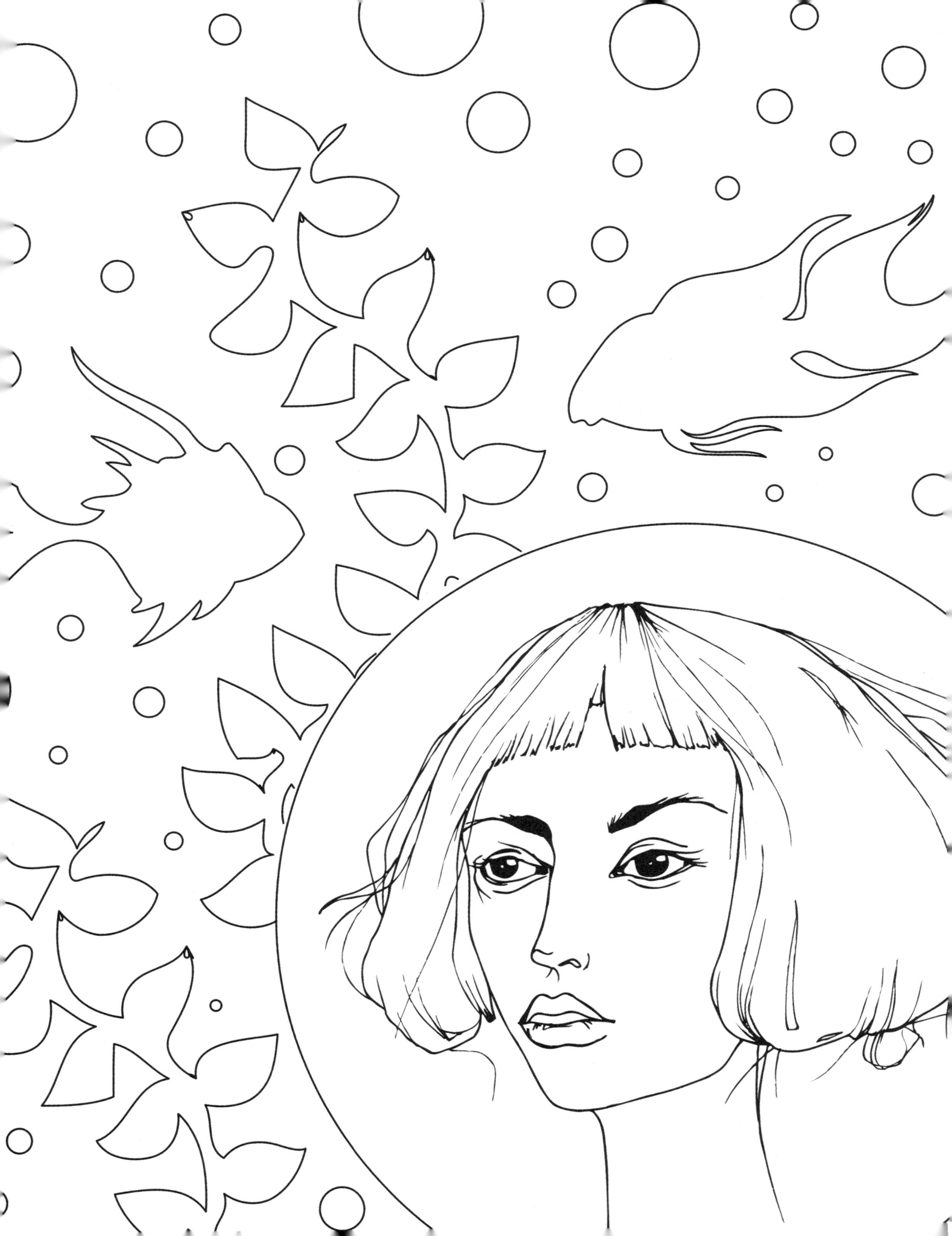

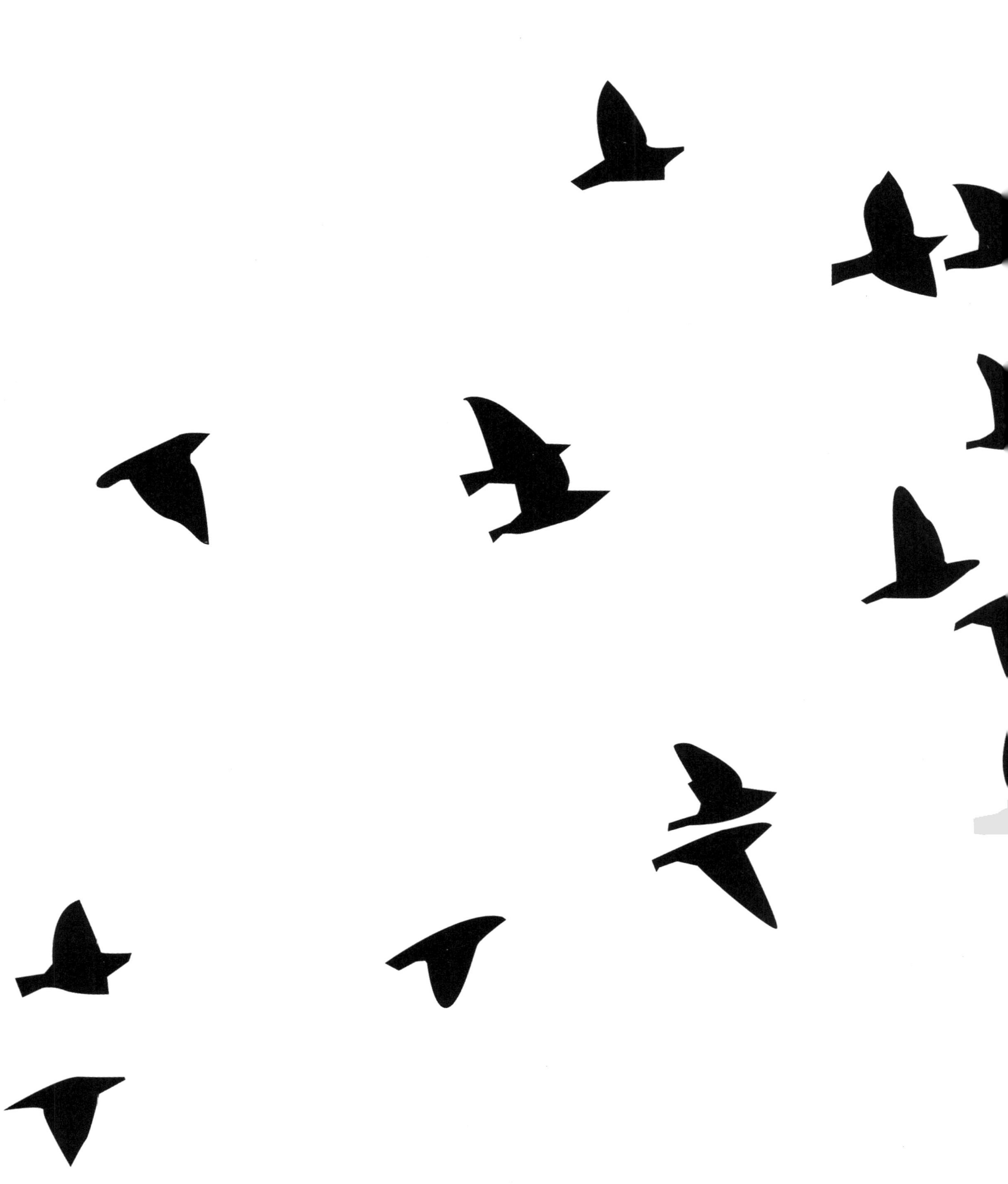

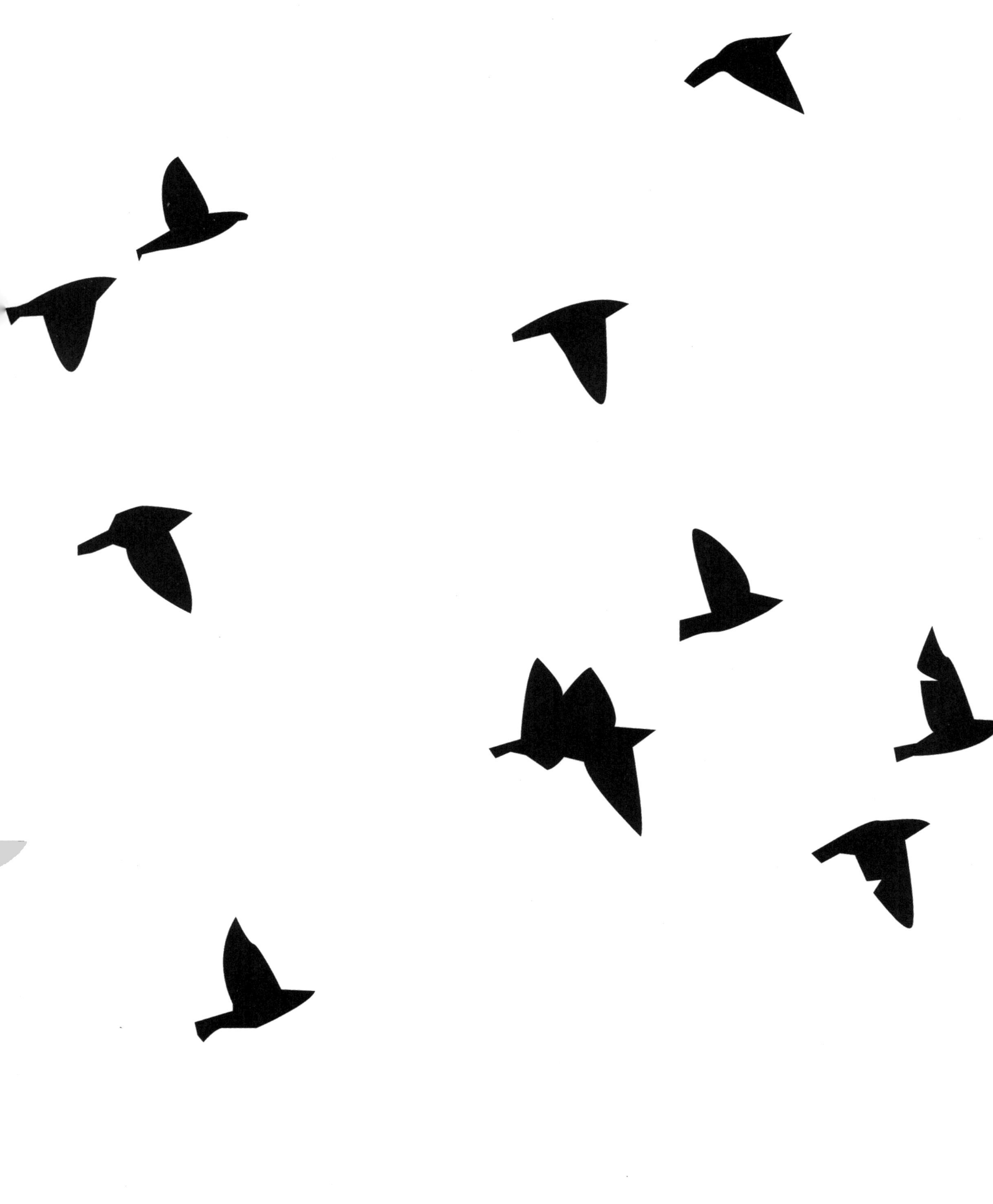

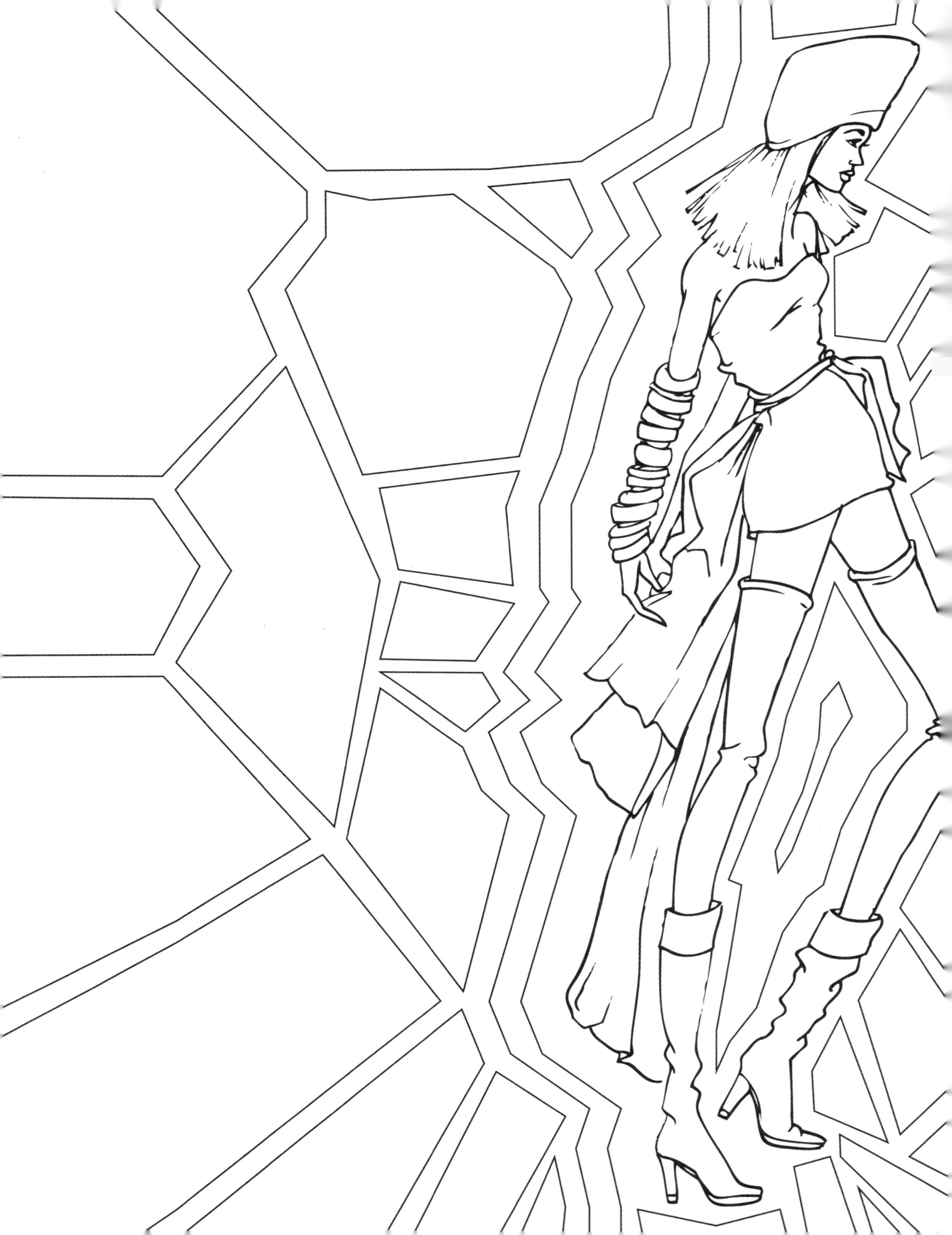

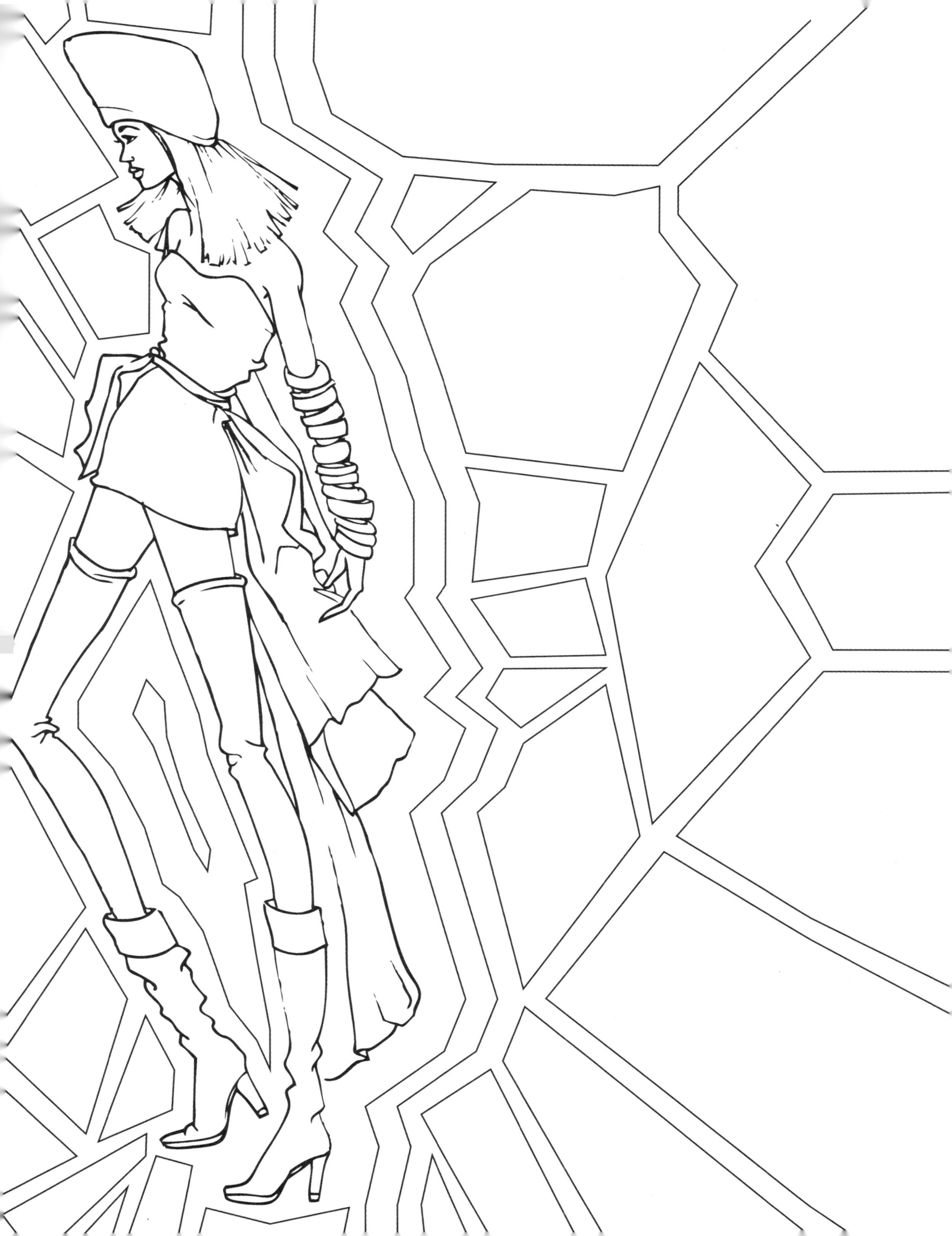

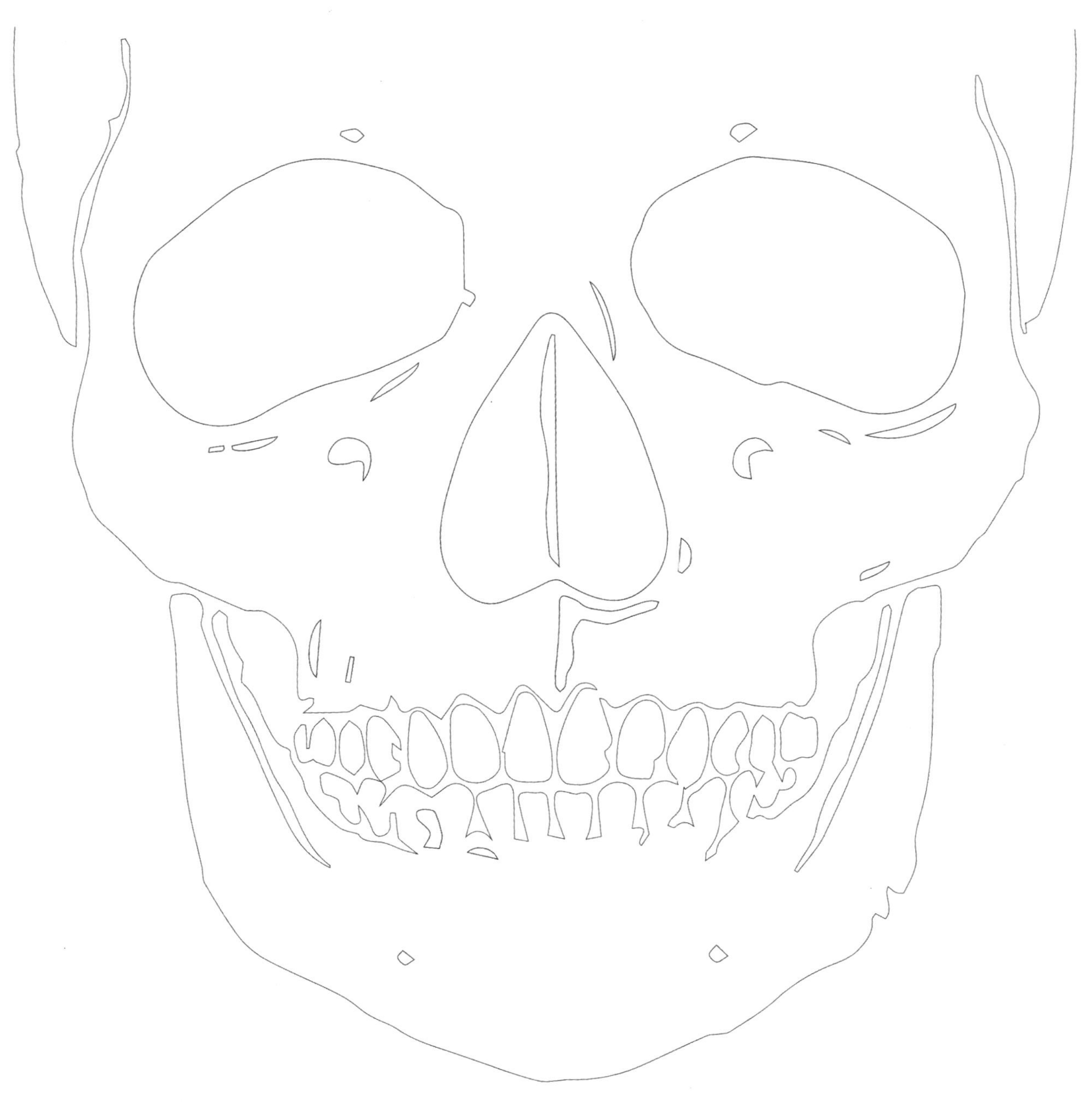

I was
three years old
when I started
drawing. I did it all my
life. - Alexander McQueen

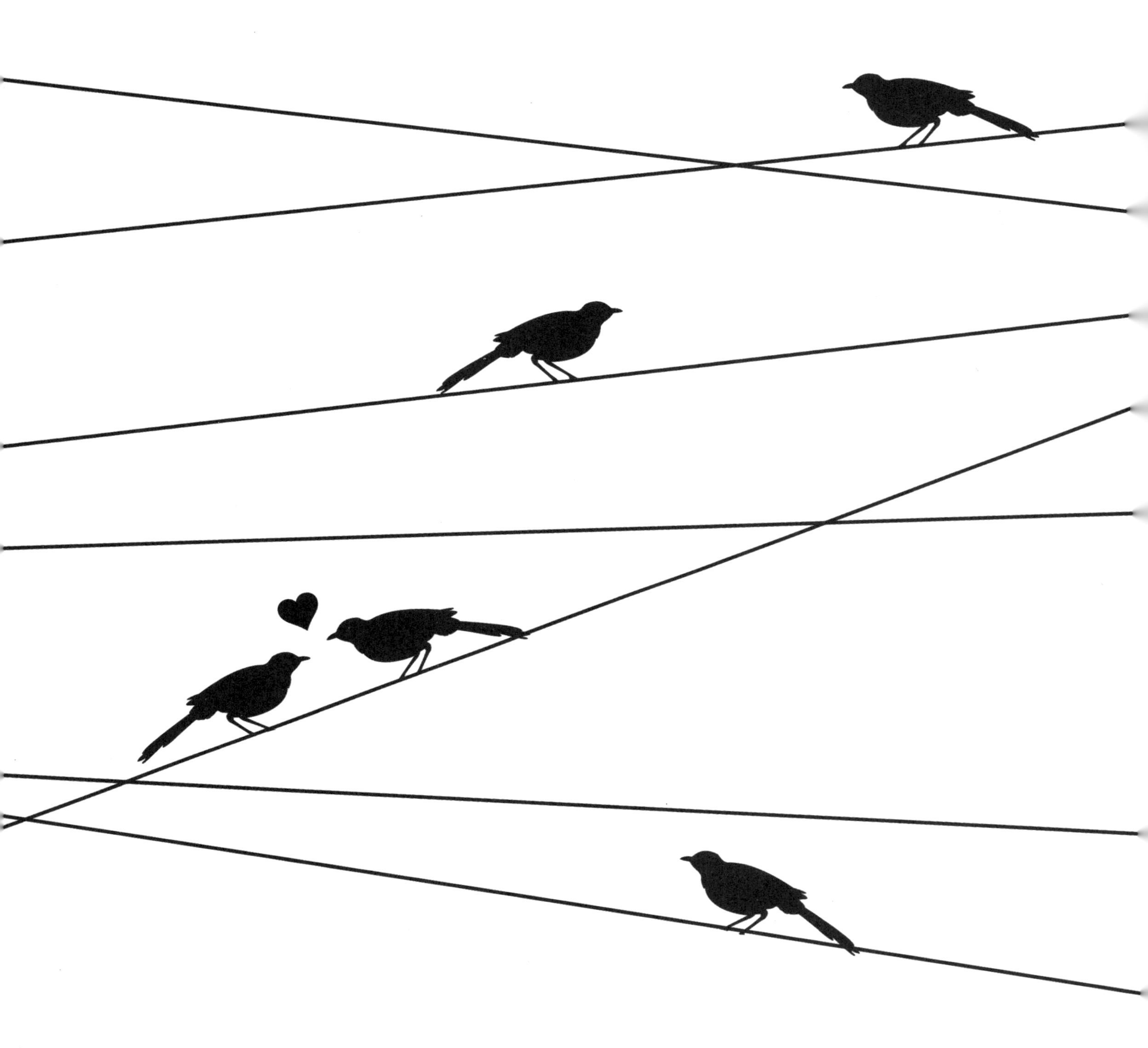

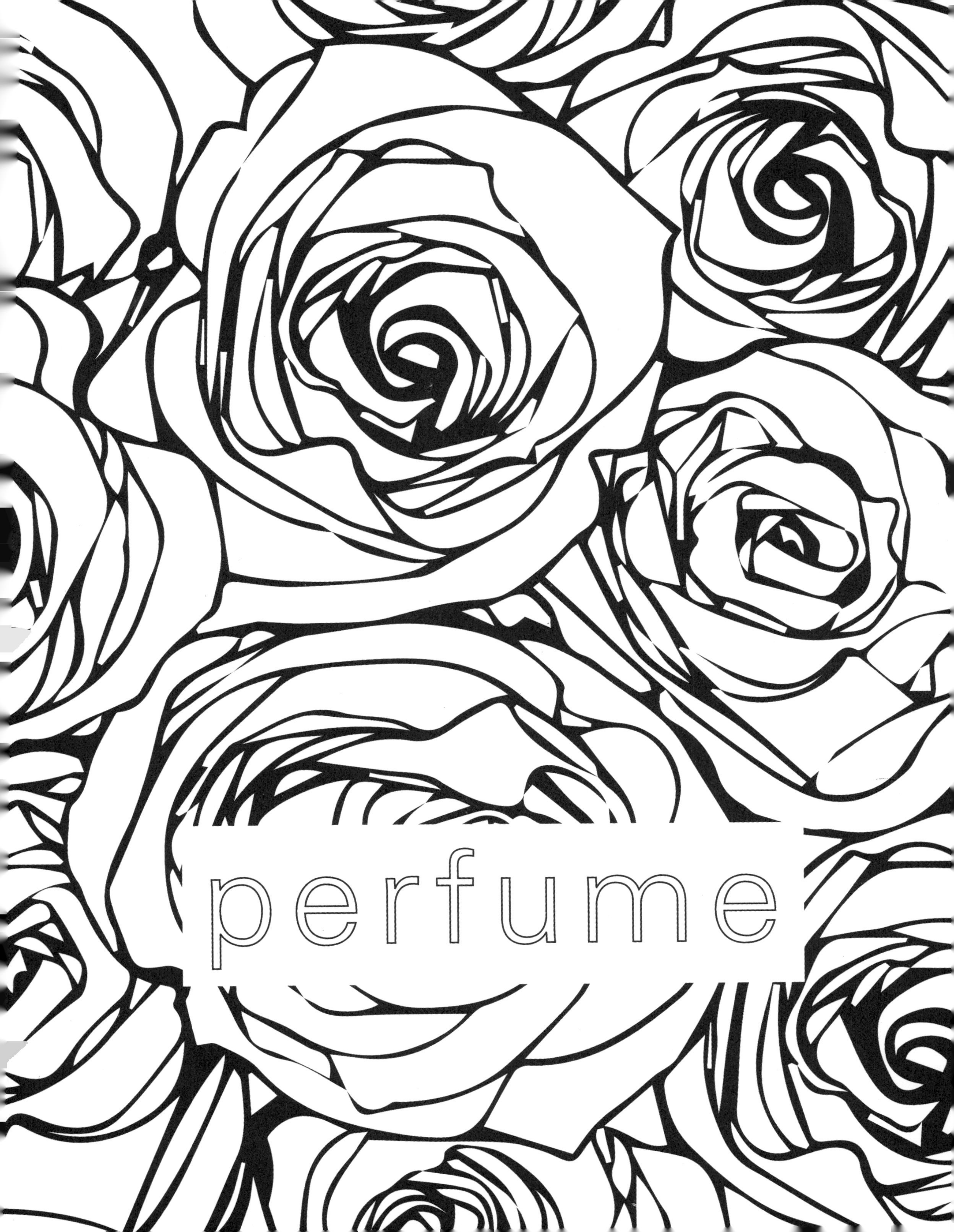
perfume

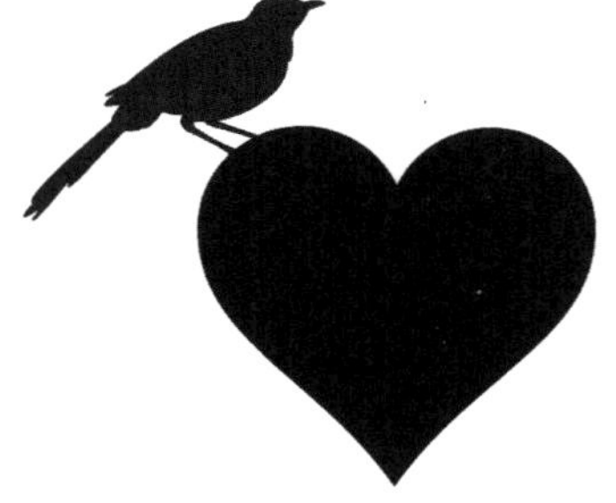

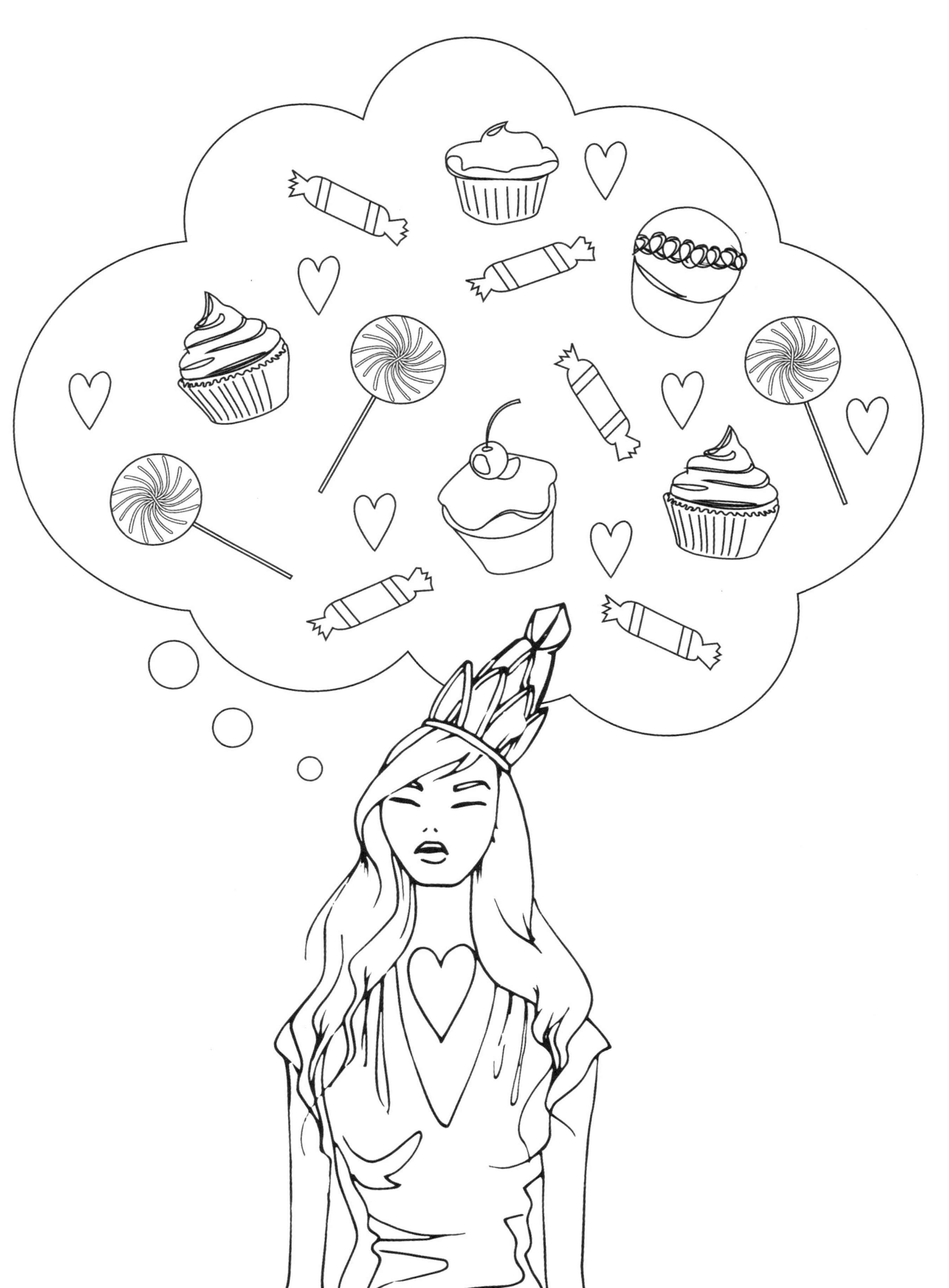

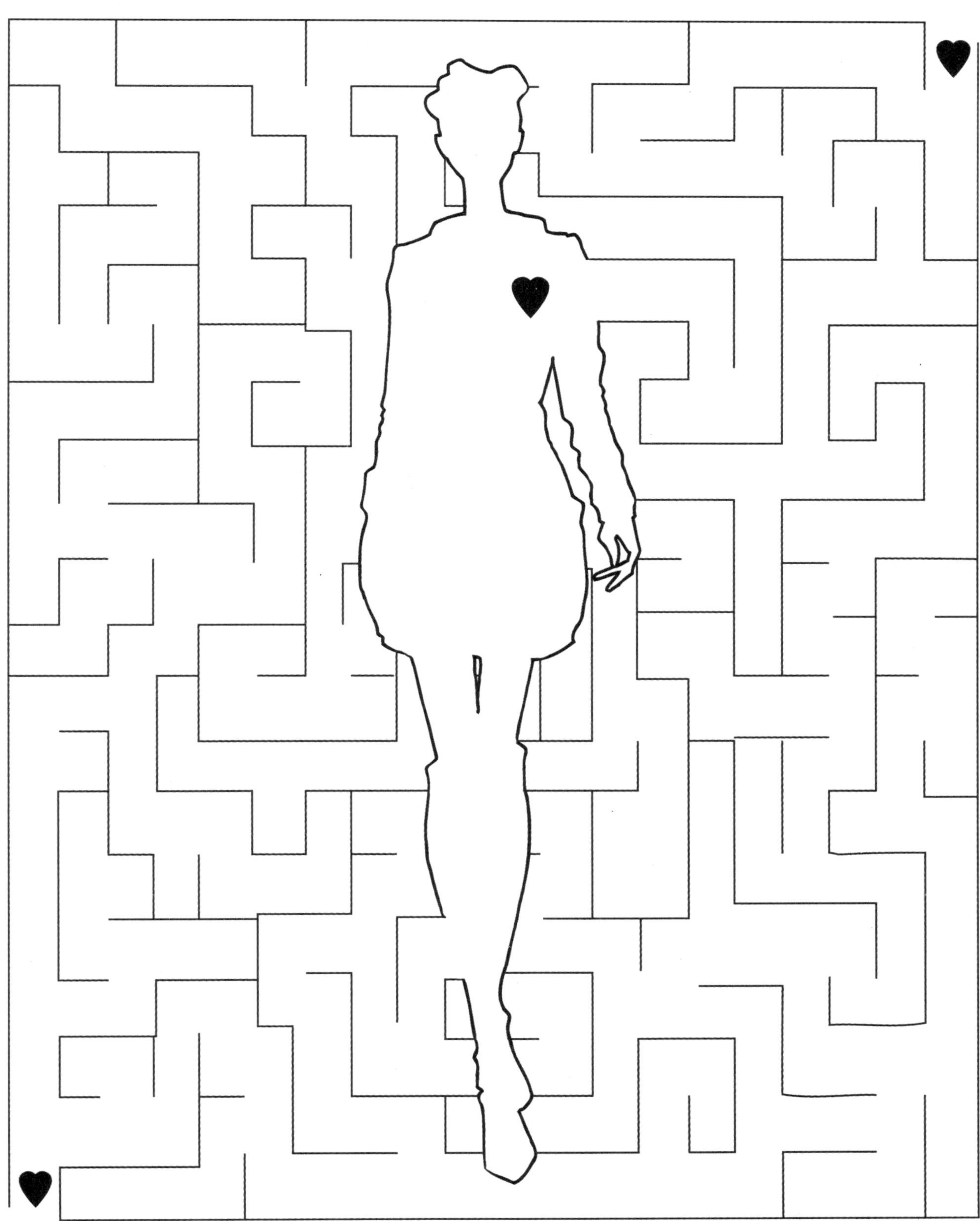

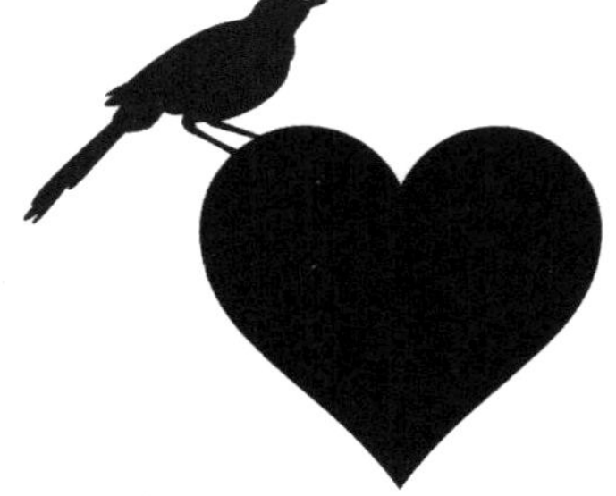

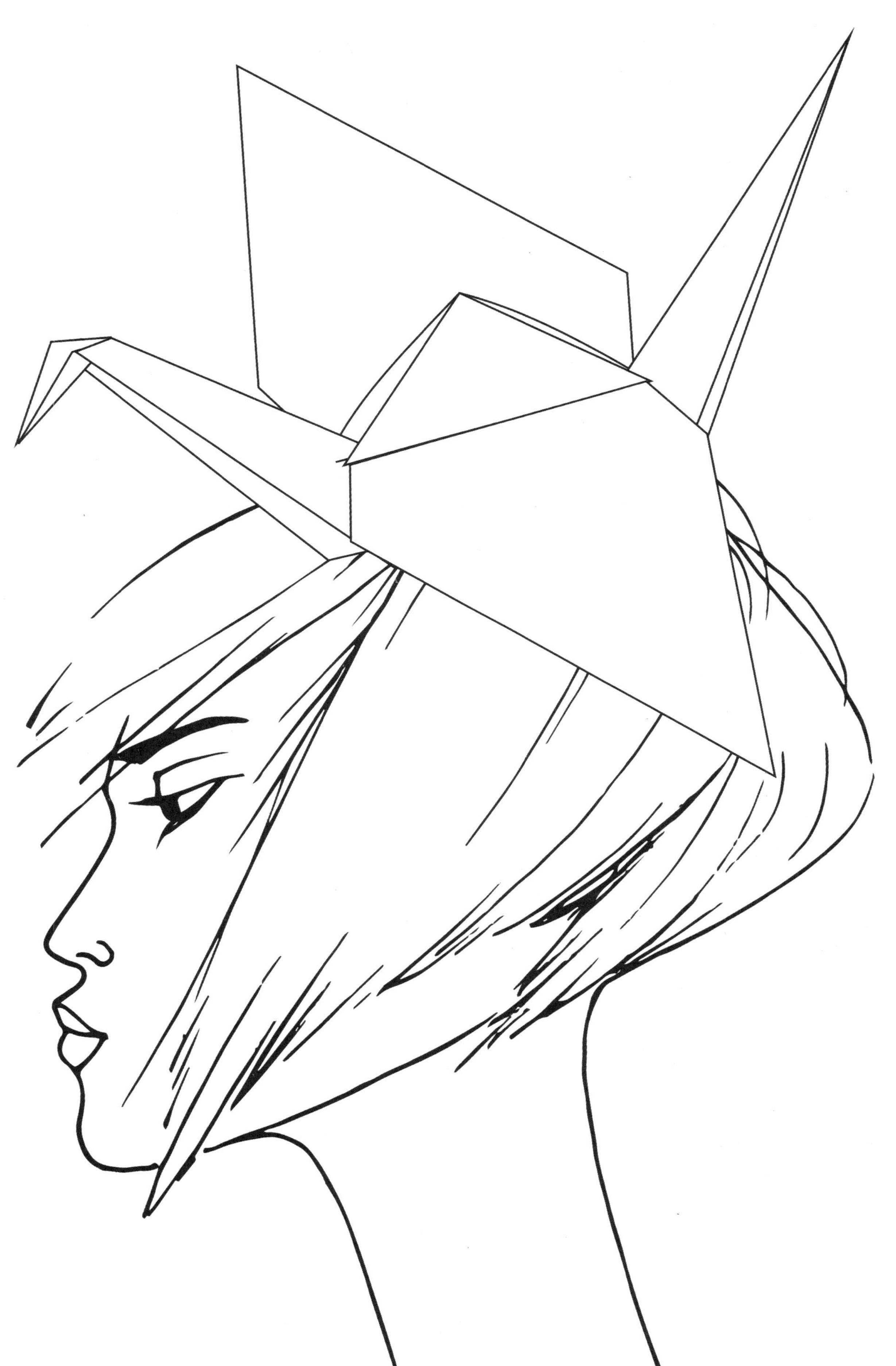

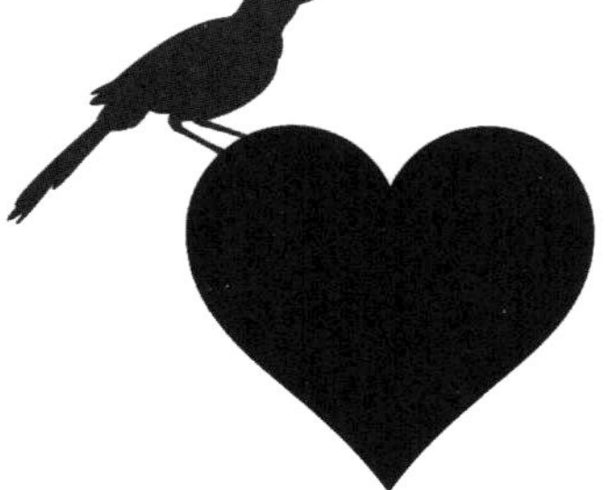

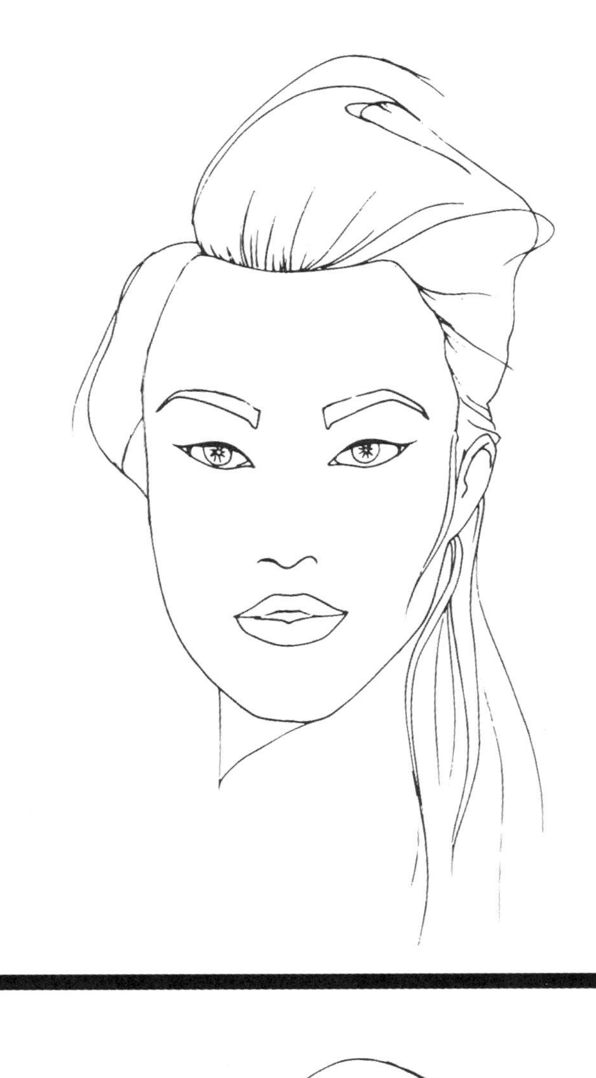
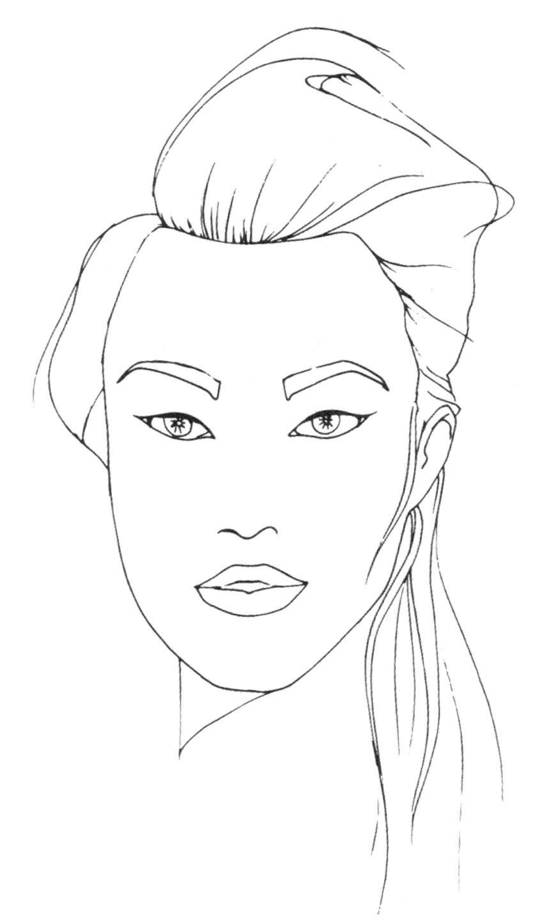
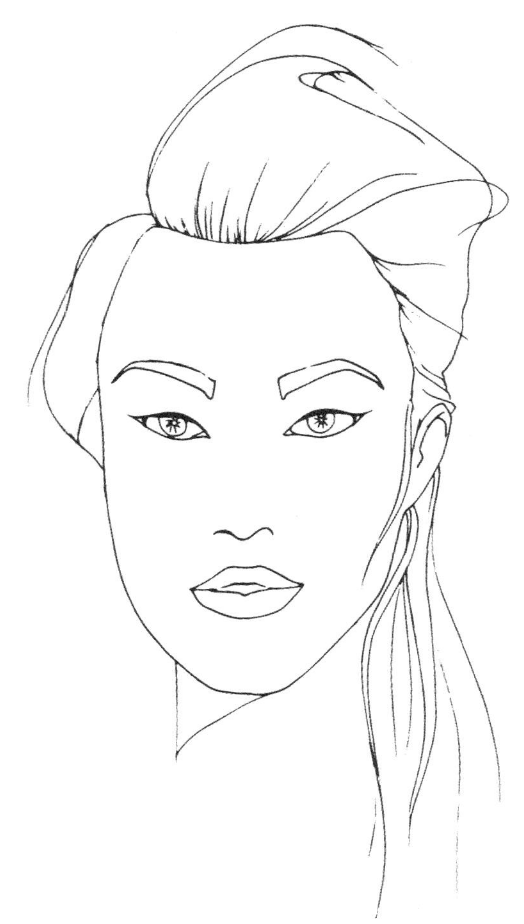
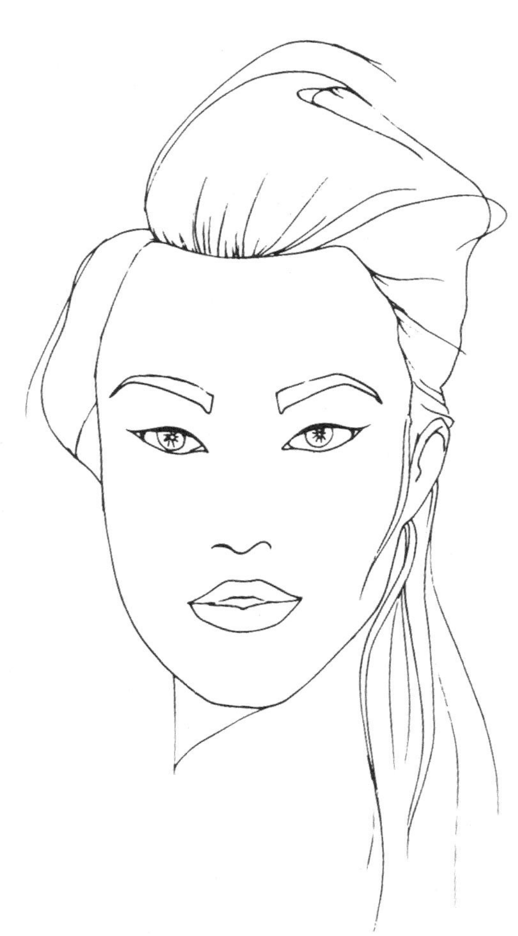

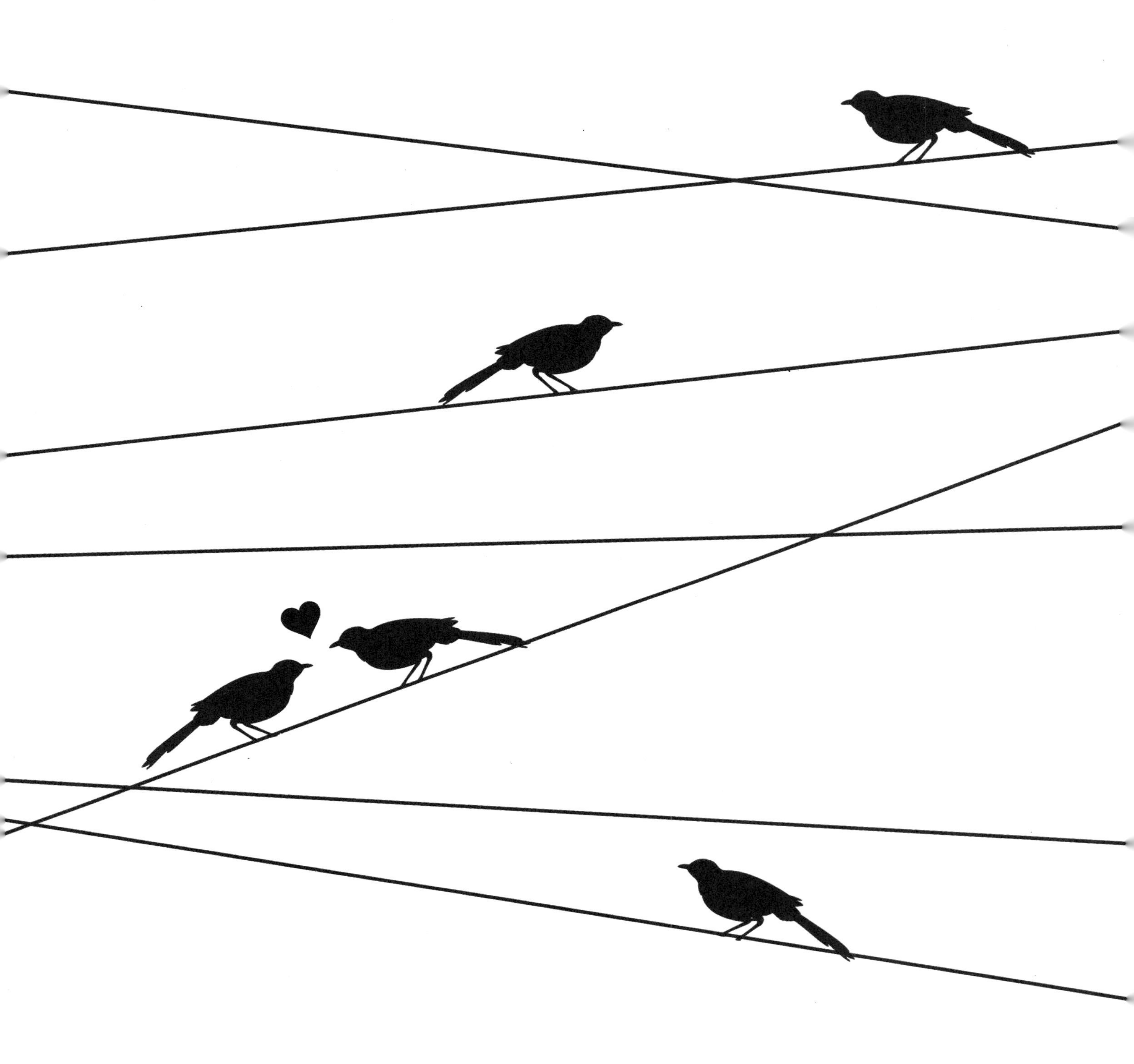

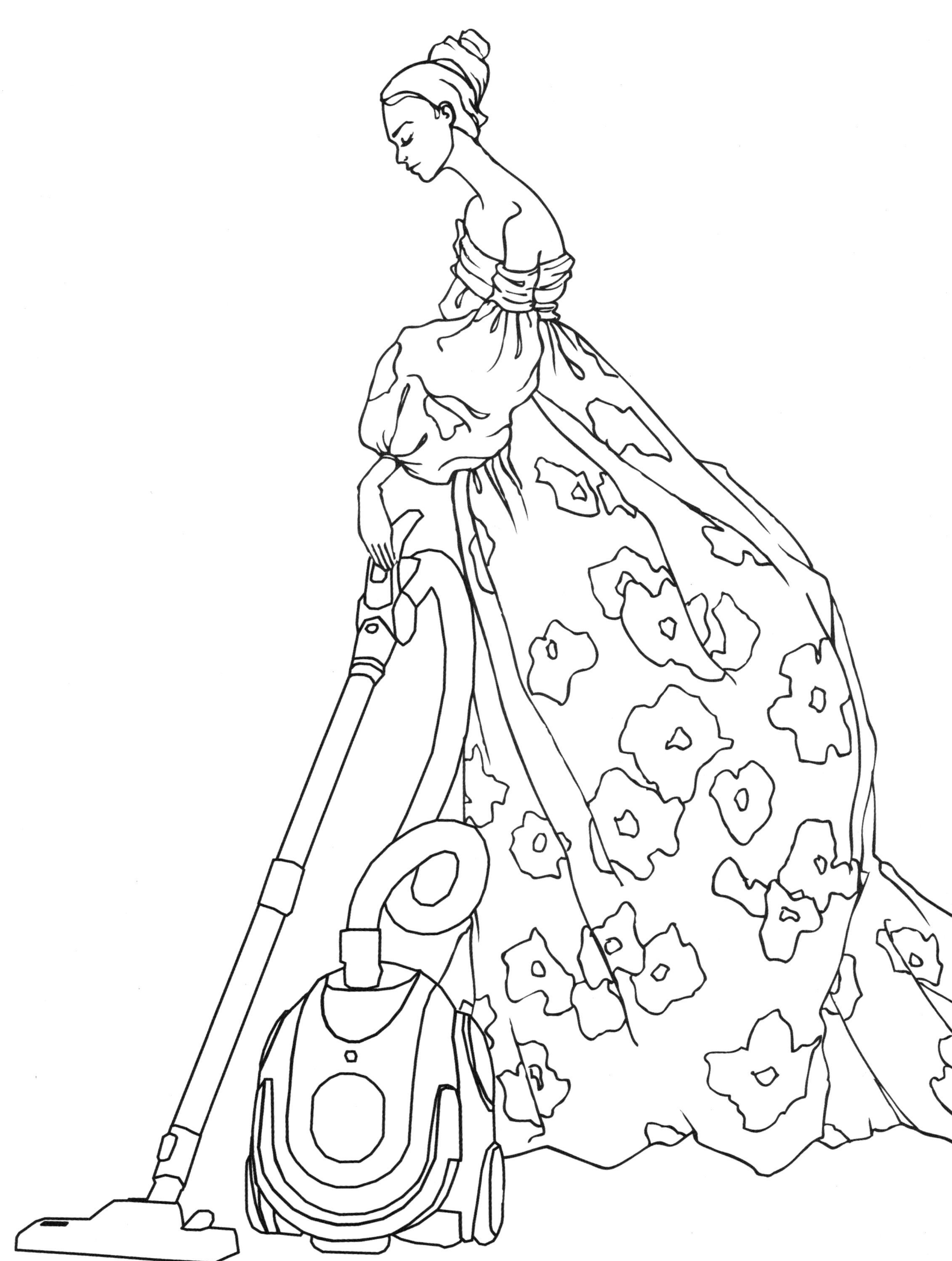

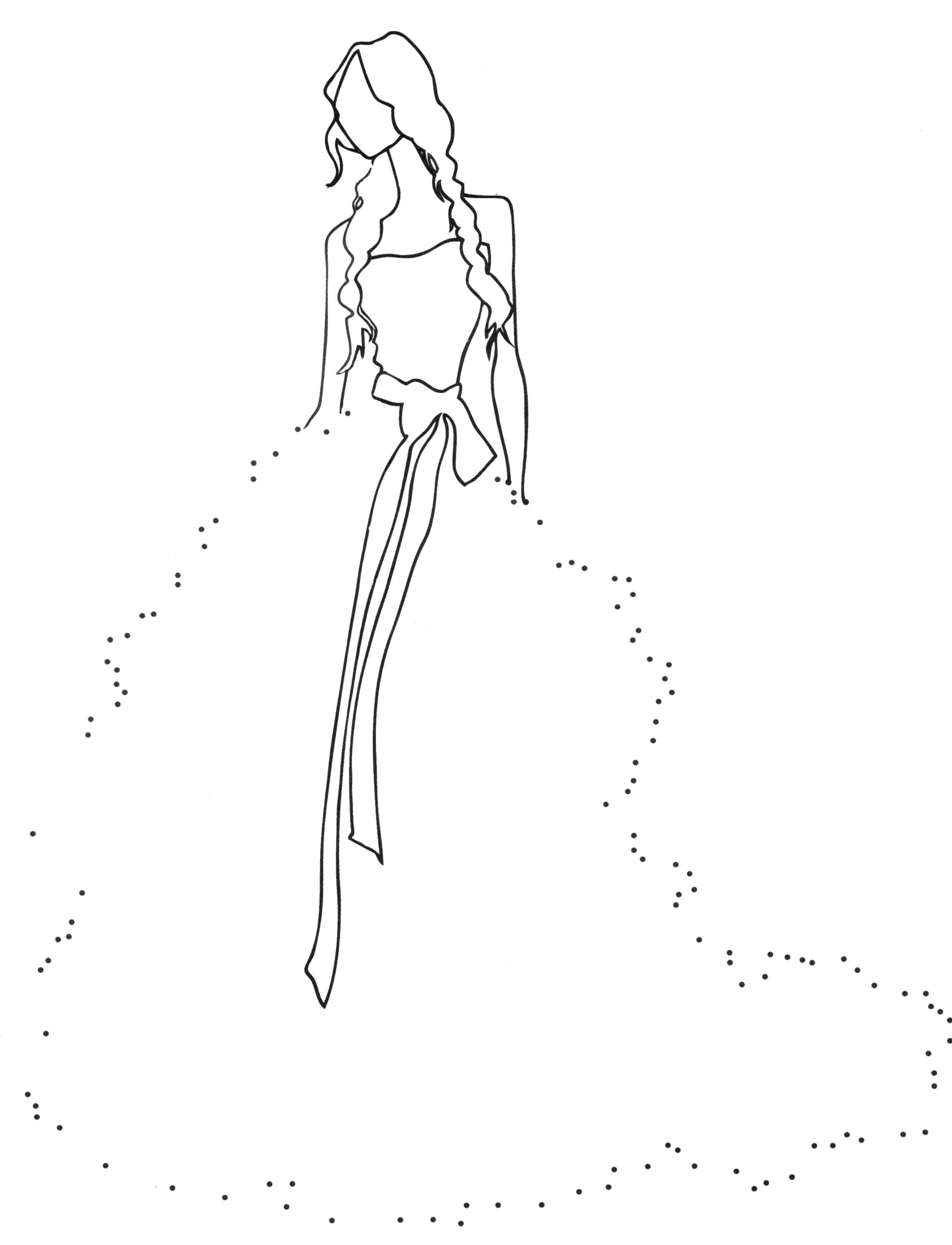

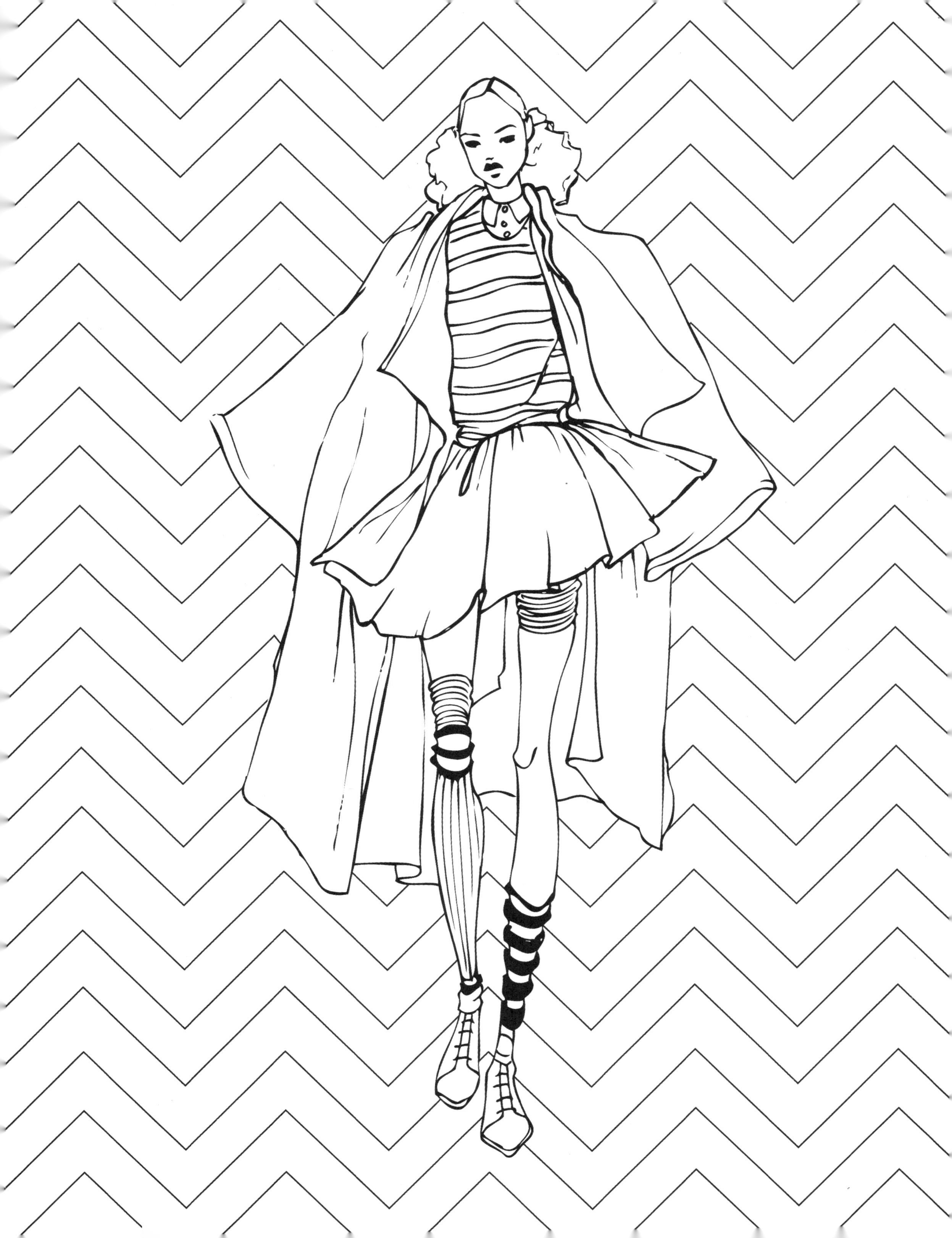

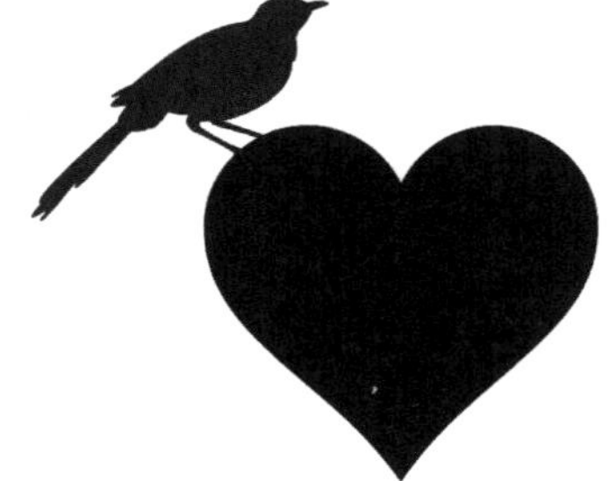

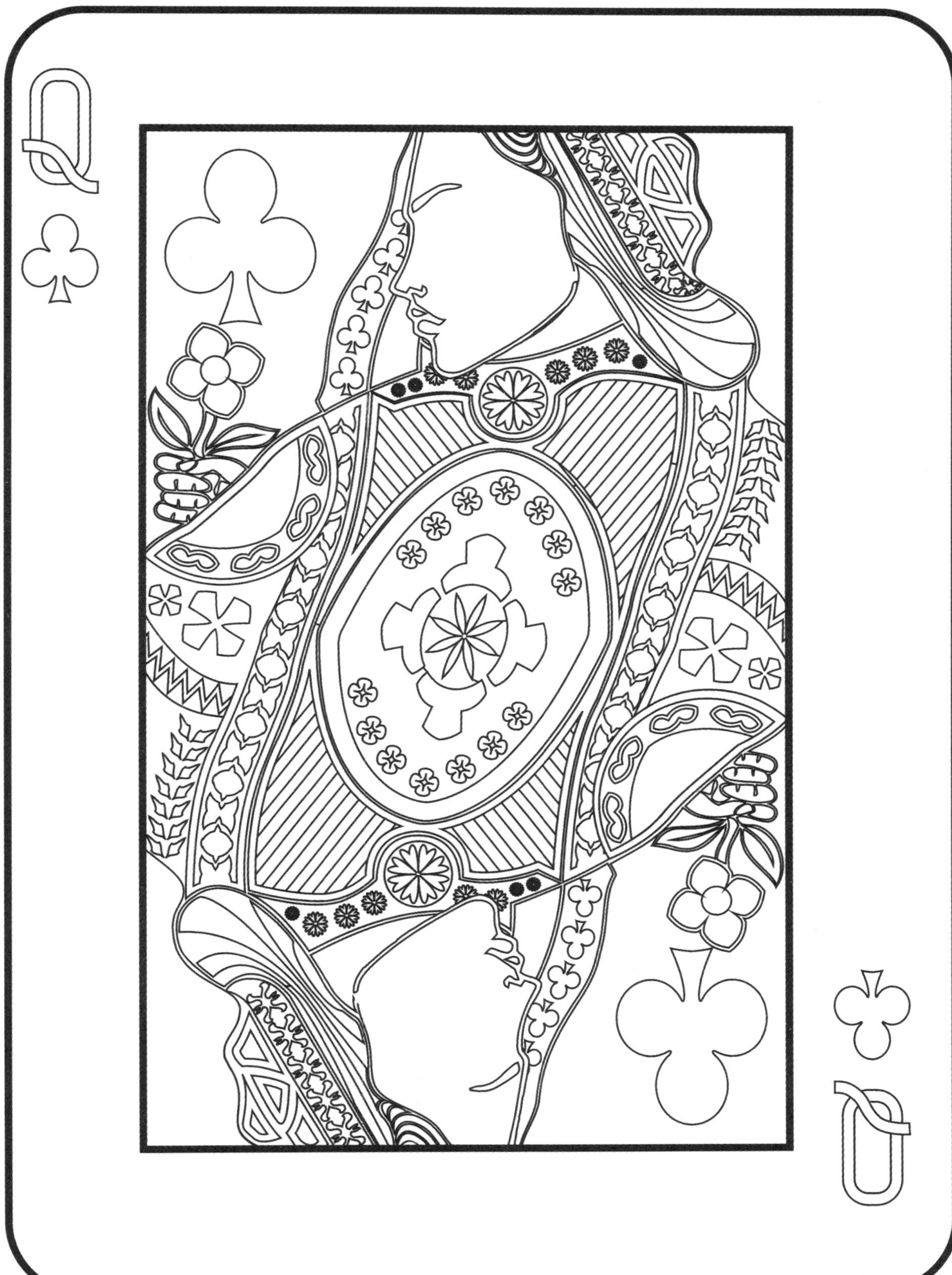

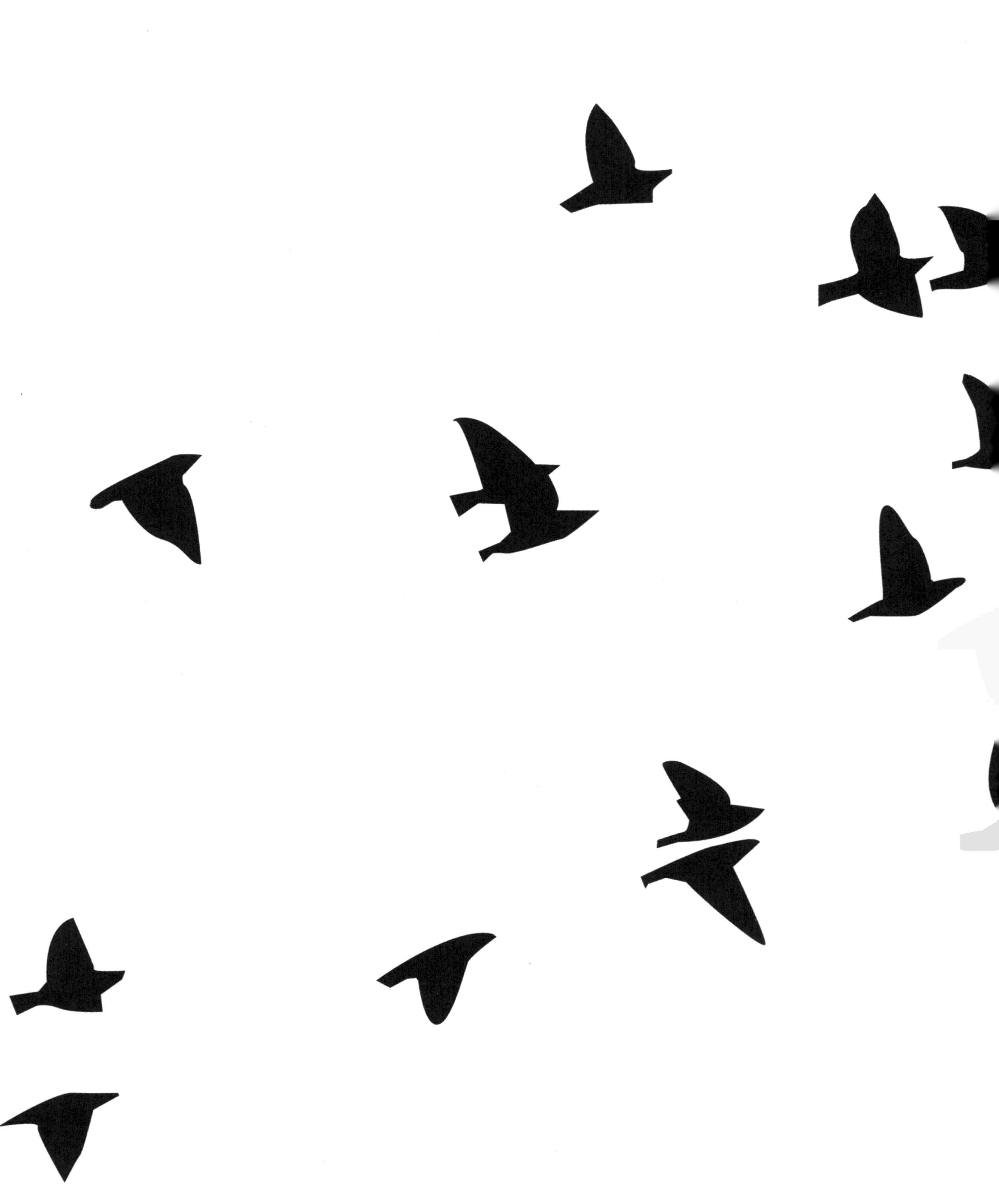

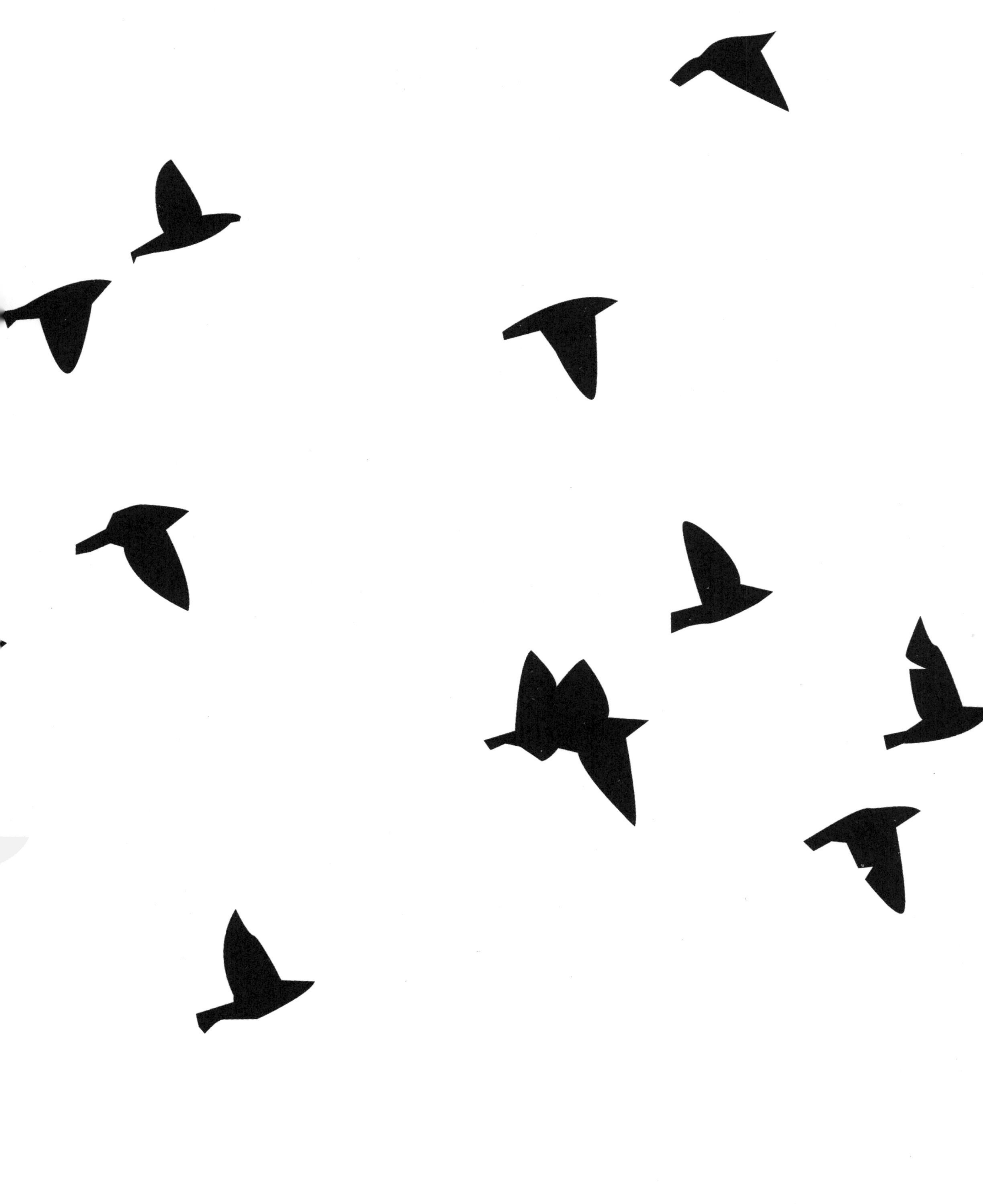

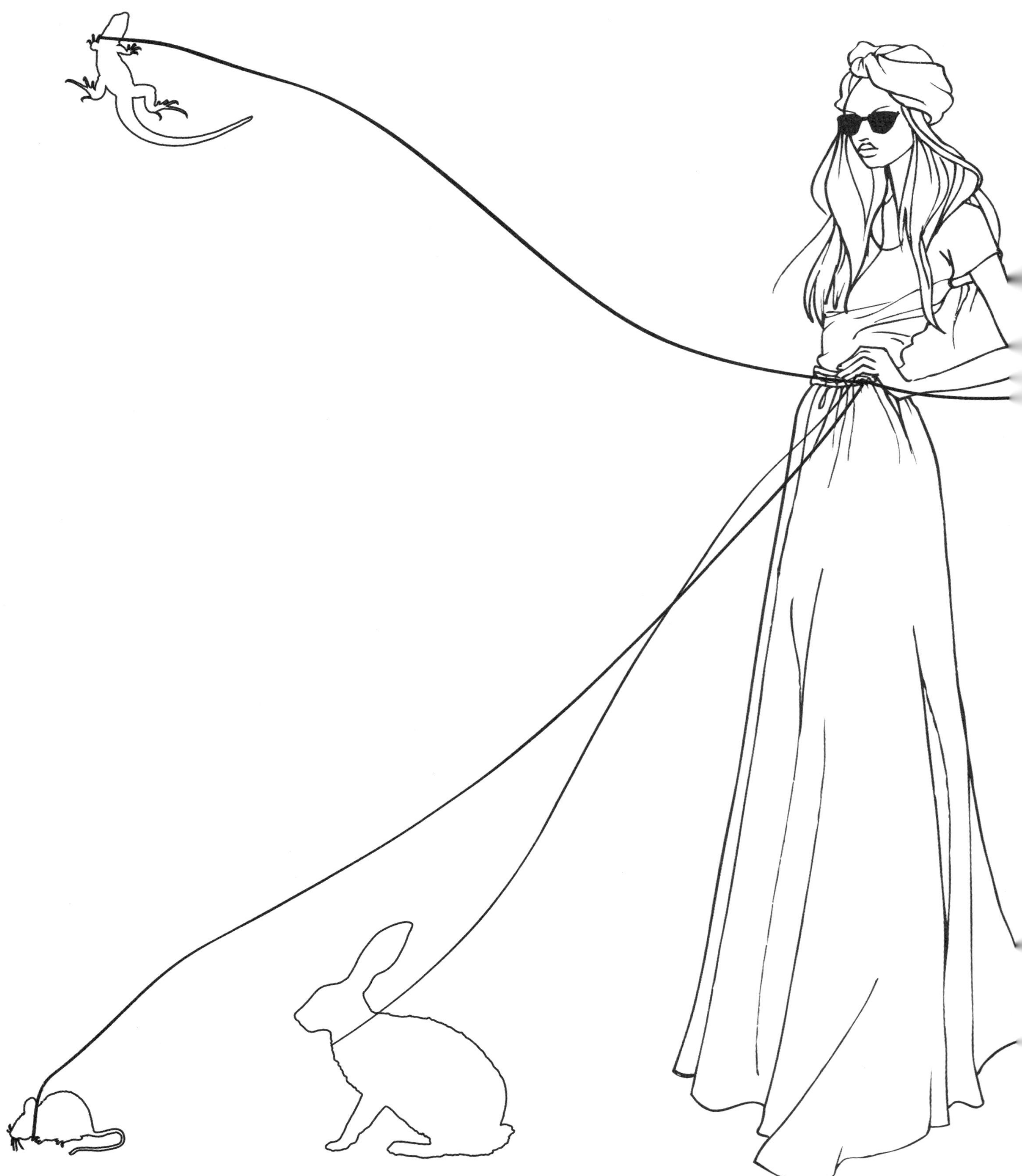

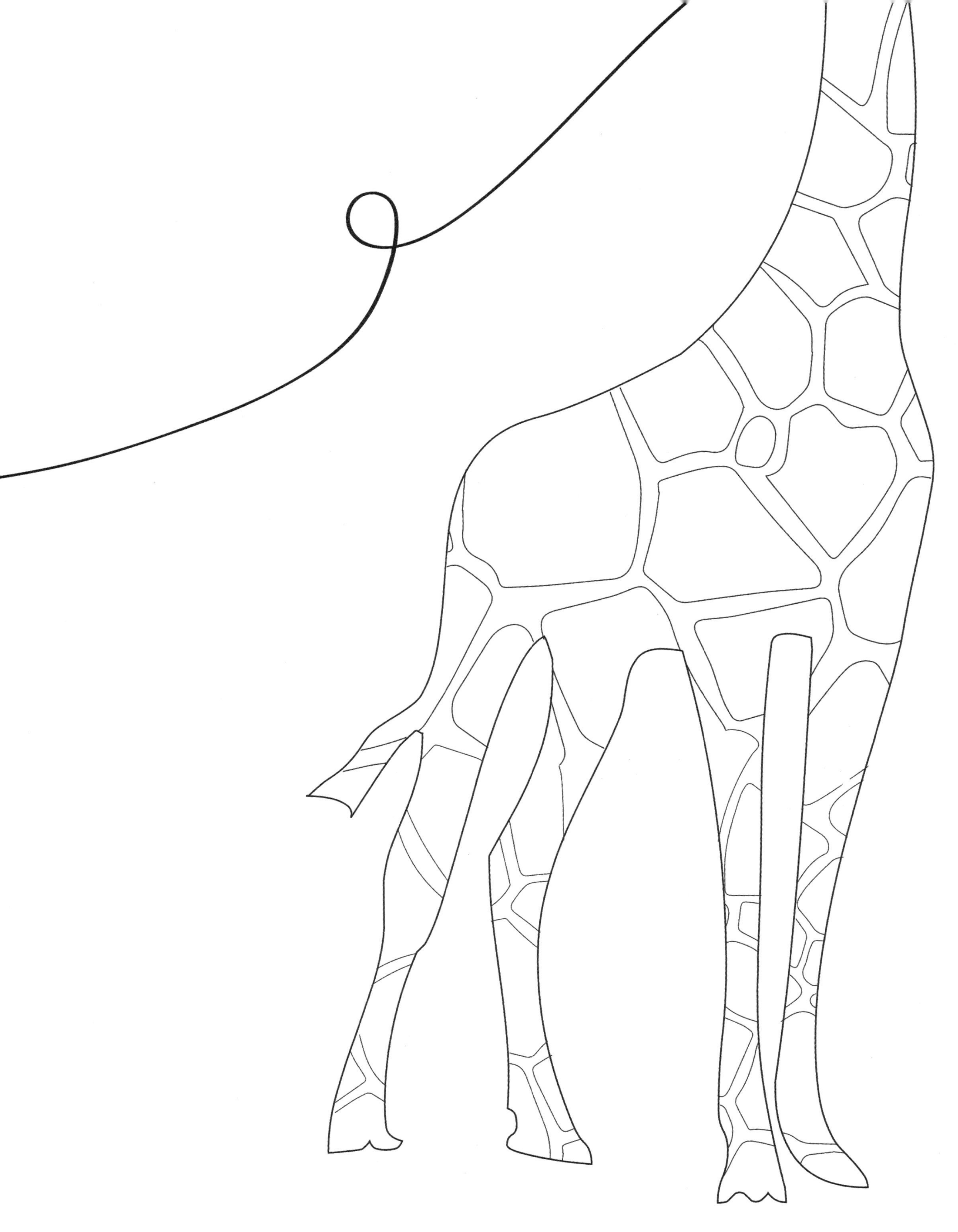

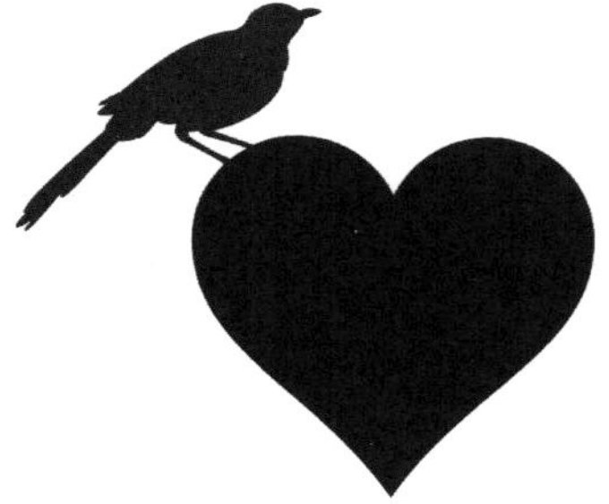

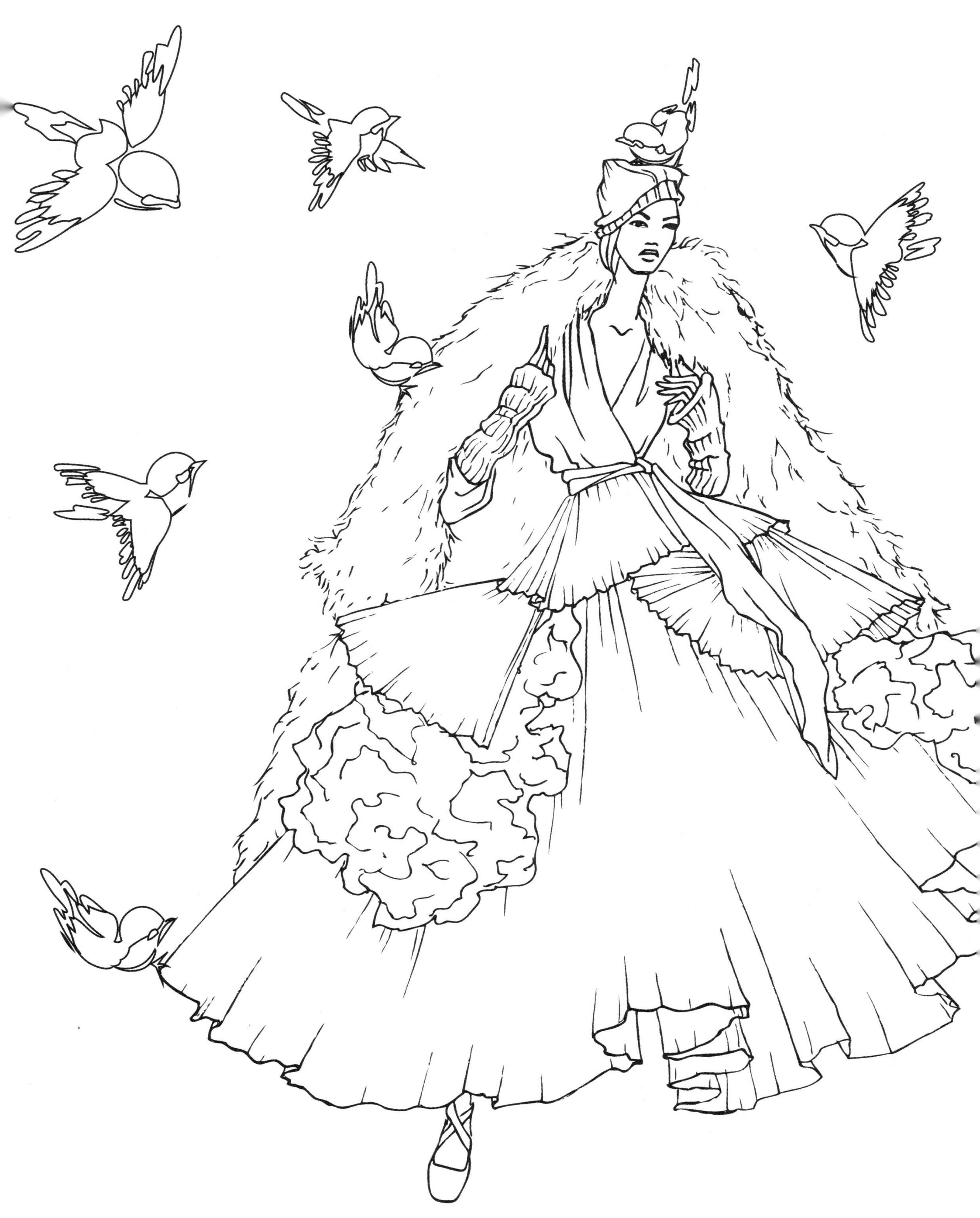

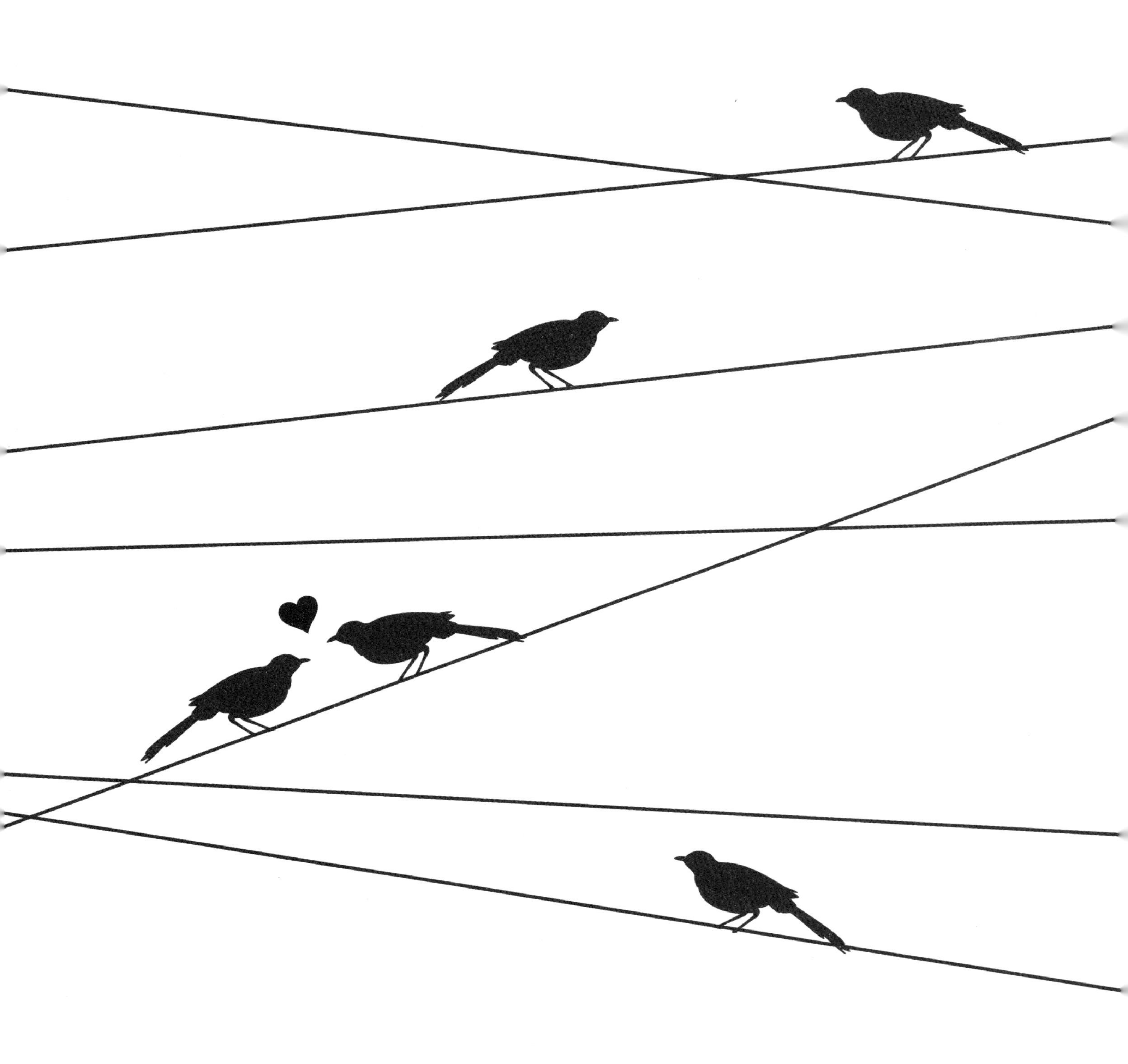

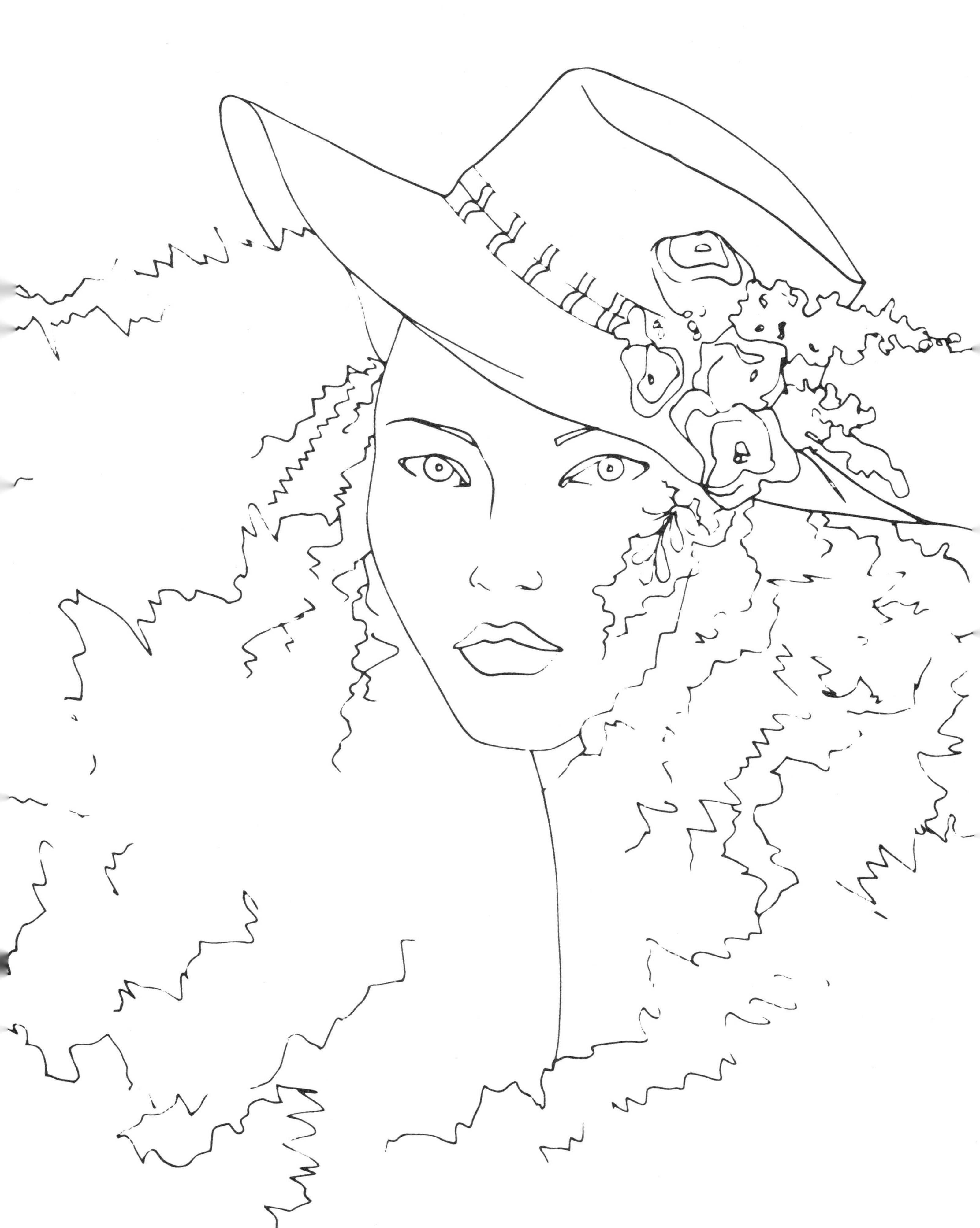

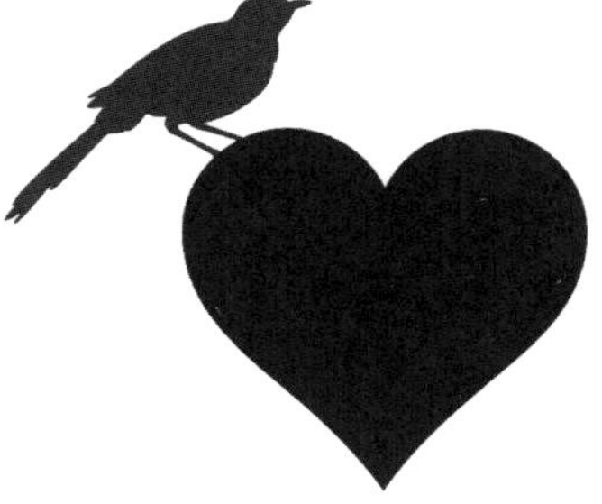

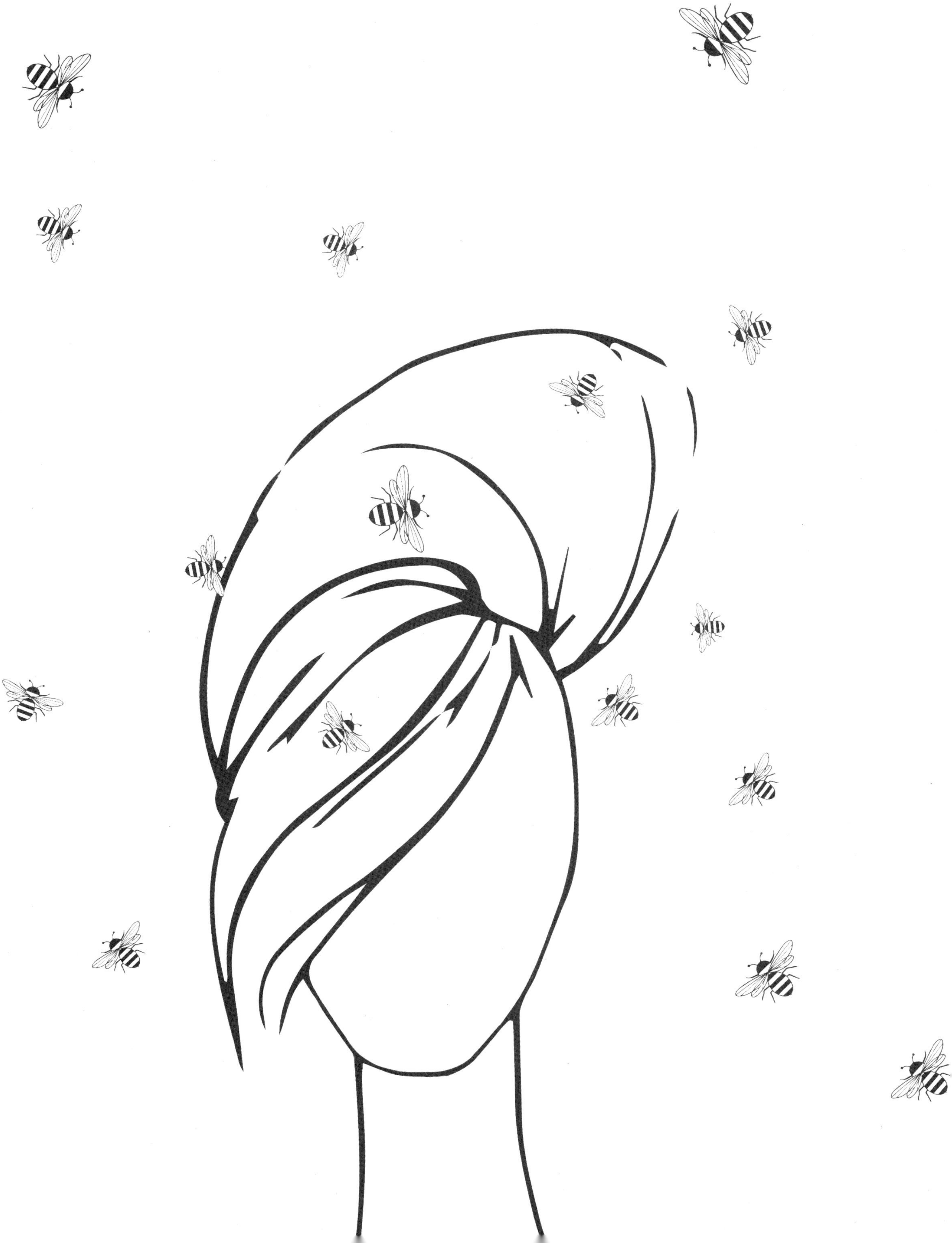

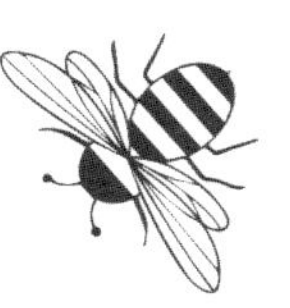

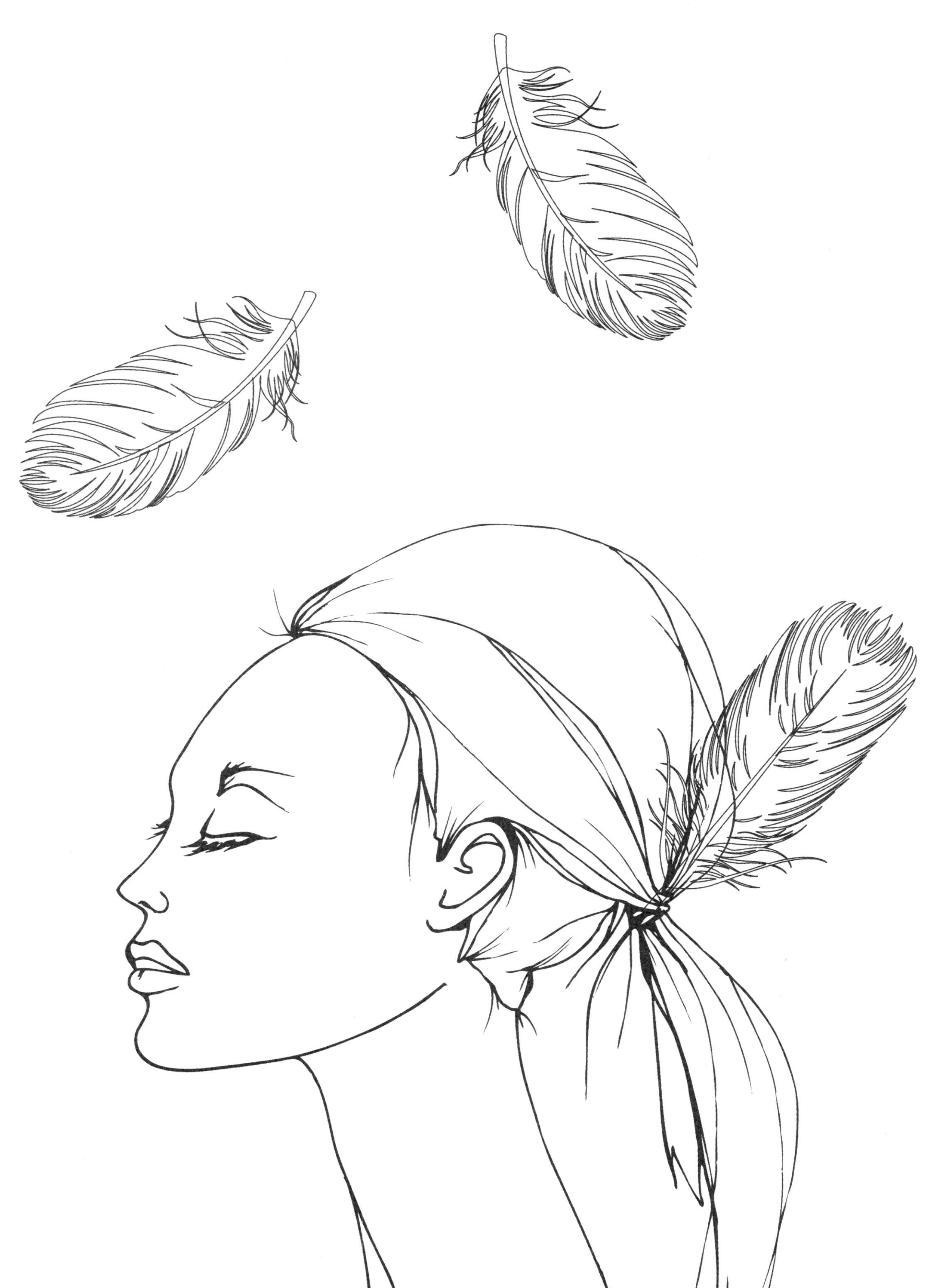

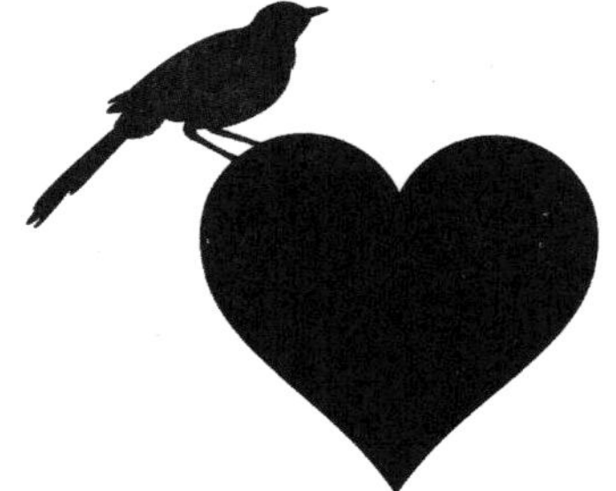

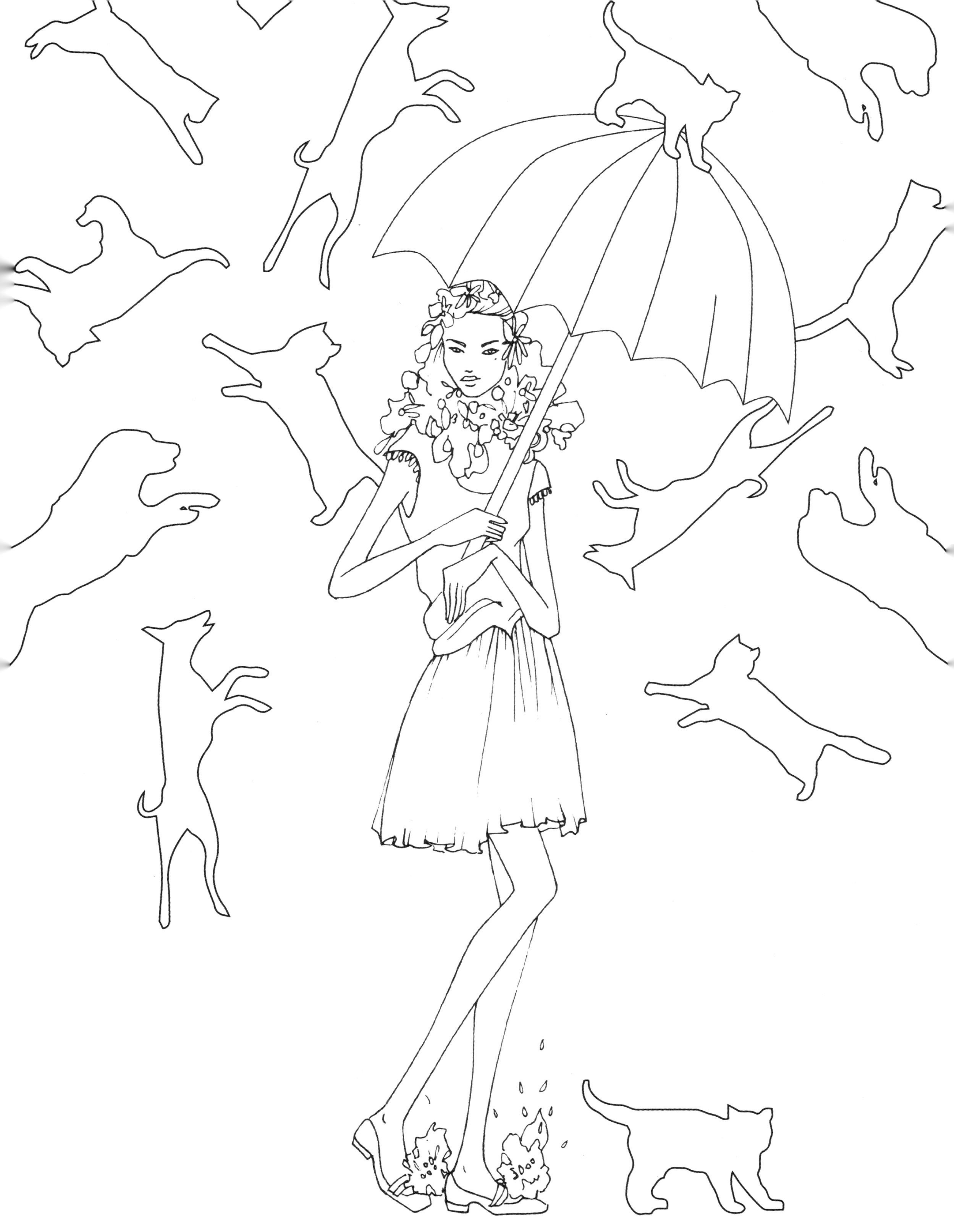

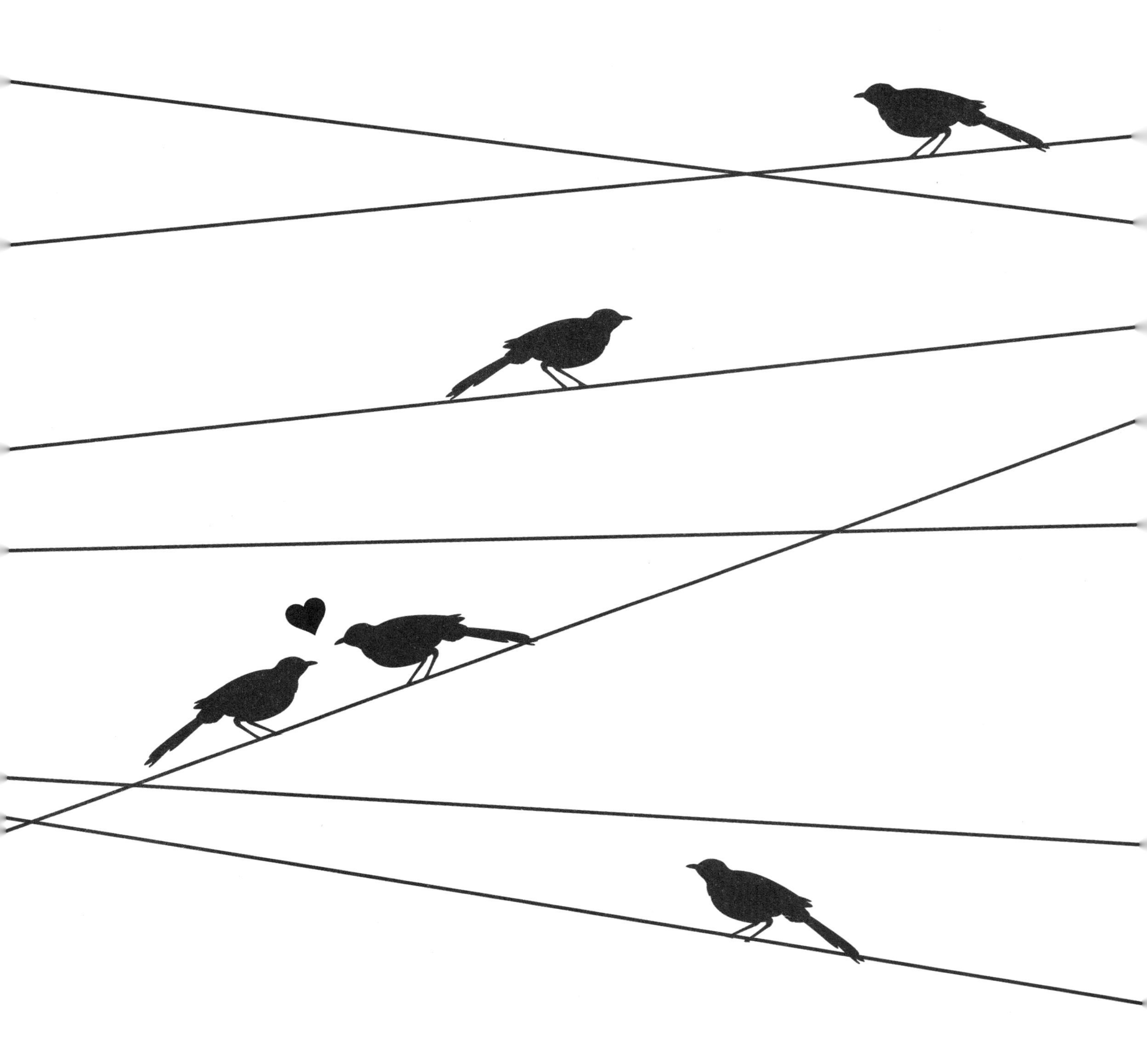

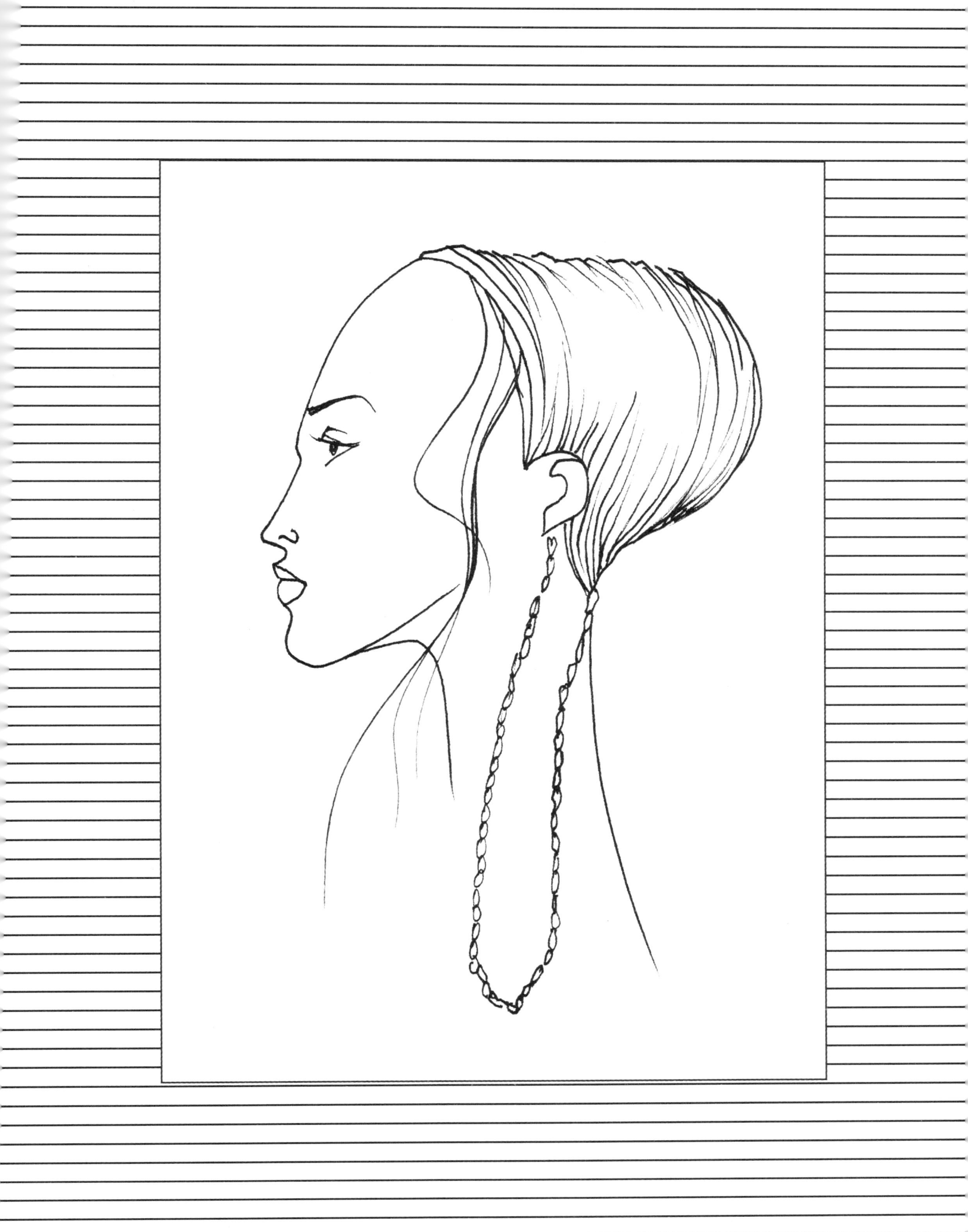

ANDROGYNOUS

BROCADE

CATWALK

DENIM

ELEGANCE

FRINGE

GINGHAM

HAUTE COUTURE

ICON

JODHPUR

KNICKERS

LEATHER

MODERN

NEUTRAL

ORGANZA

PREPPY

QUALITY

REVERSIBLE

STYLE

TASTE

UTILITARIAN

VOGUE

WEAVE

XOXO

YOKE

ZEITGEIST

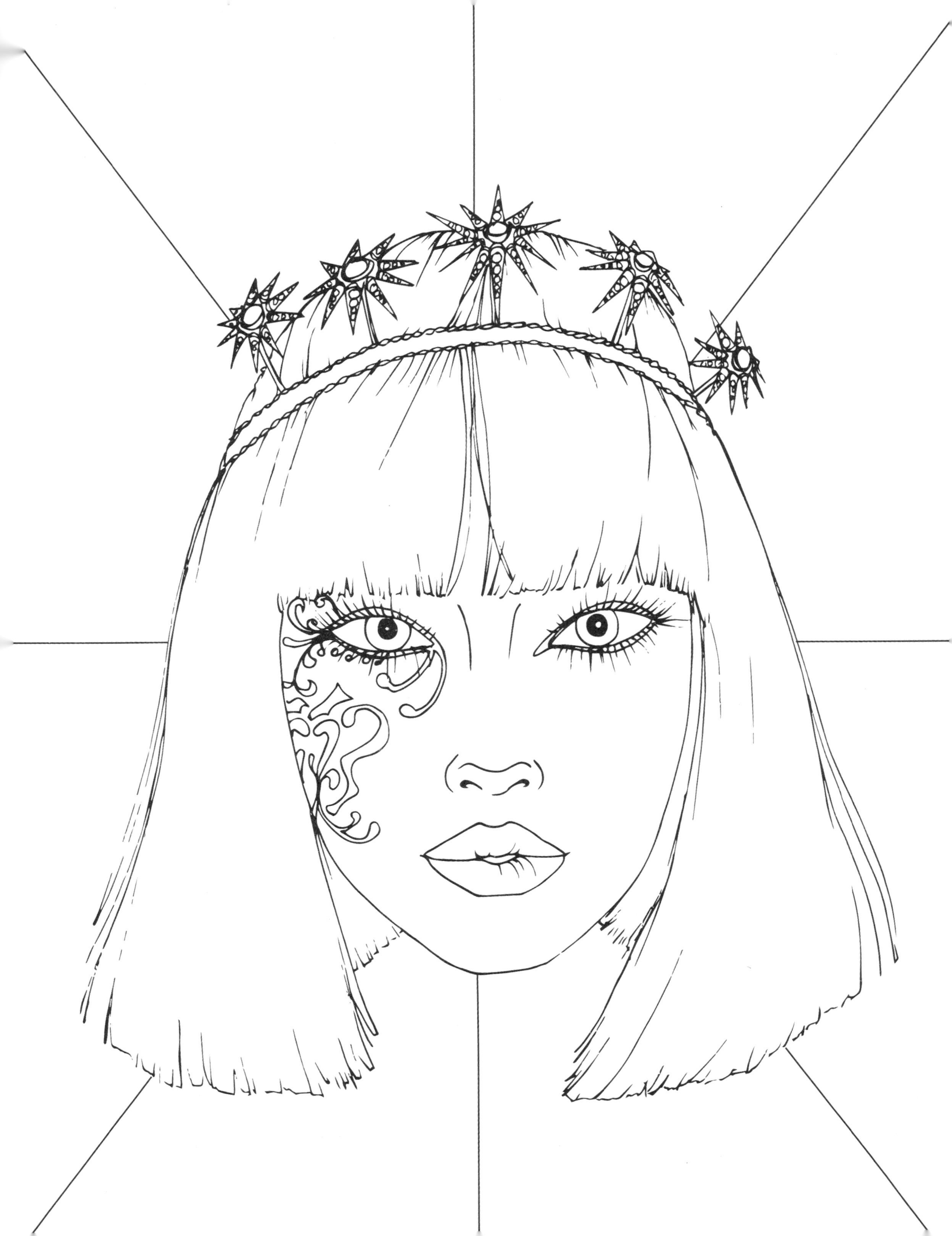

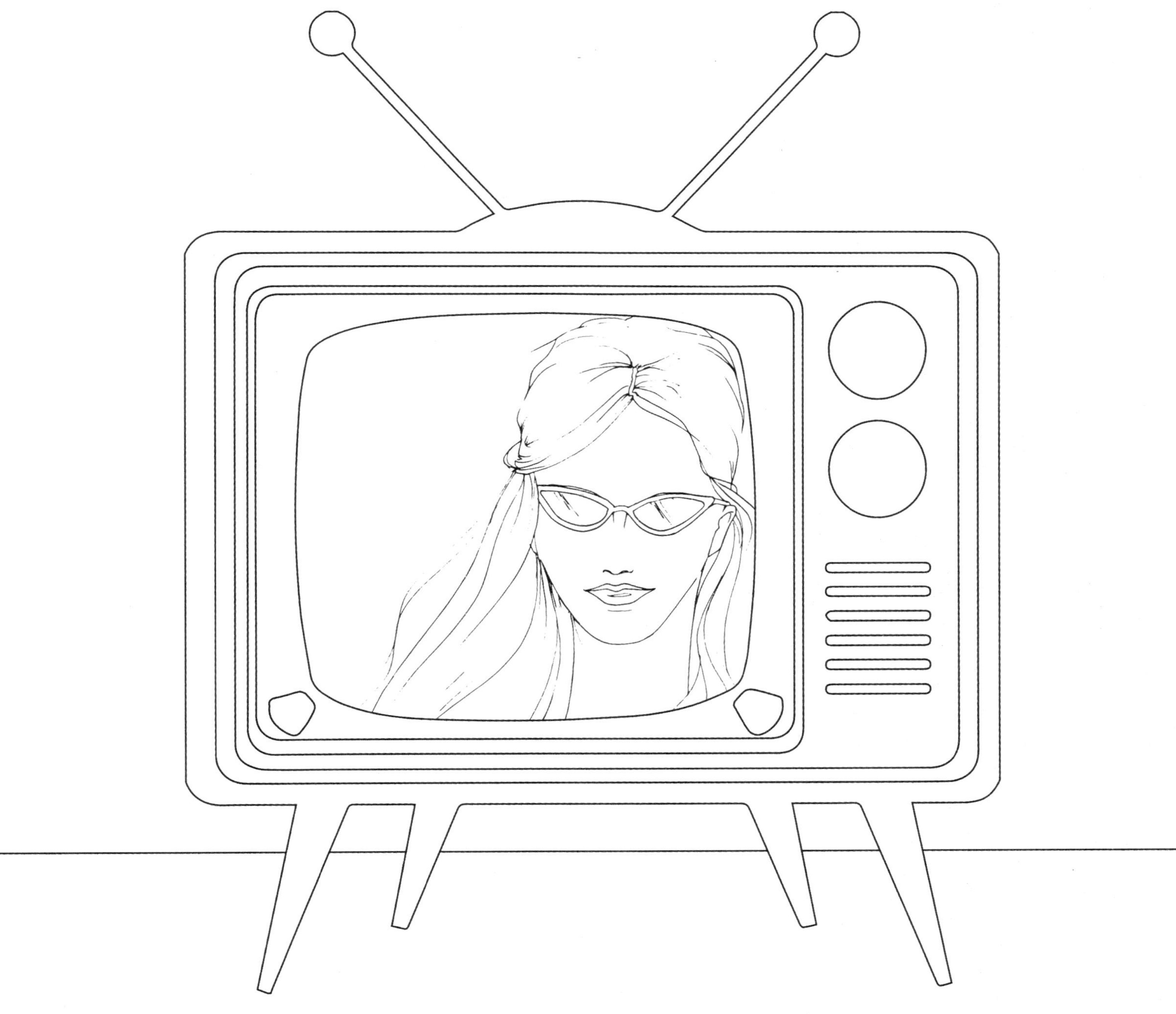

A DRAWING IS SIMPLY A LINE GOING FOR A WALK.

PAUL KLEE

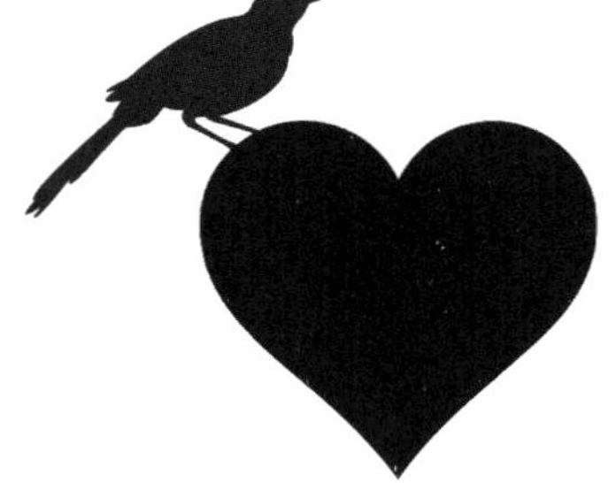

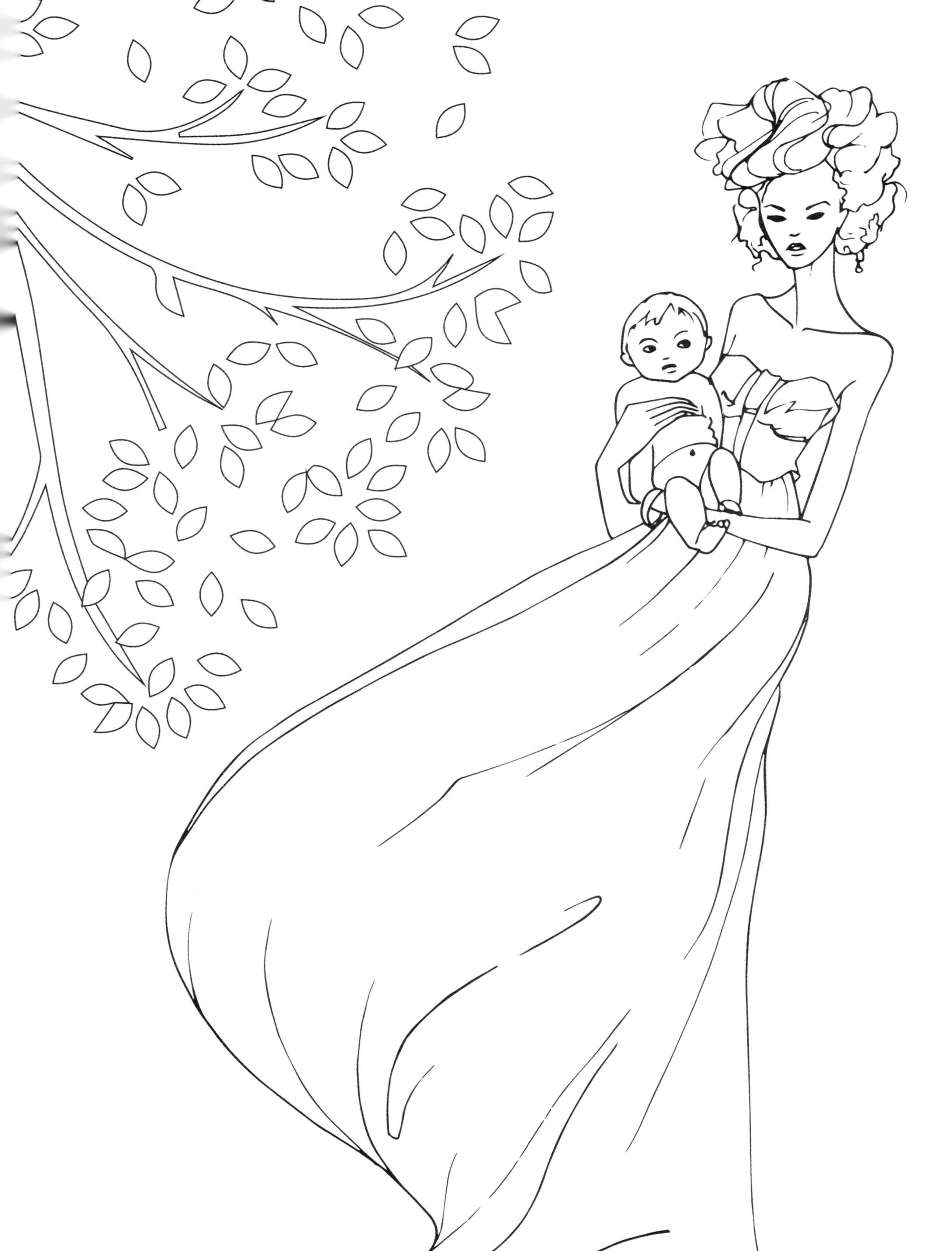

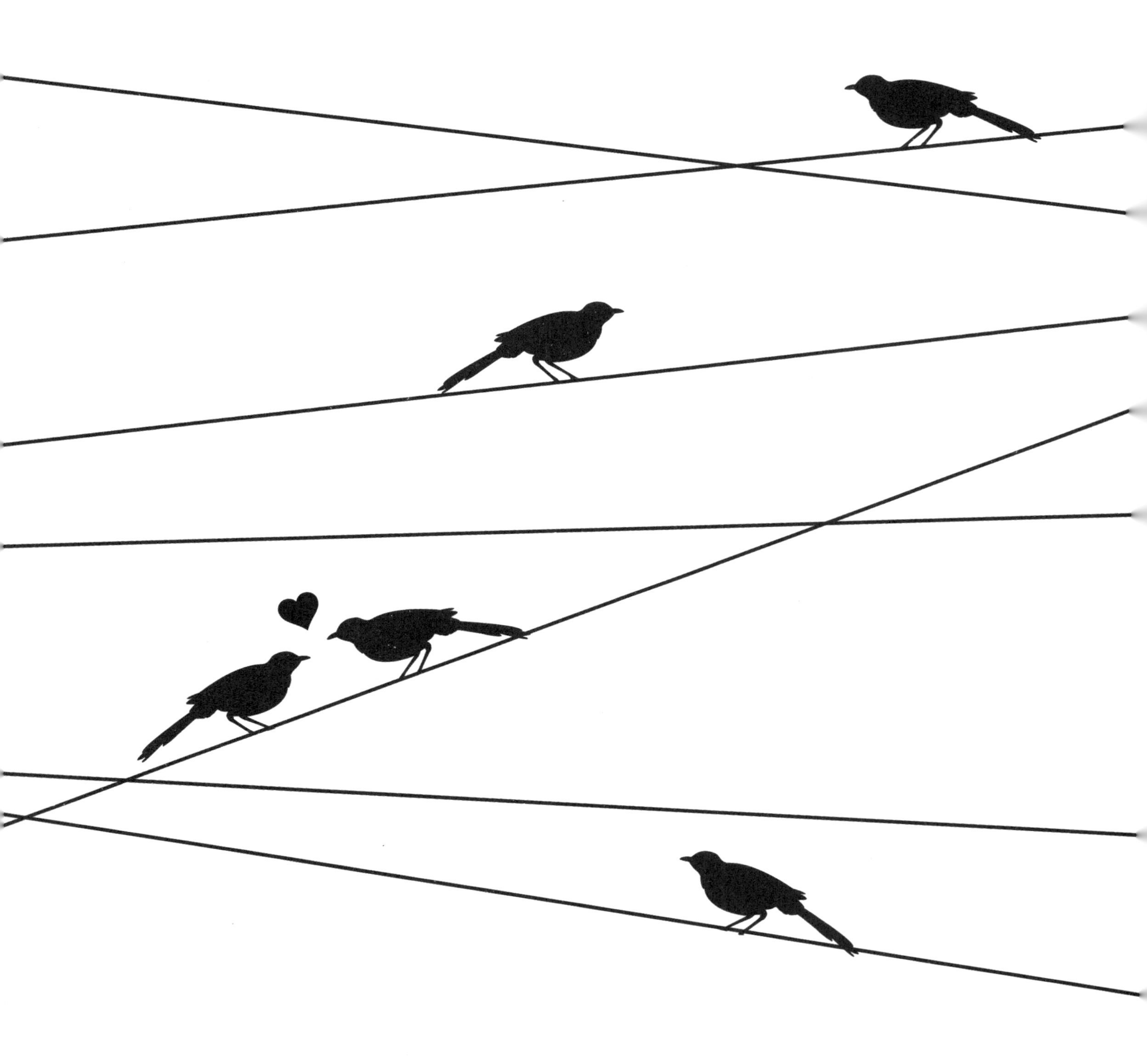

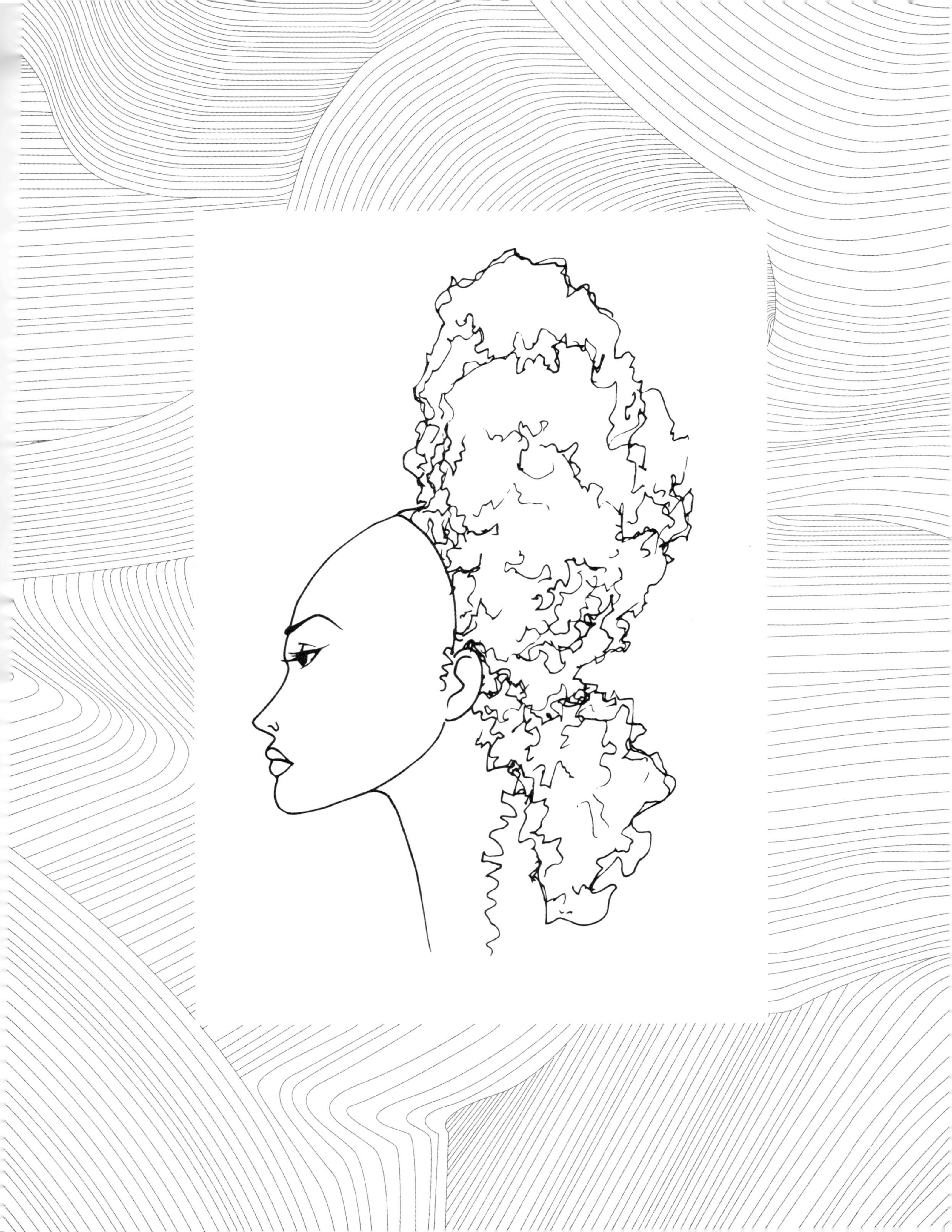

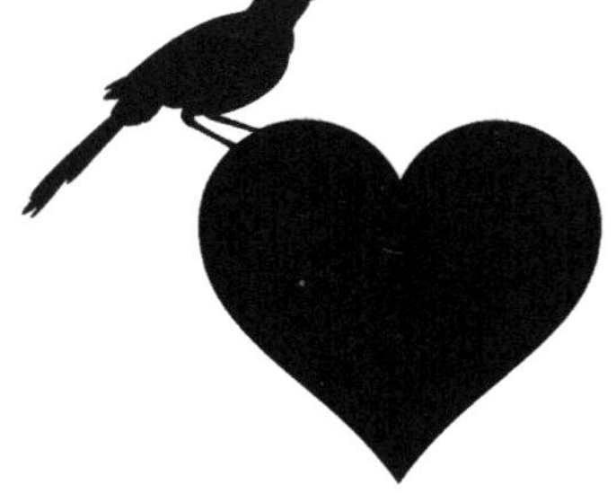

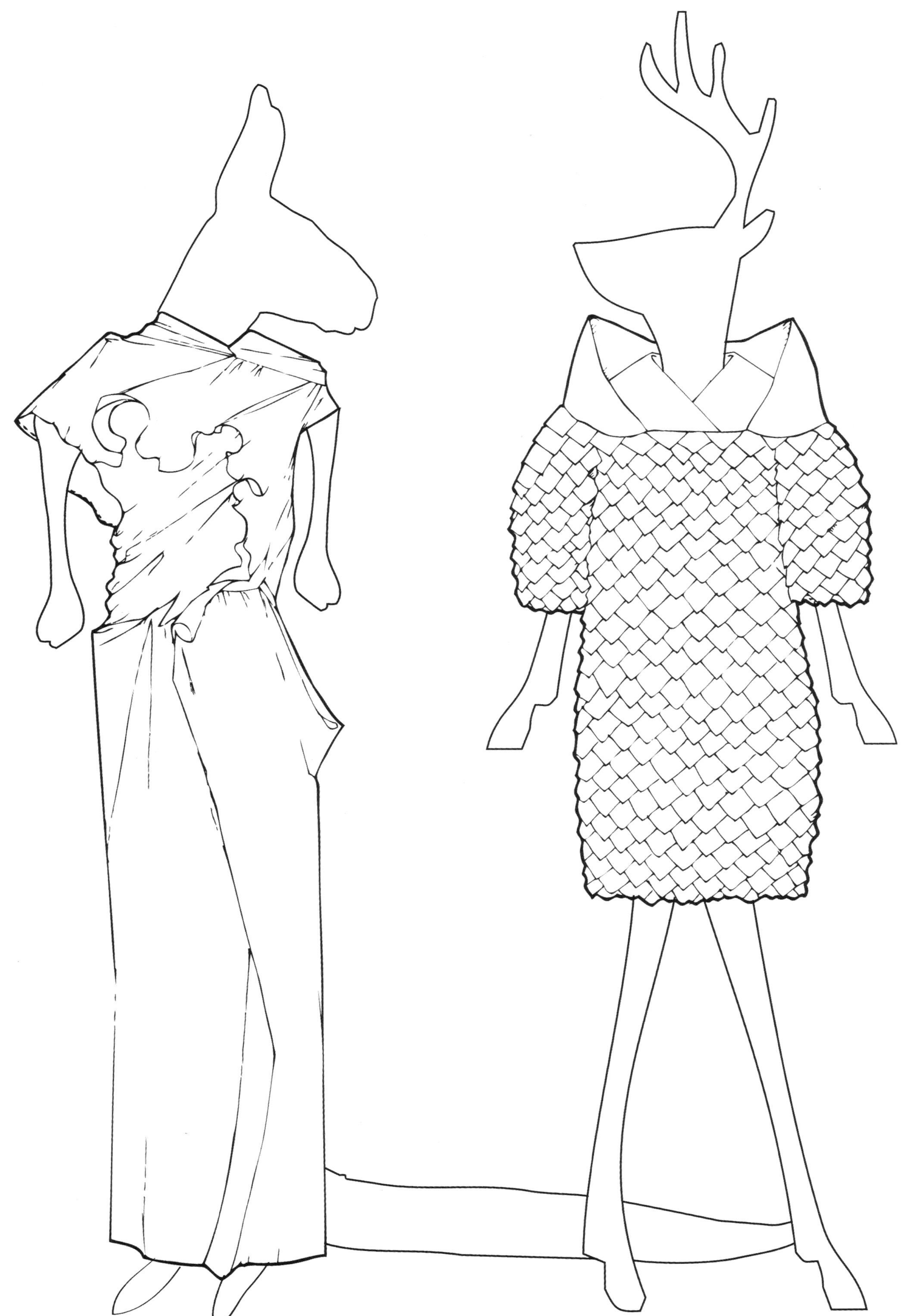

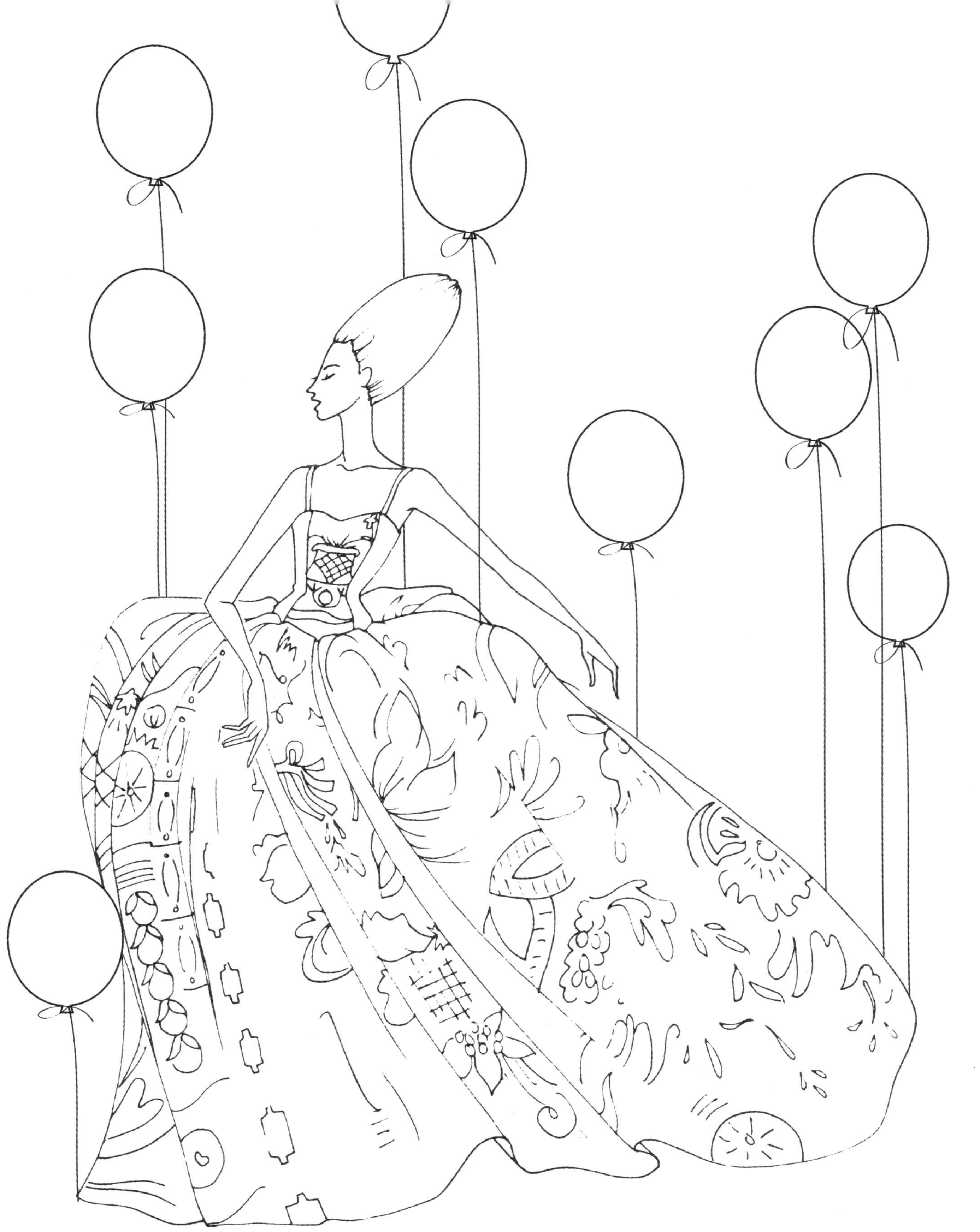

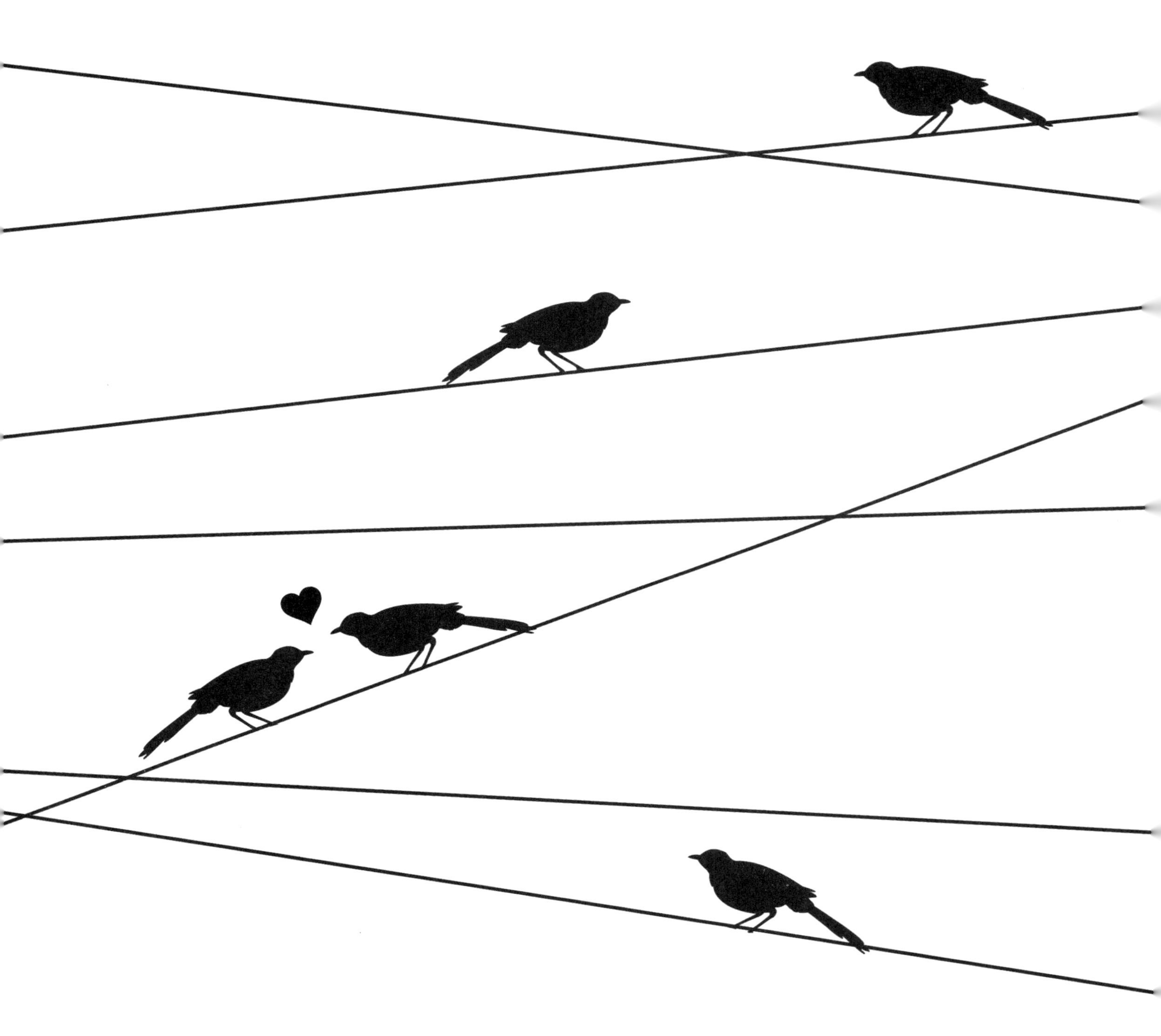

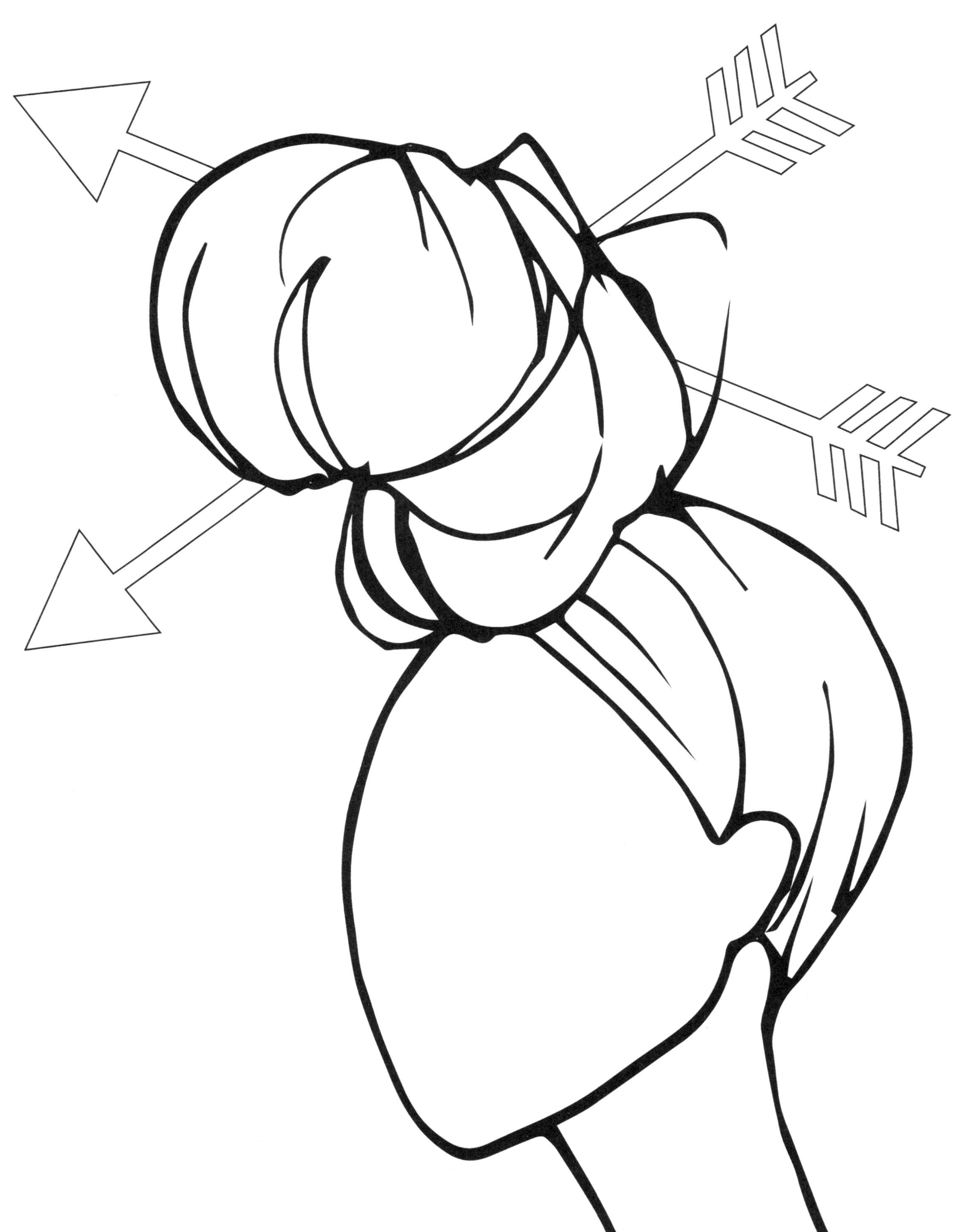

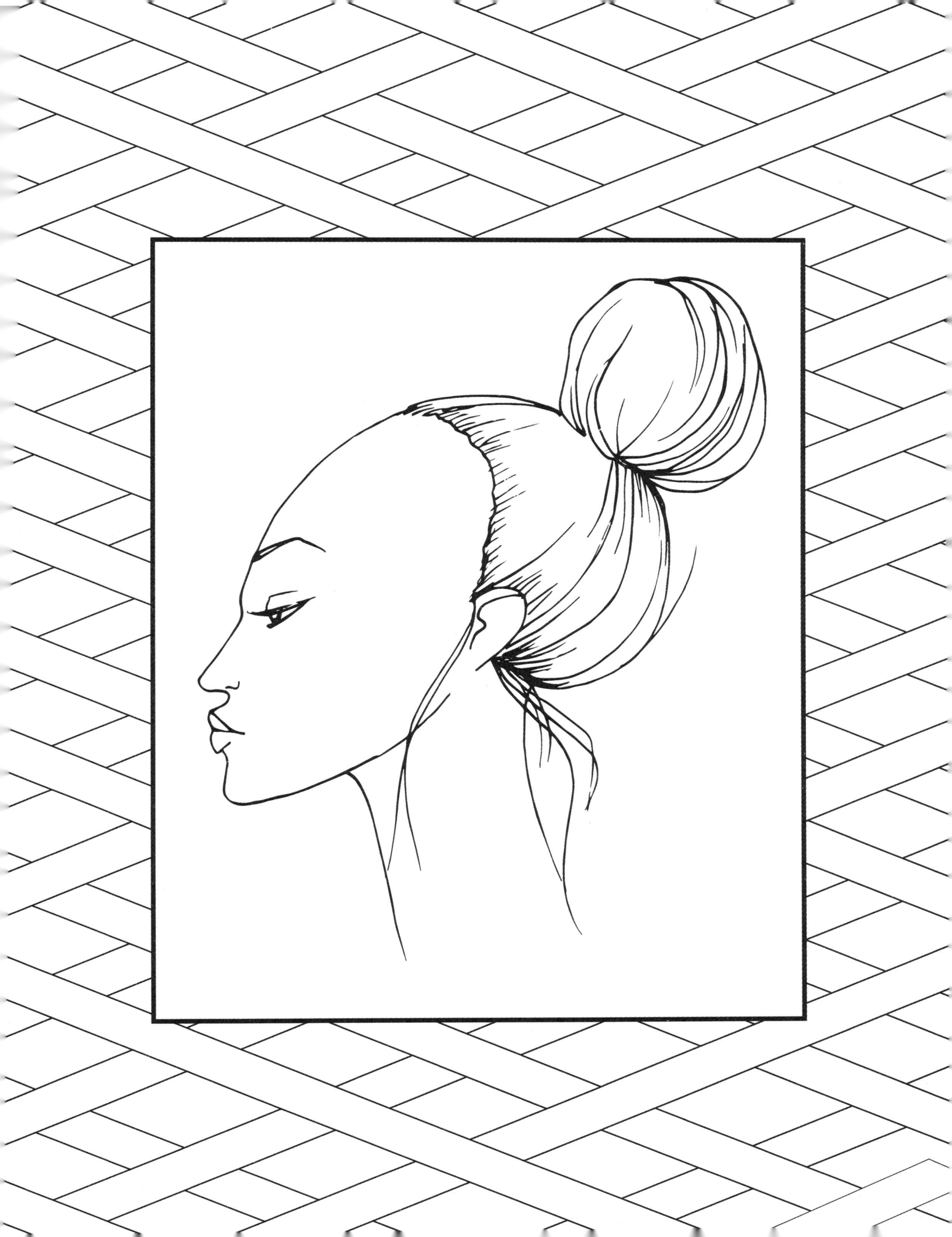

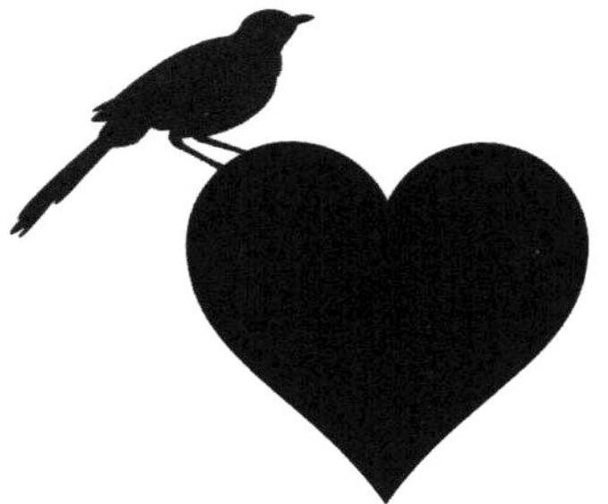

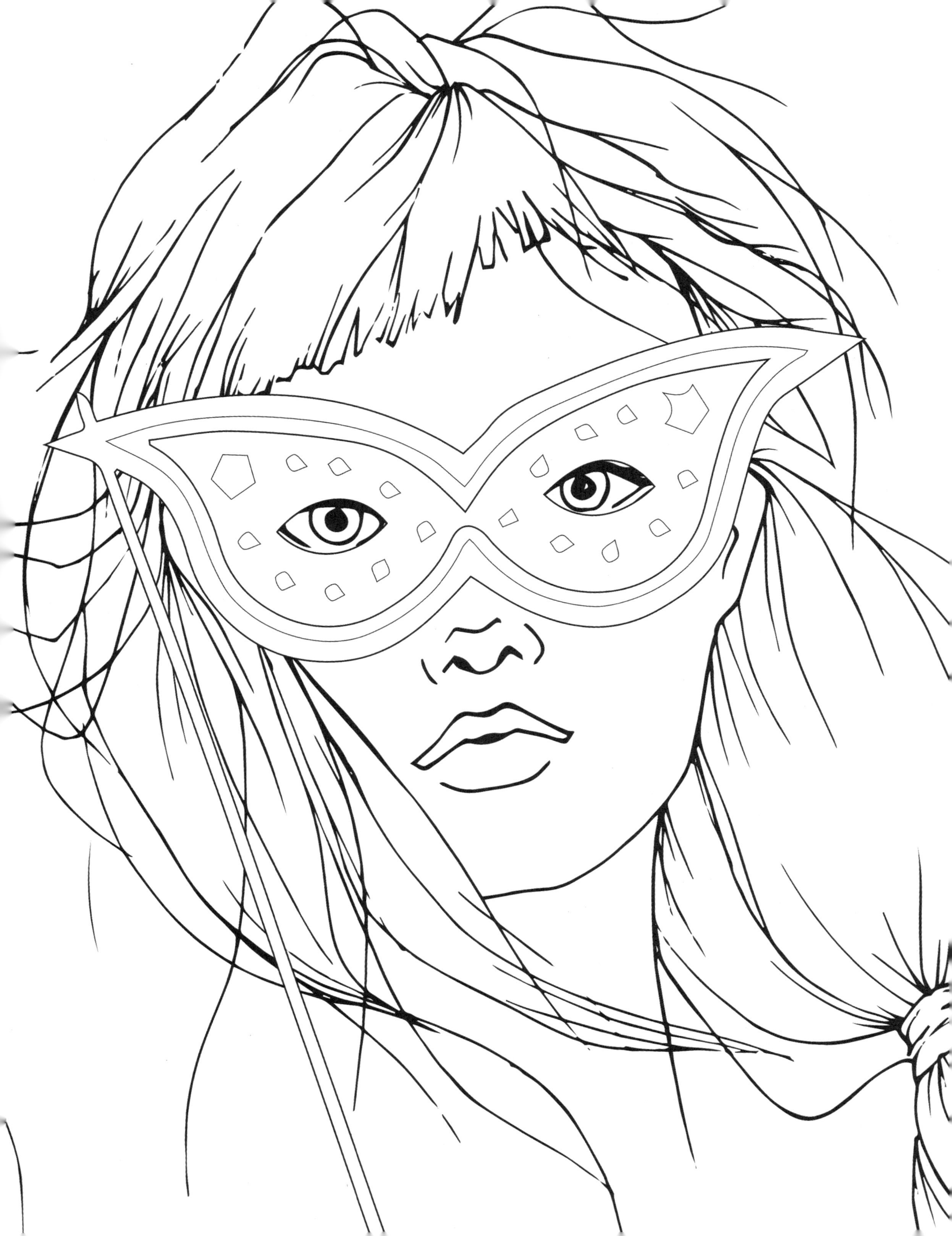

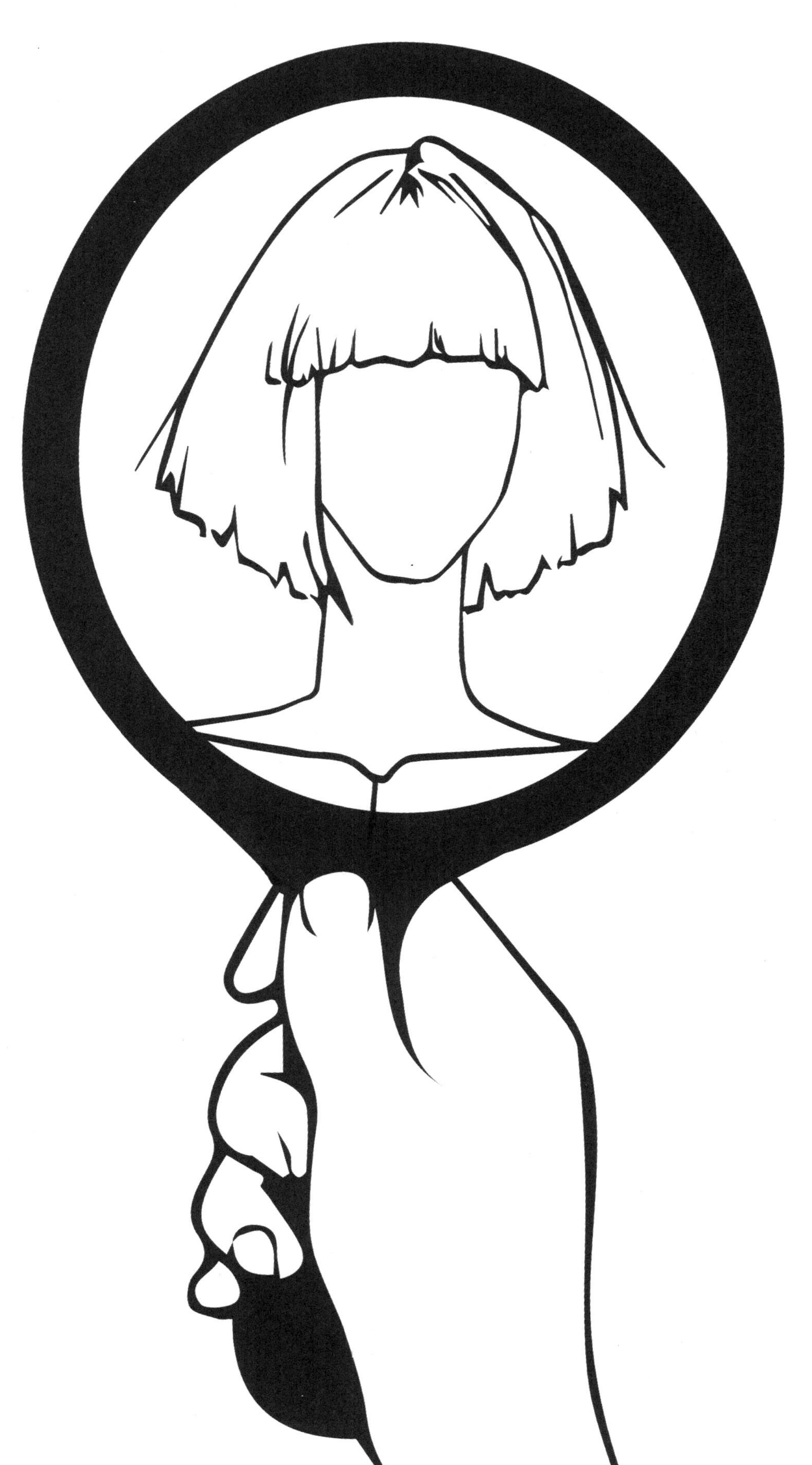

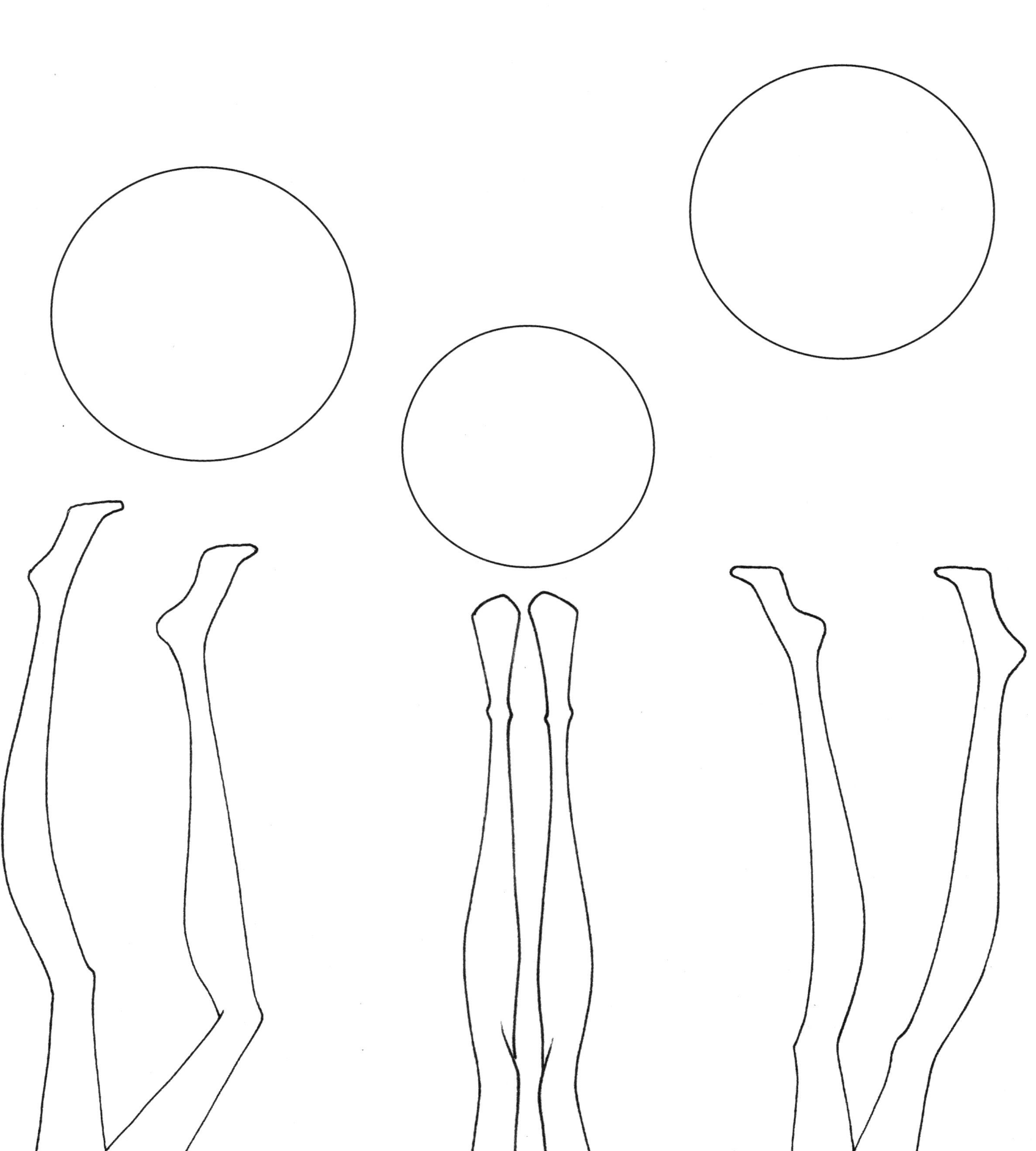

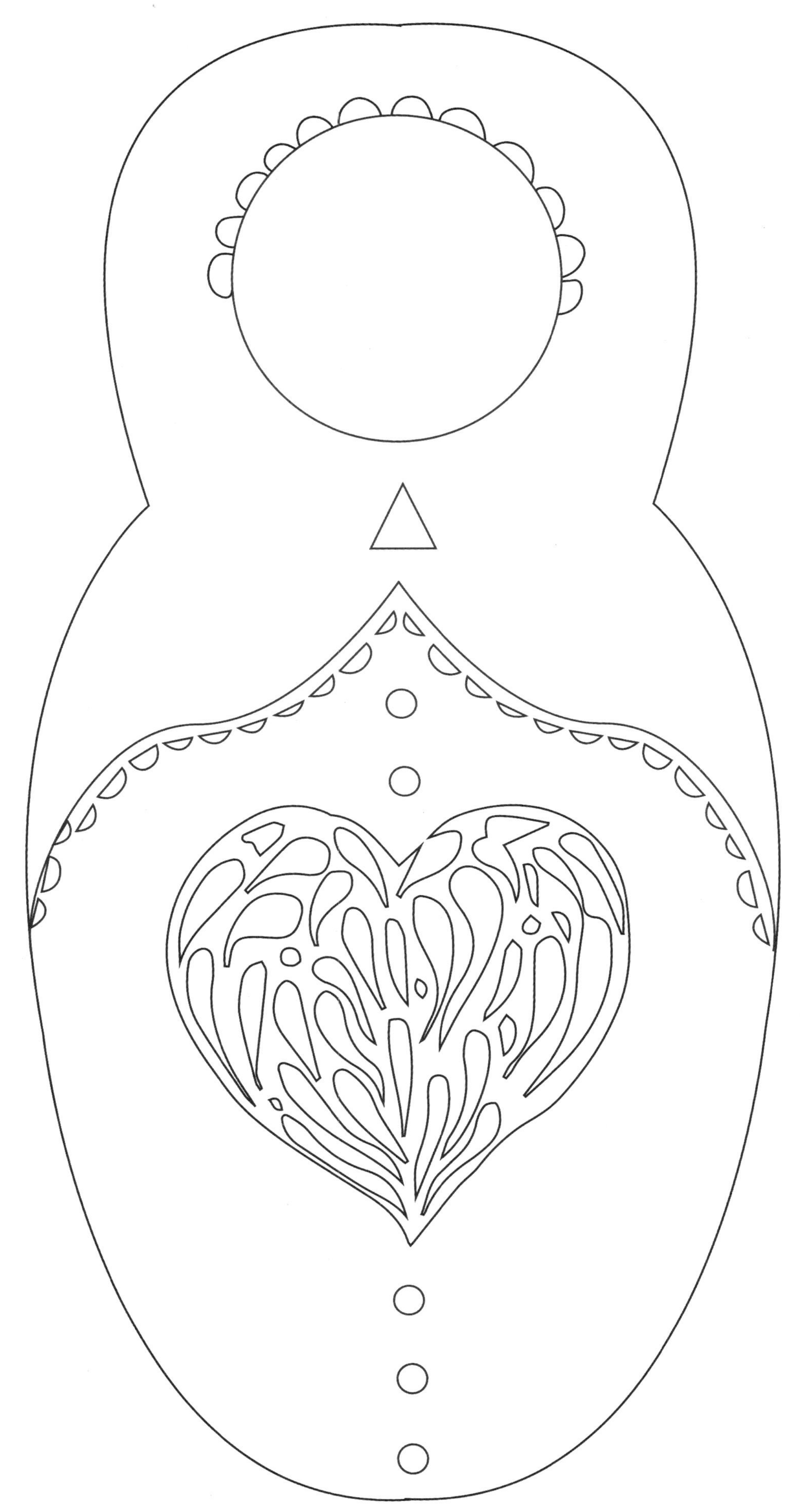

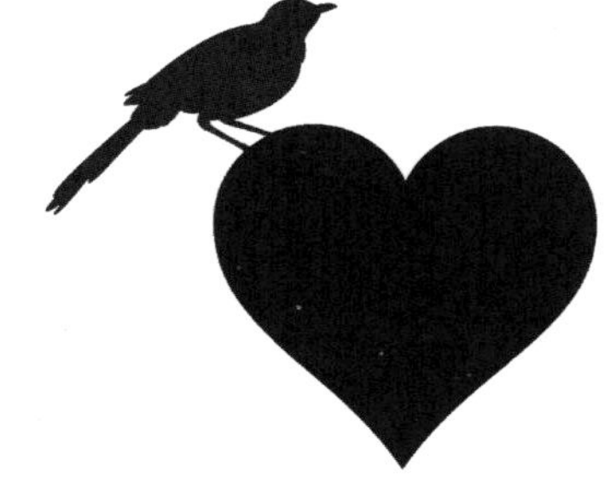

MODERN &

NERVOUS

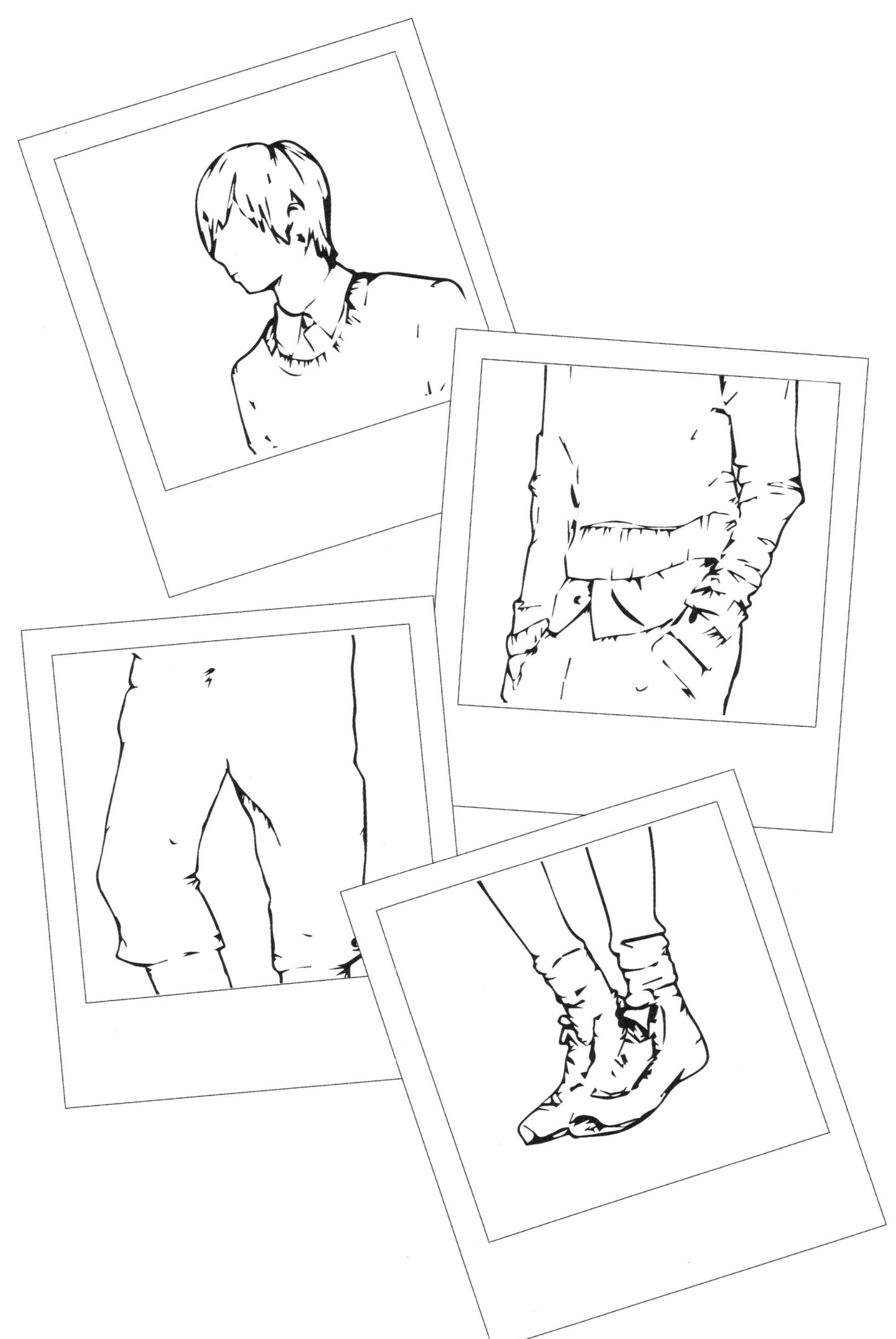

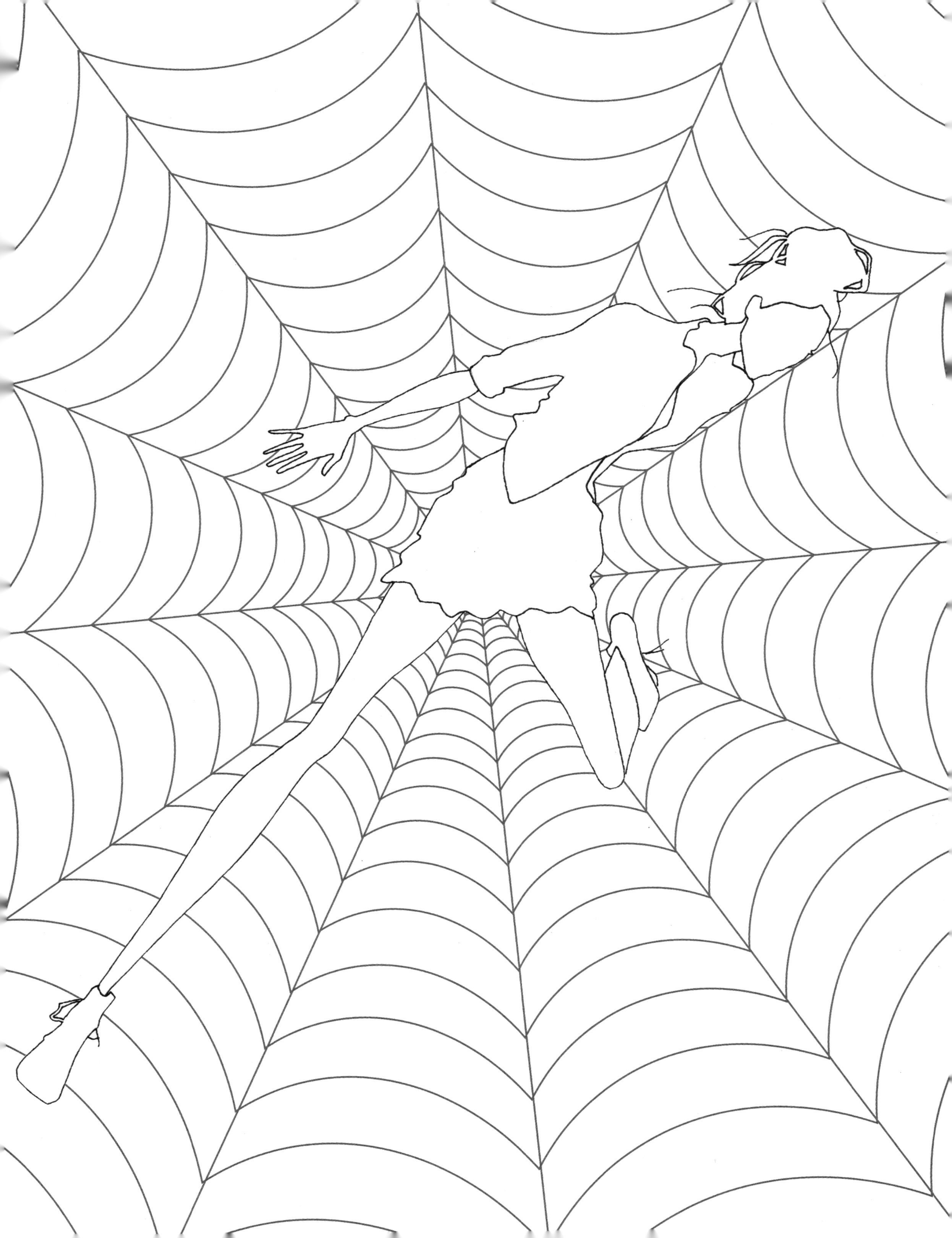

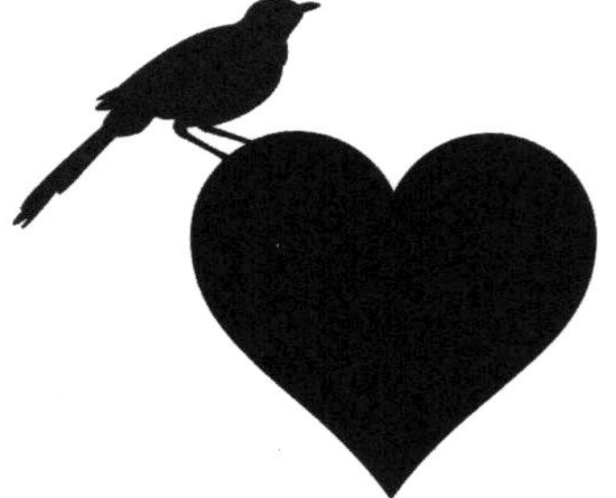

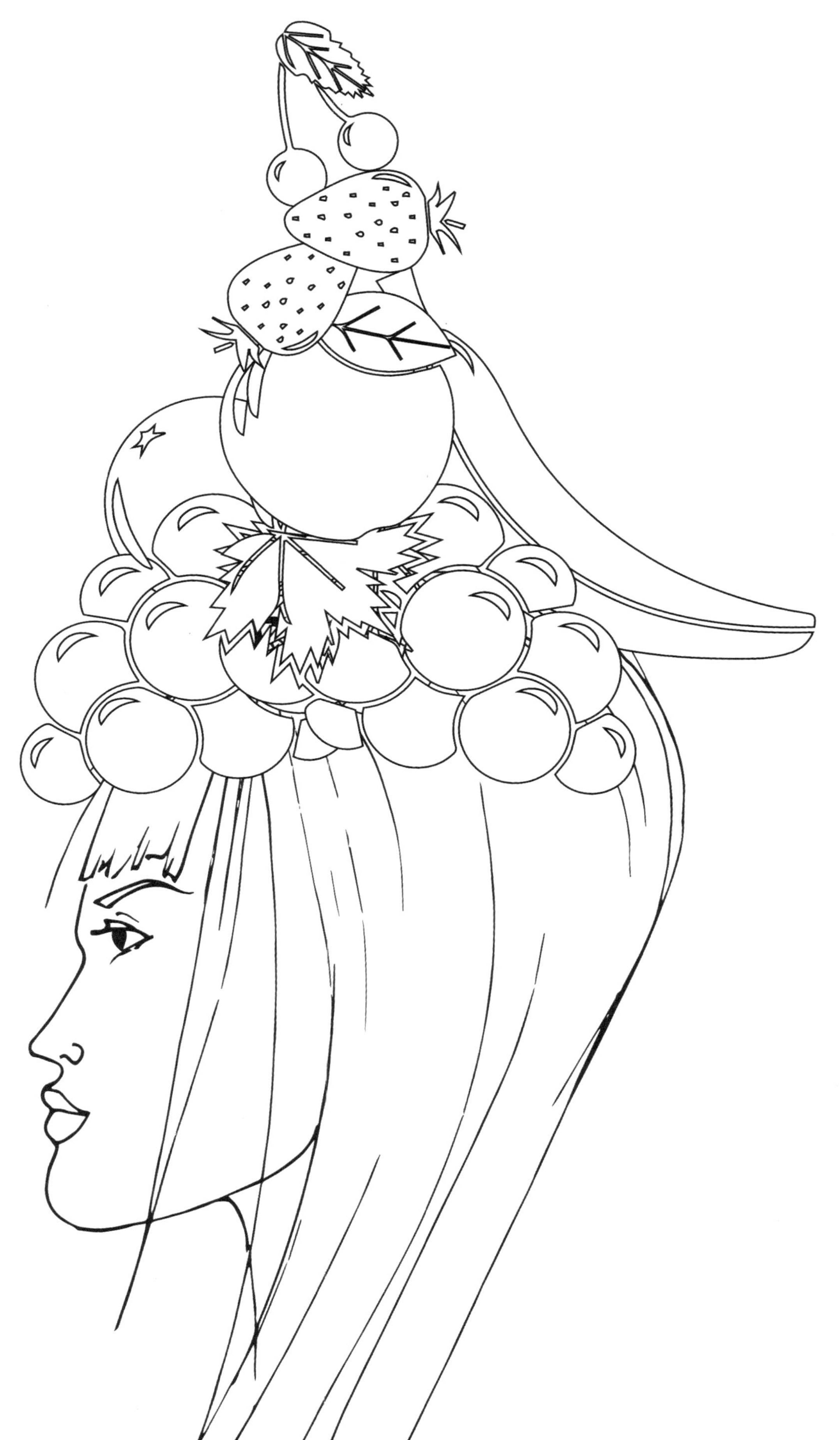

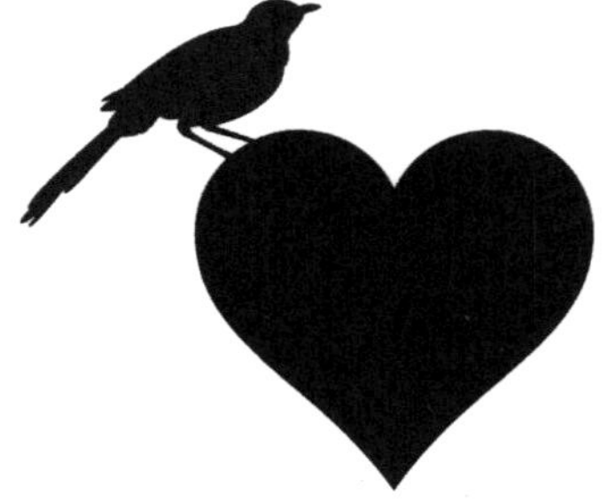

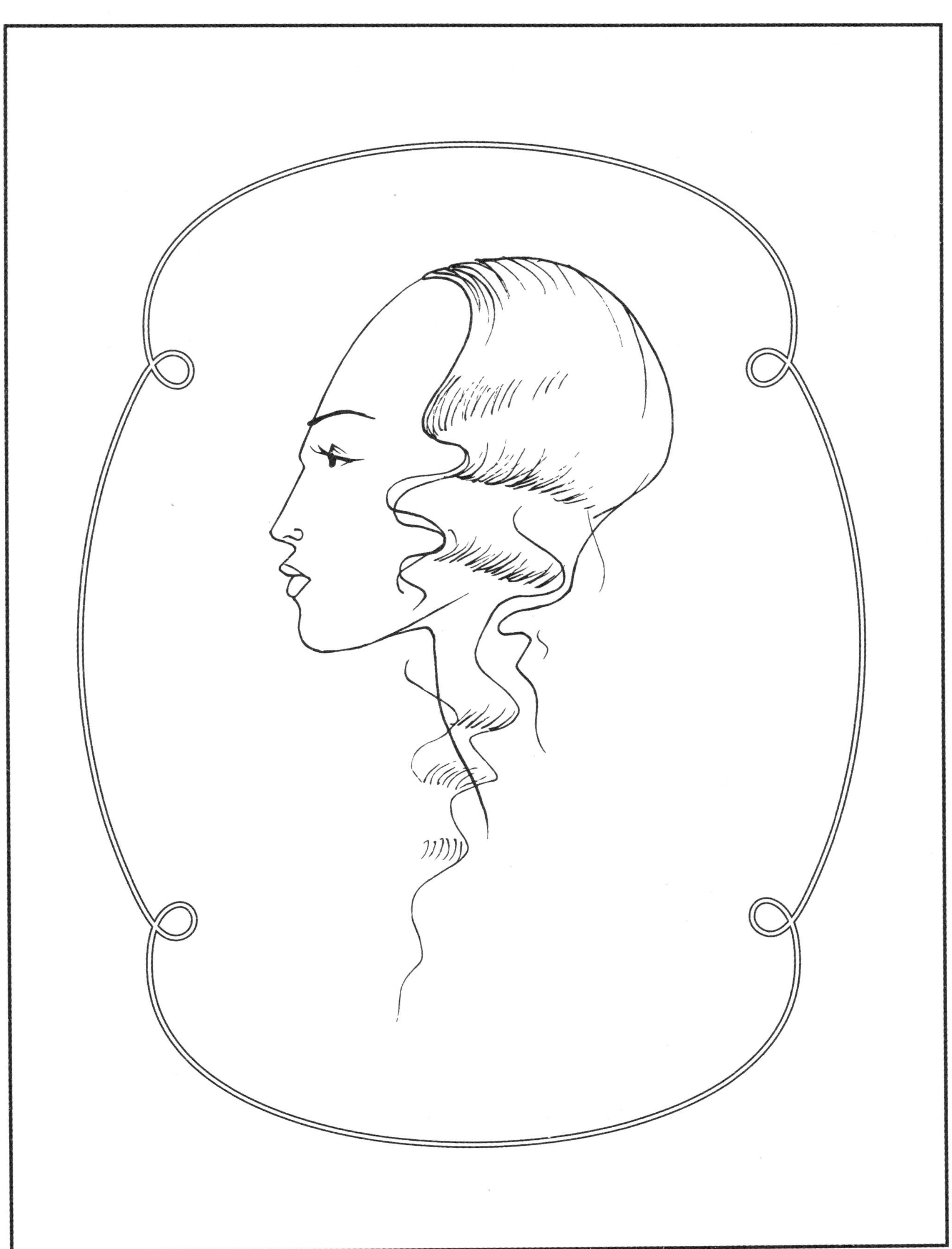

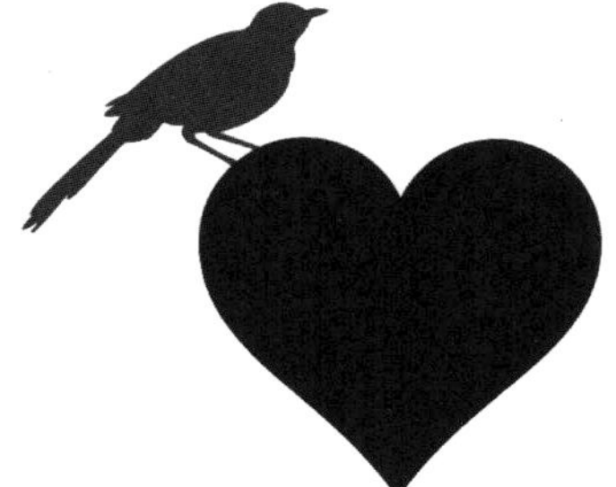

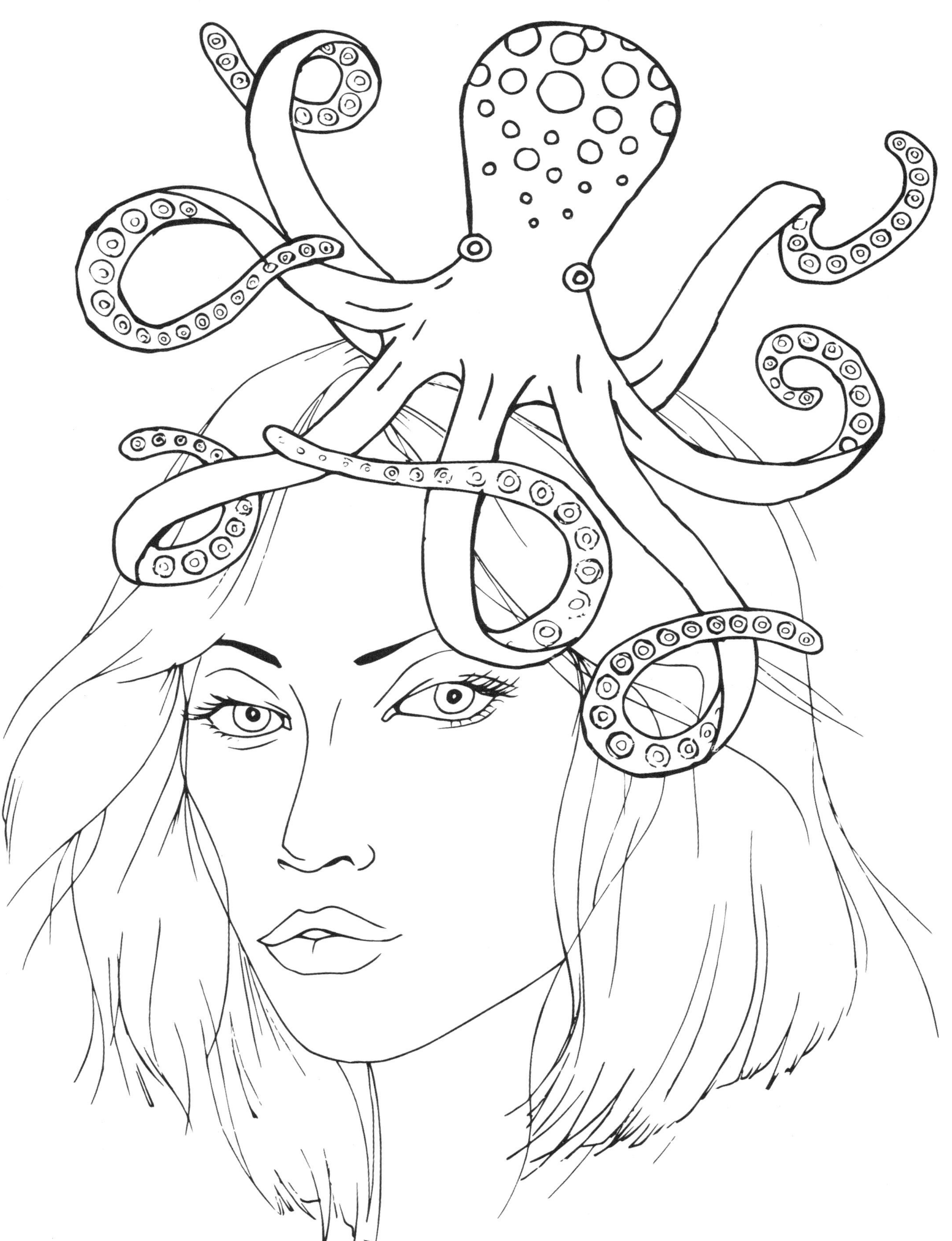

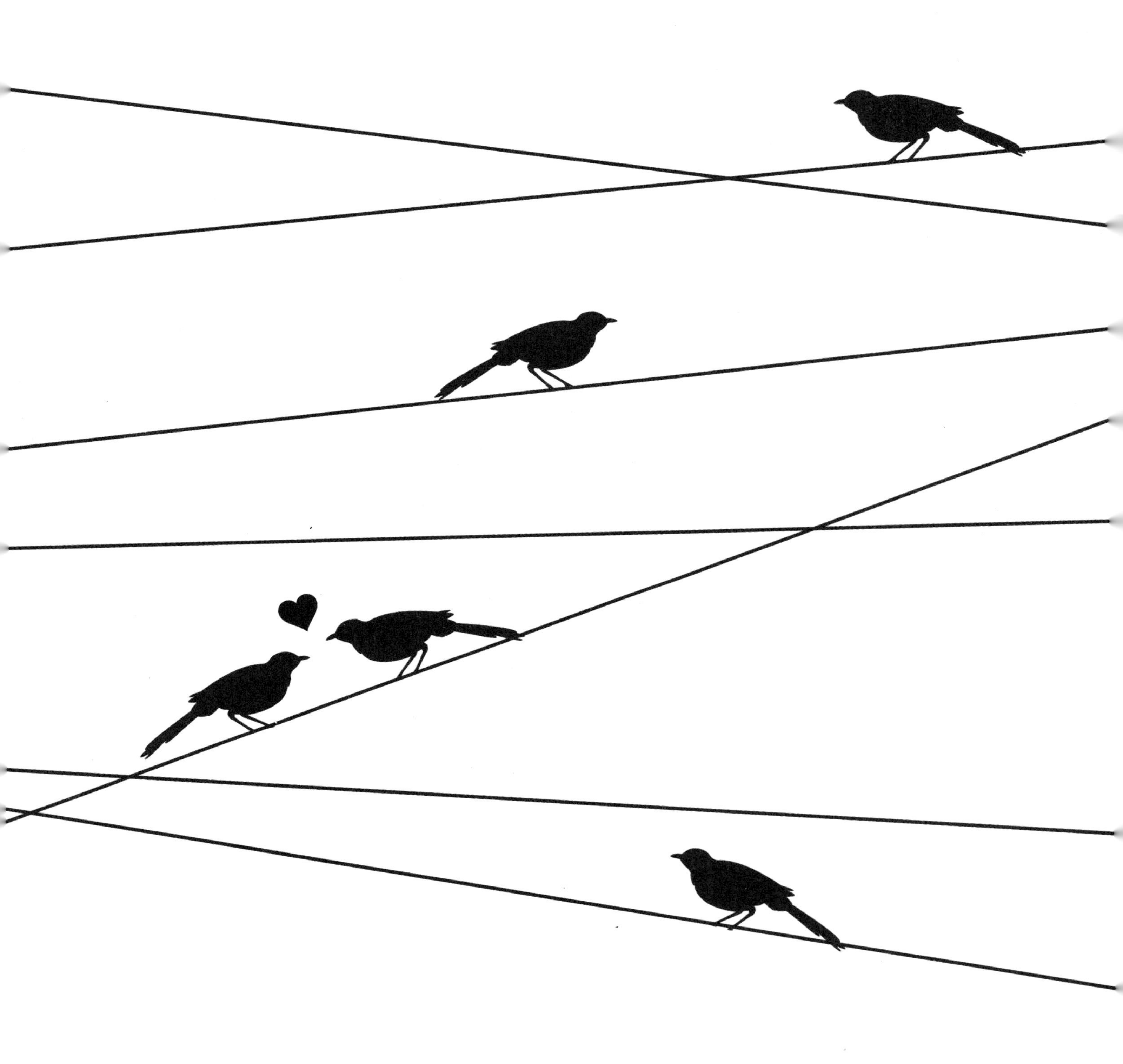

Drawing makes you
see things
clearer,
and clearer
and clearer
still,
until your eyes ache.

- David Hockney

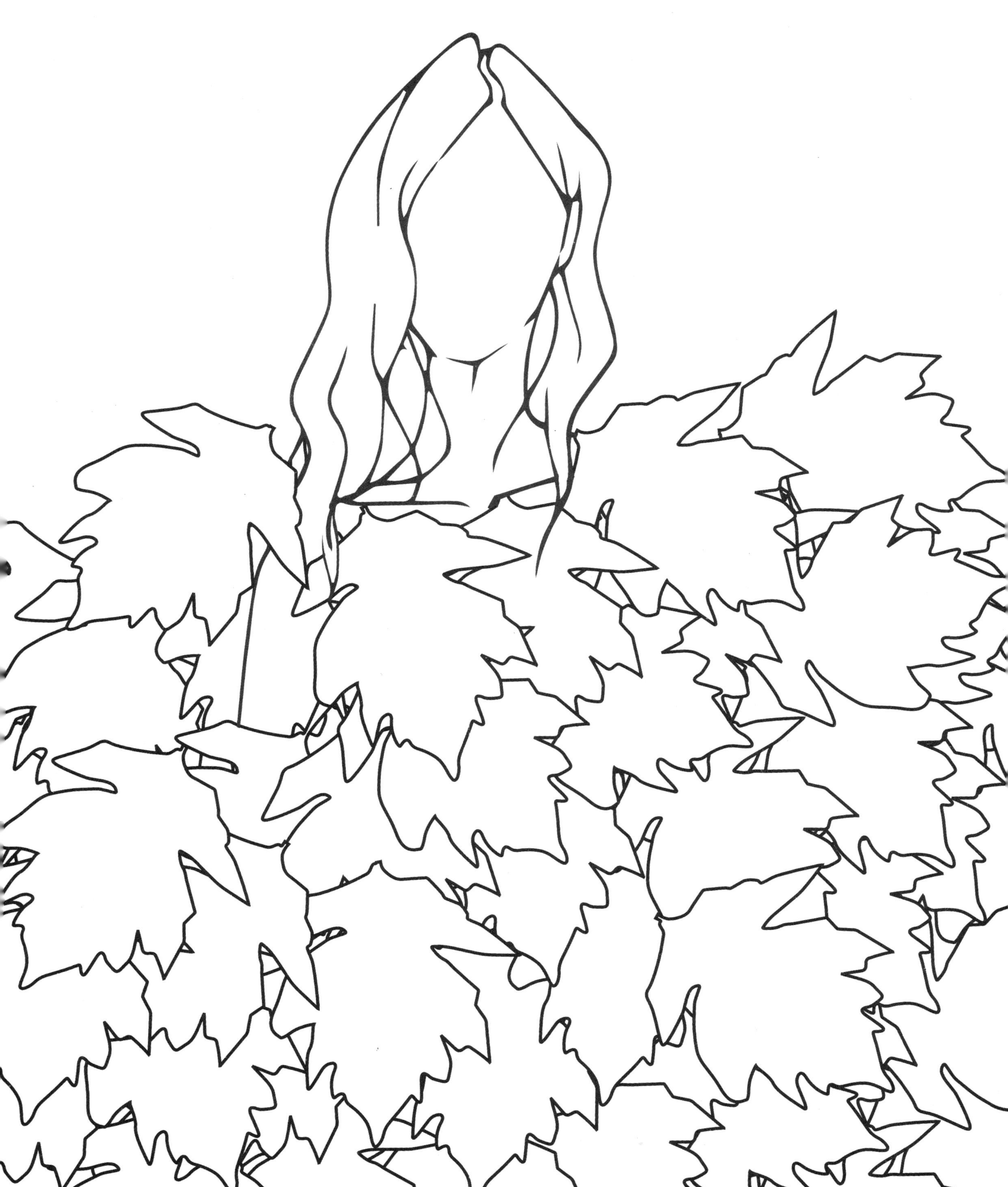

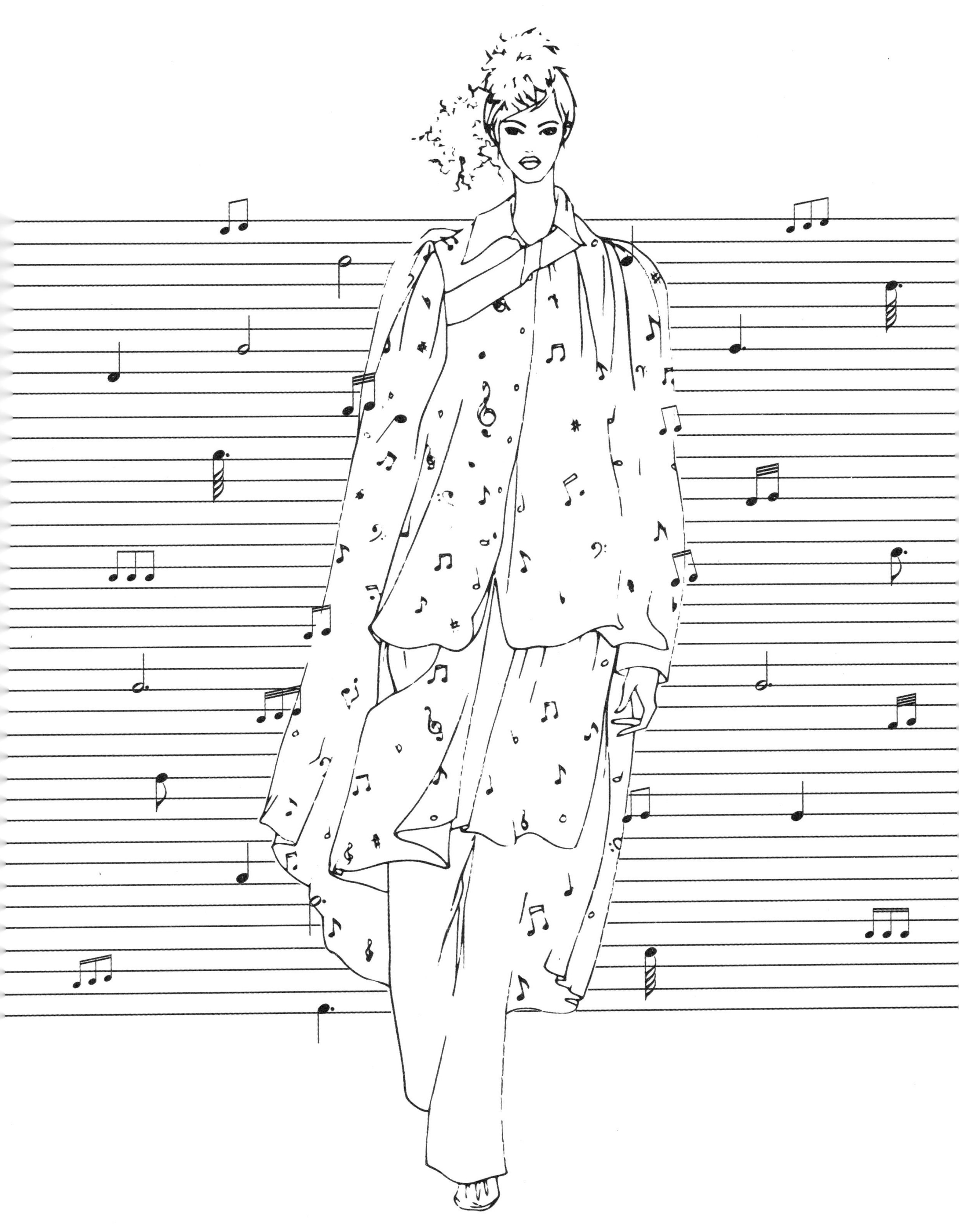

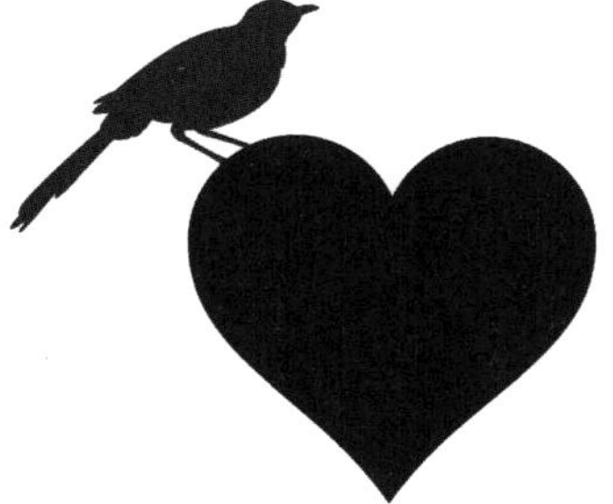

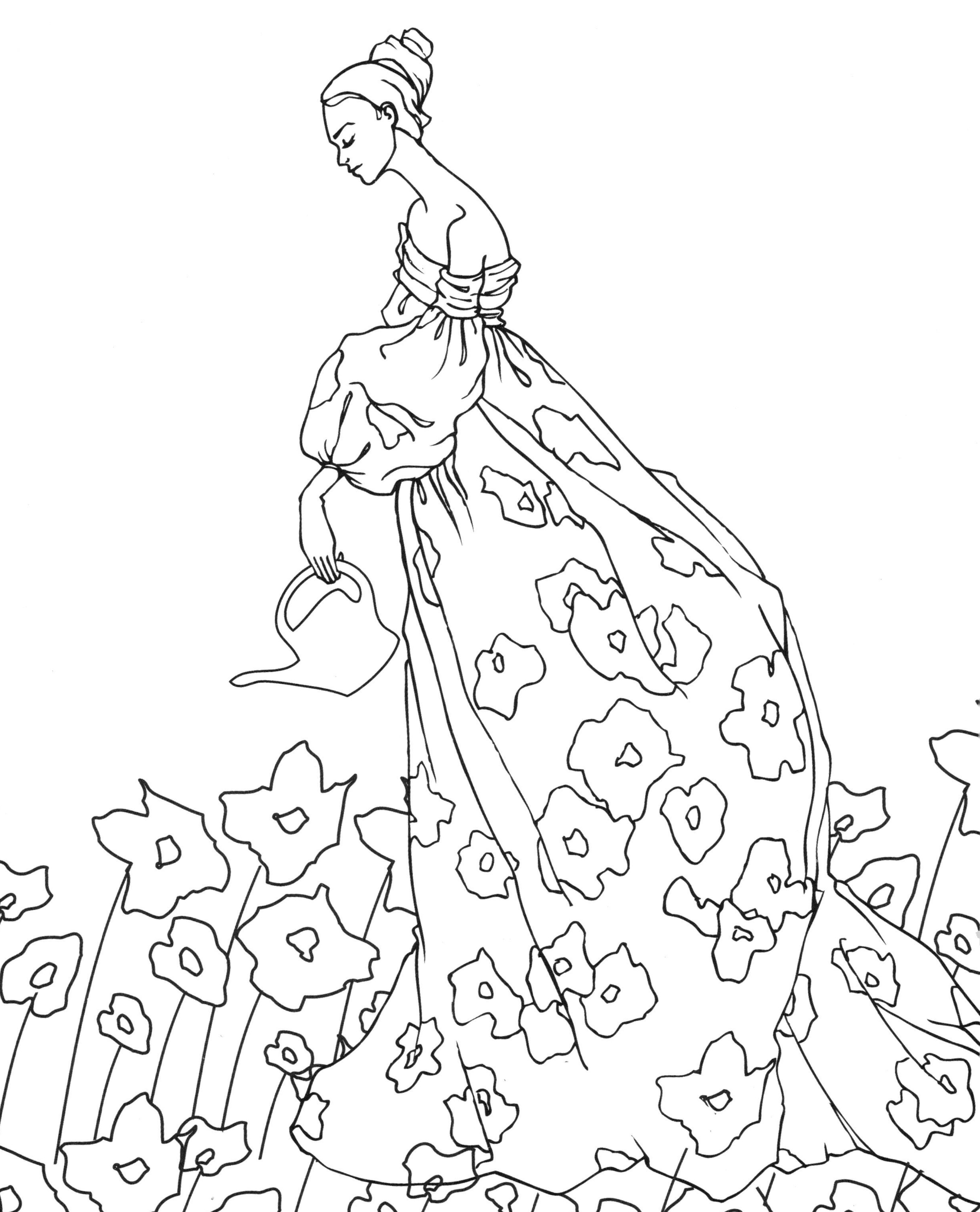

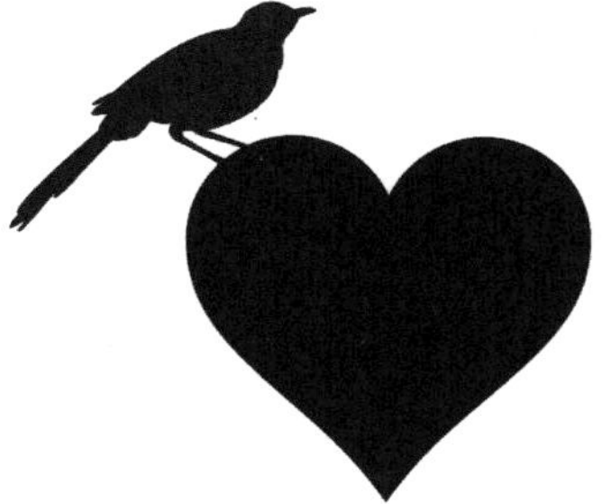

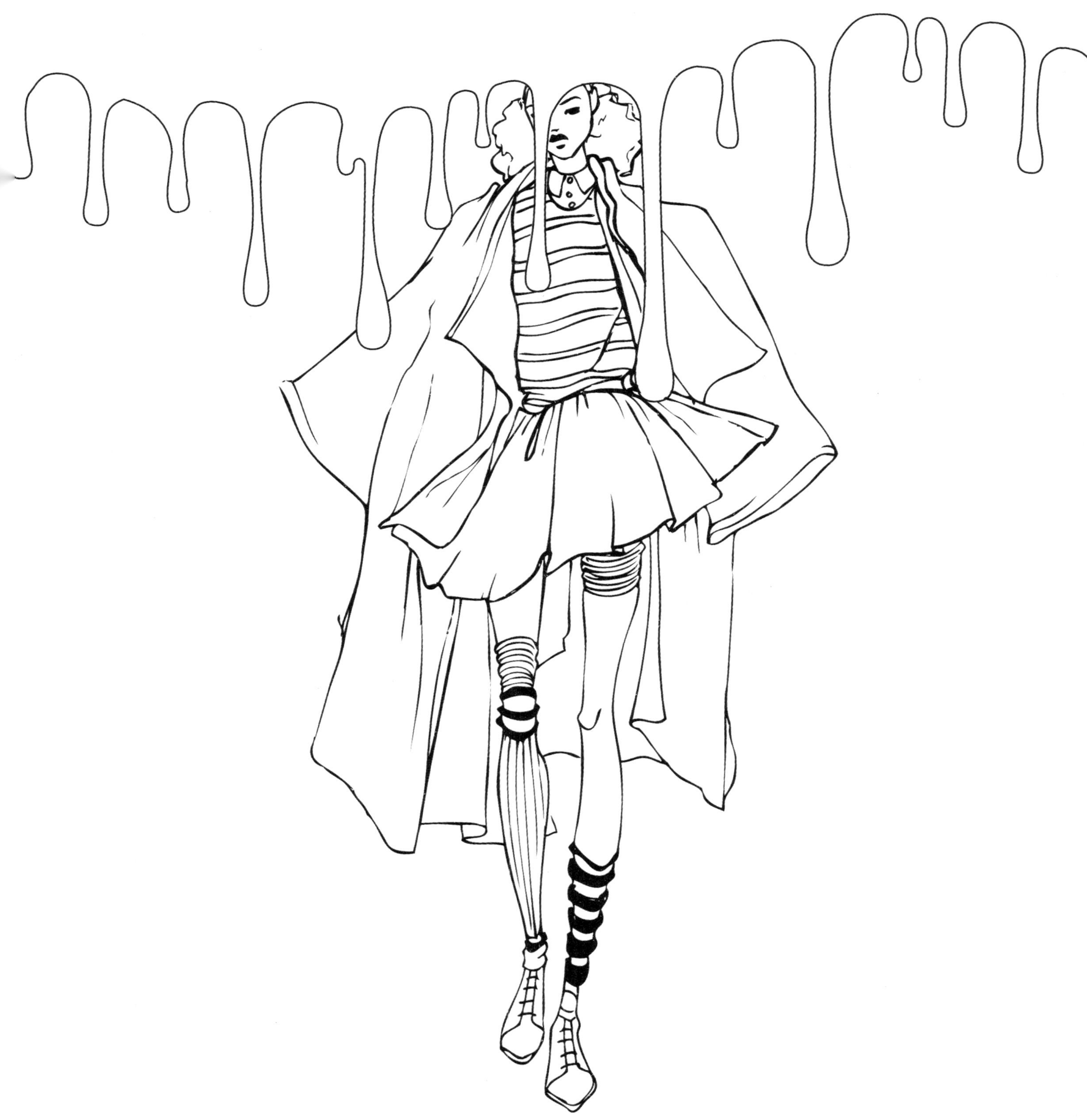

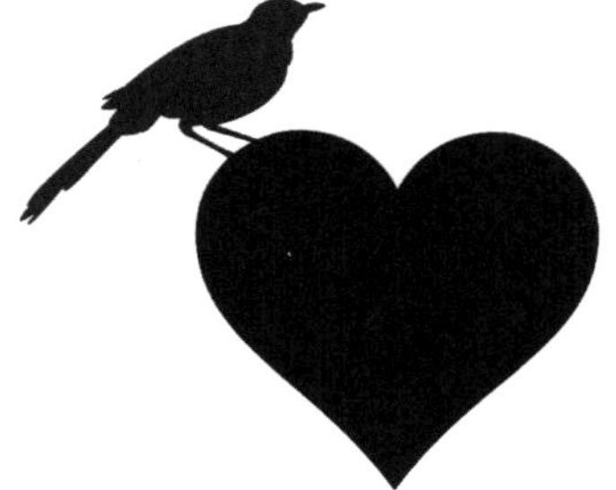

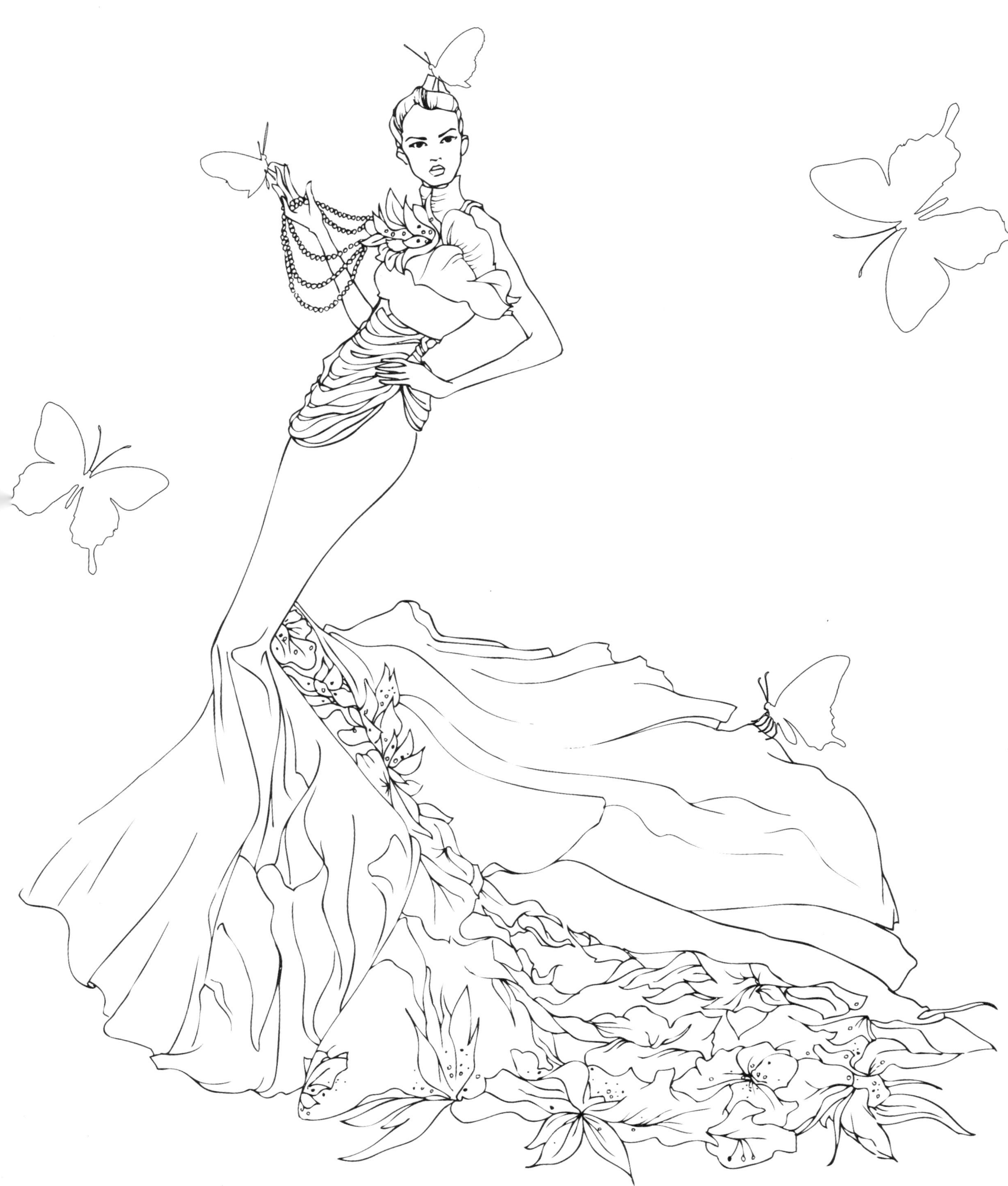

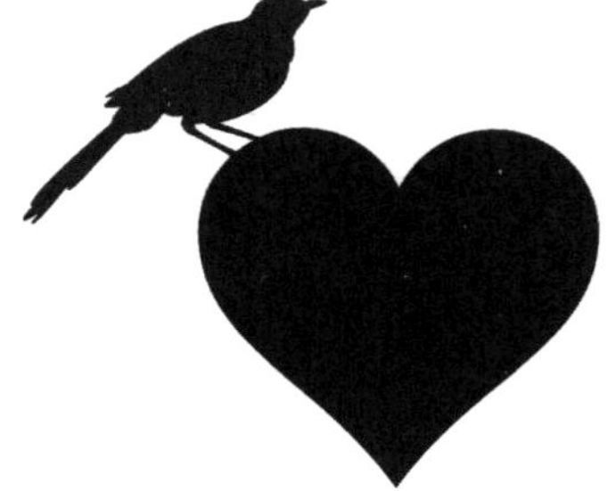

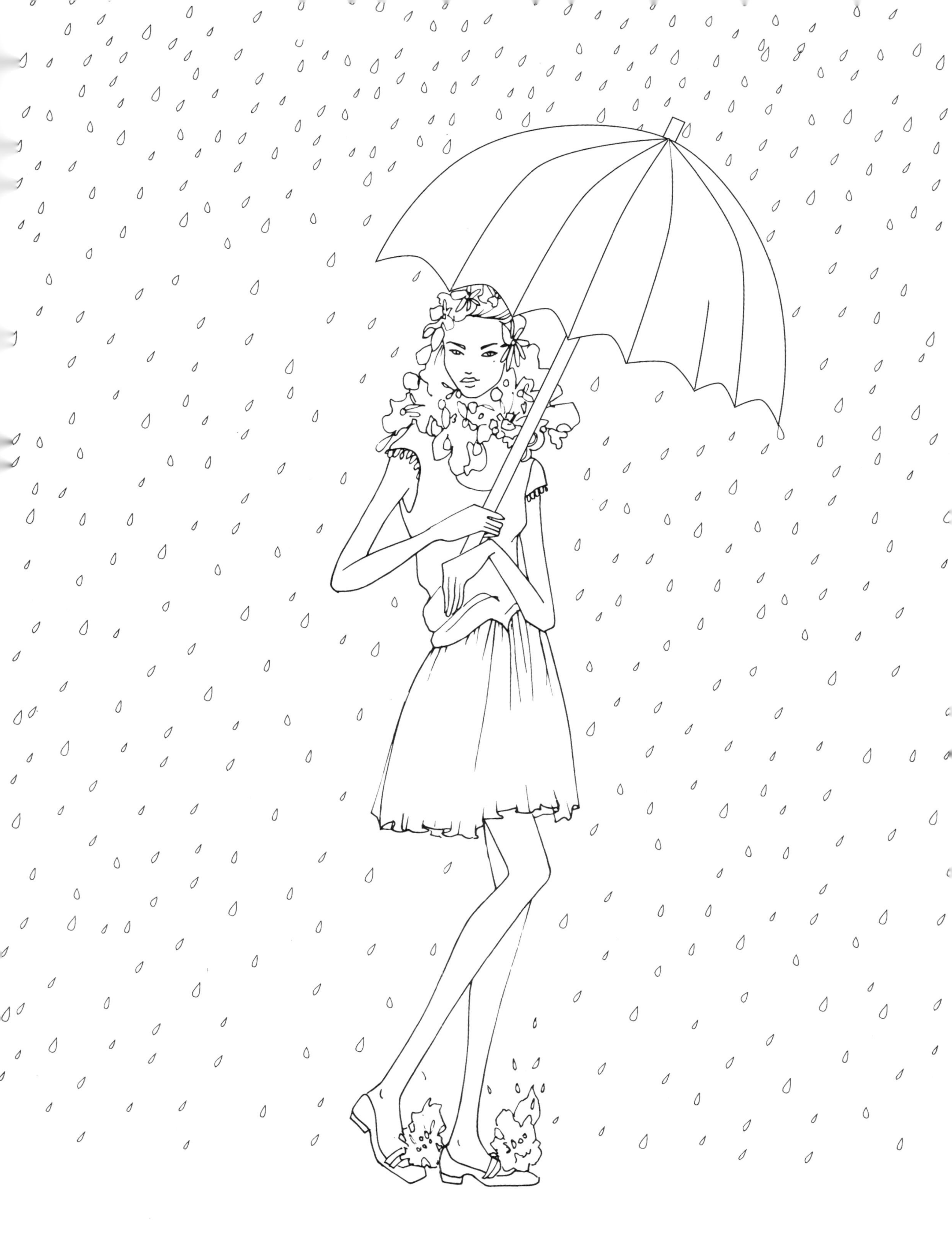

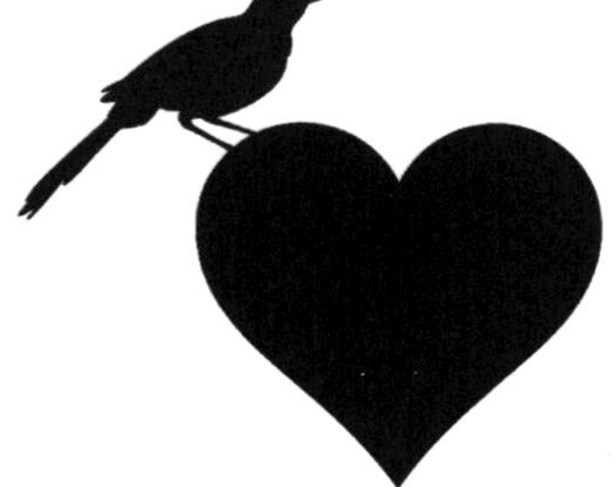

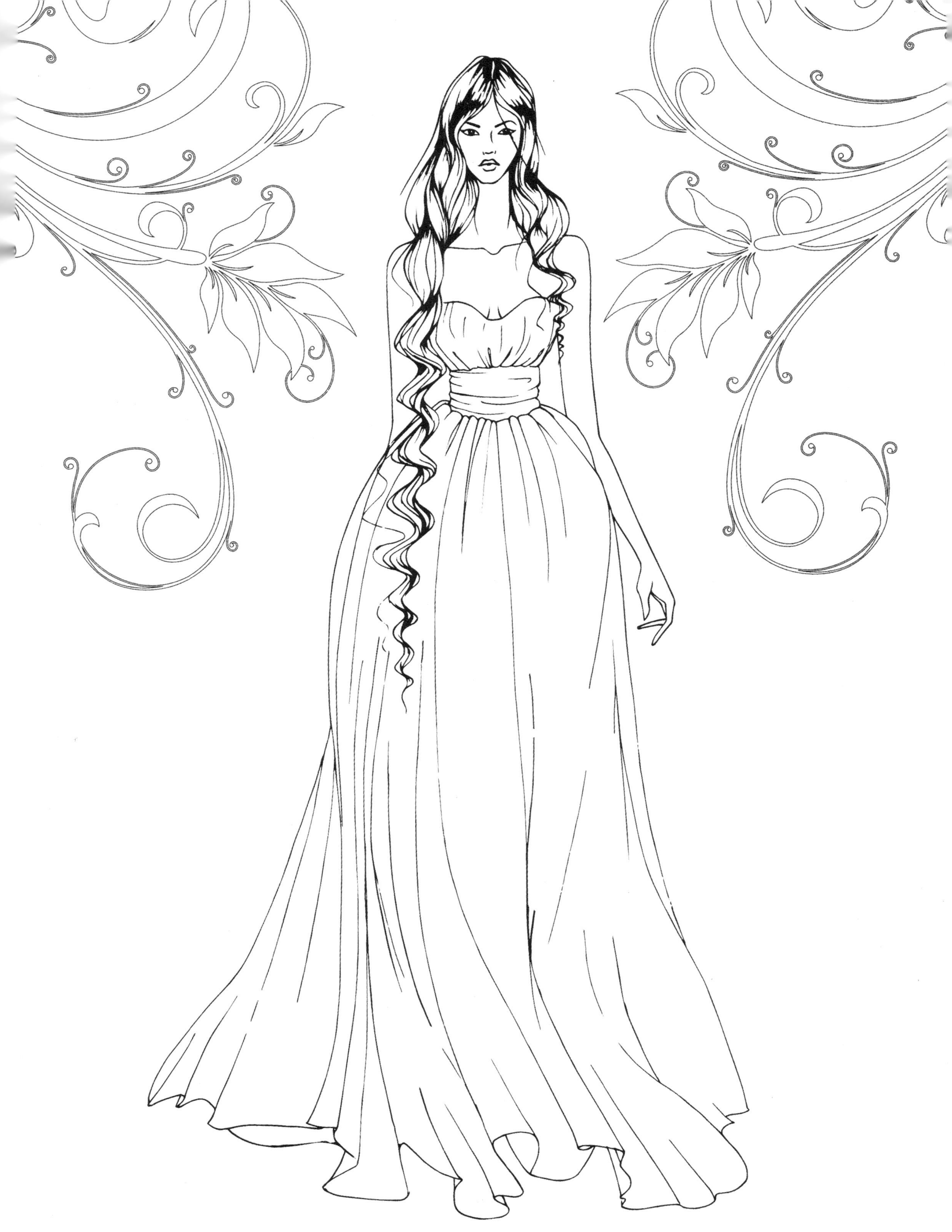

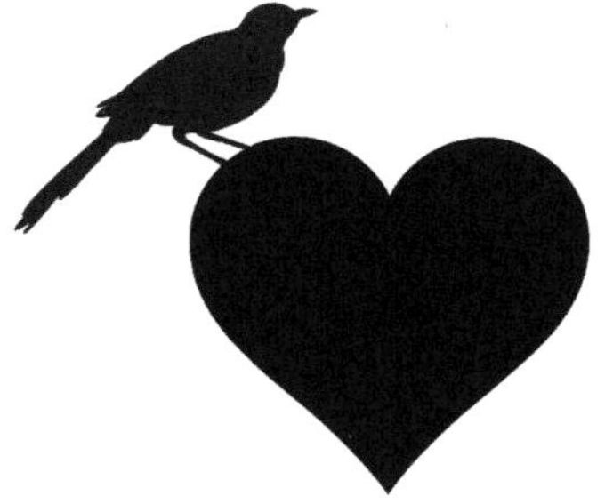

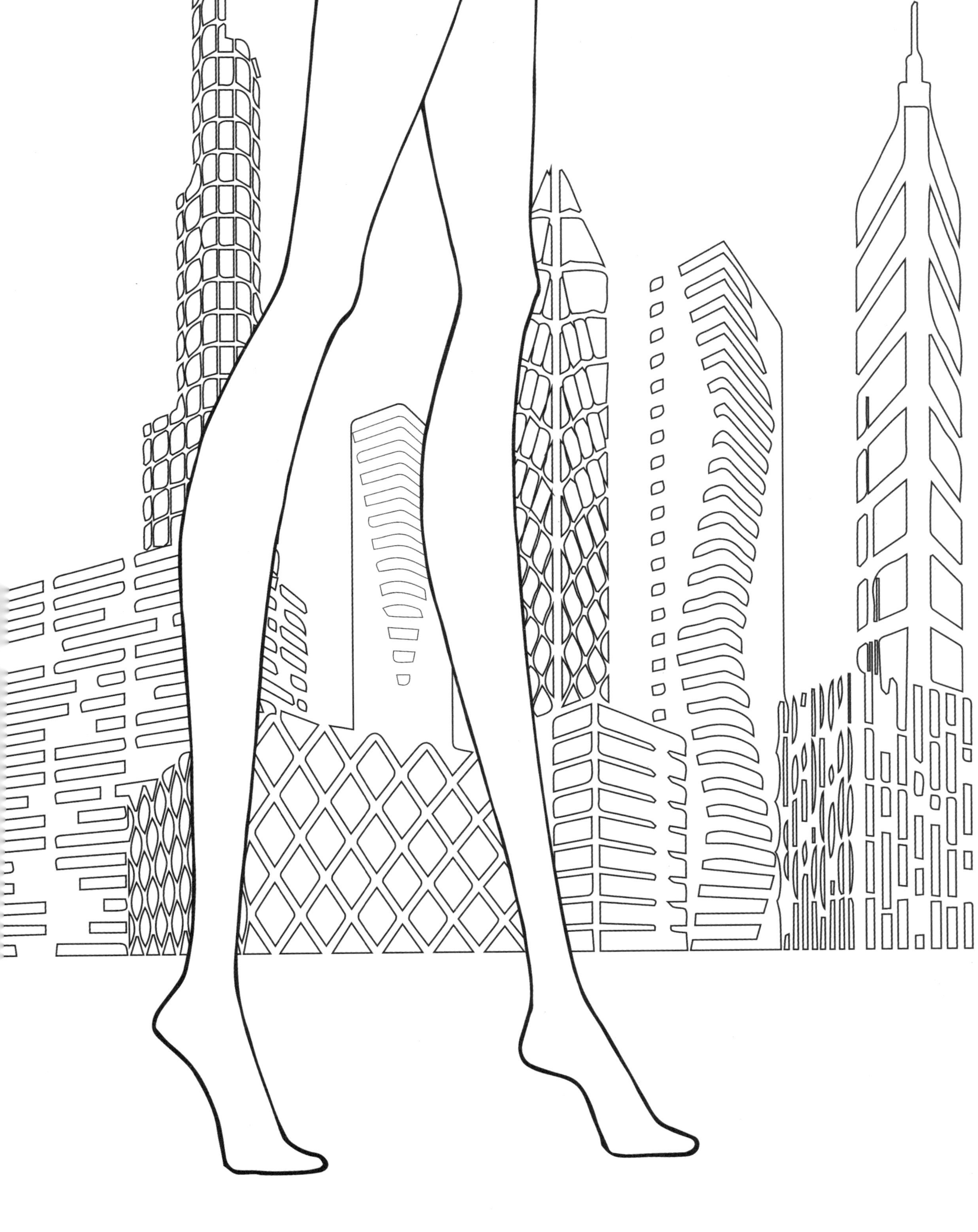

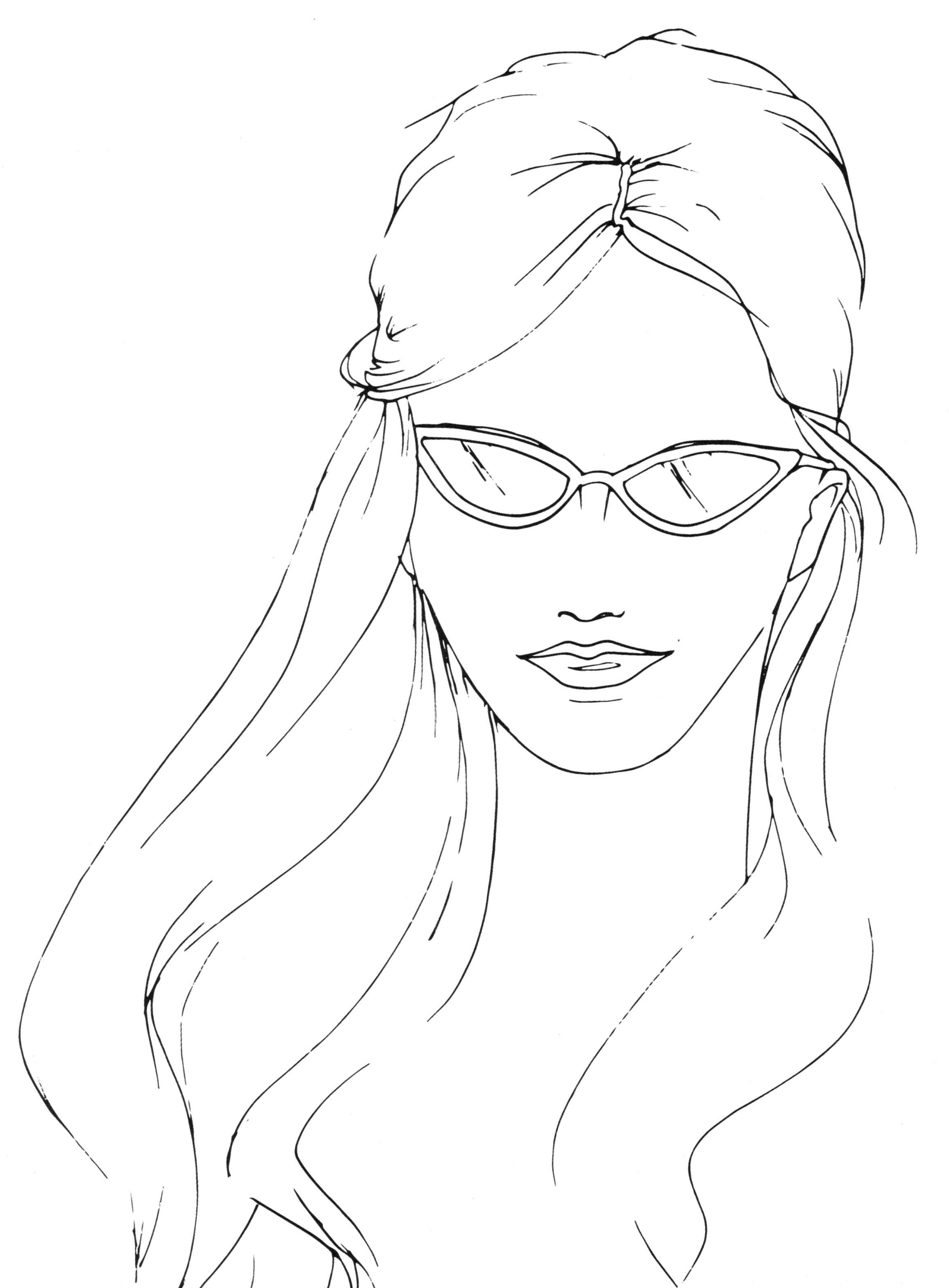

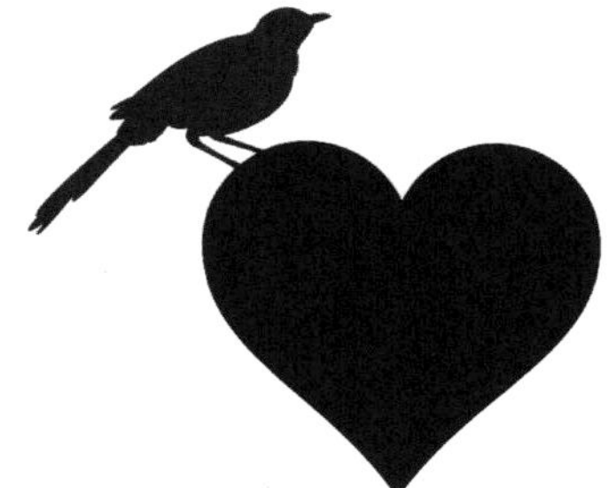

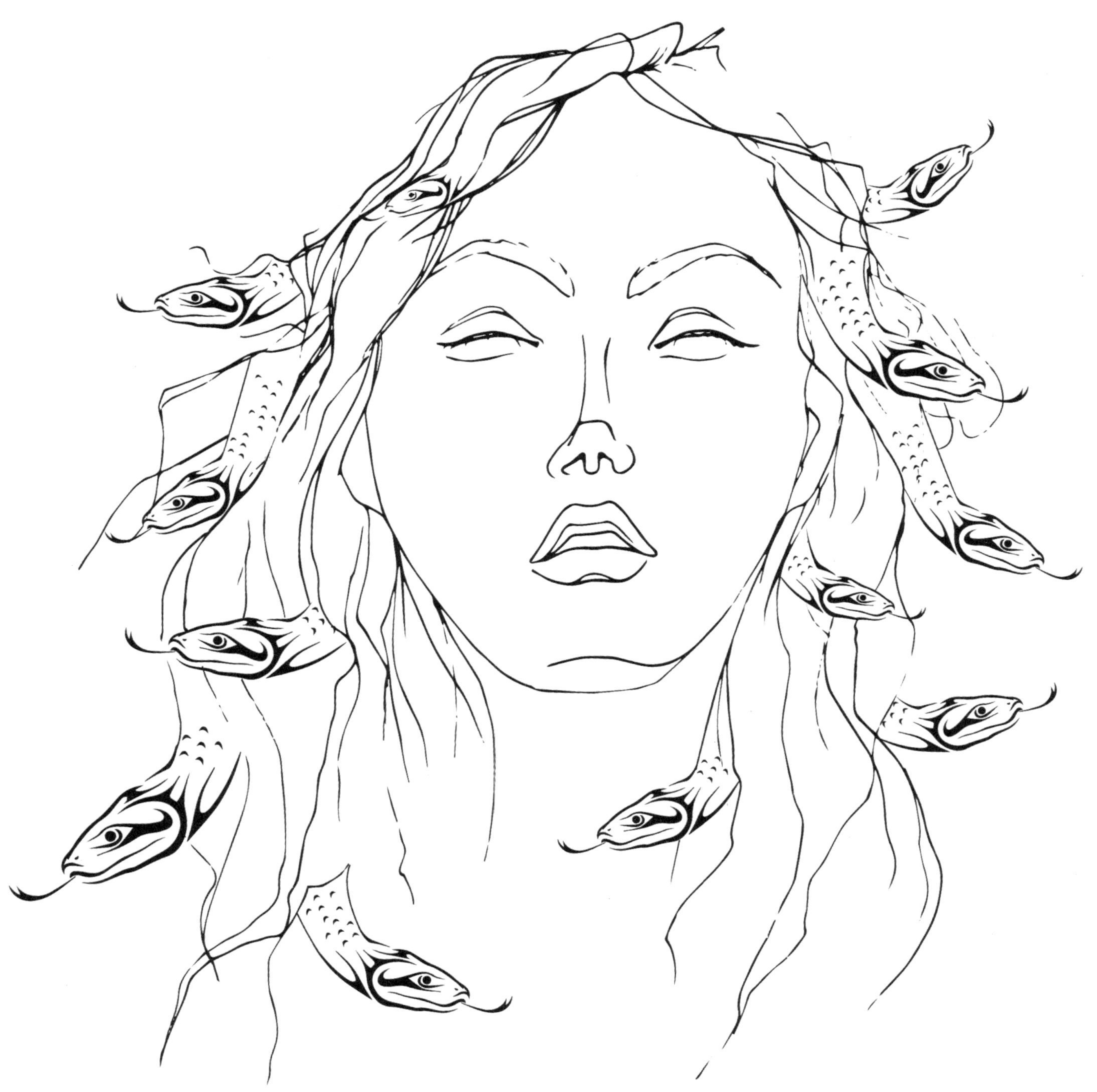

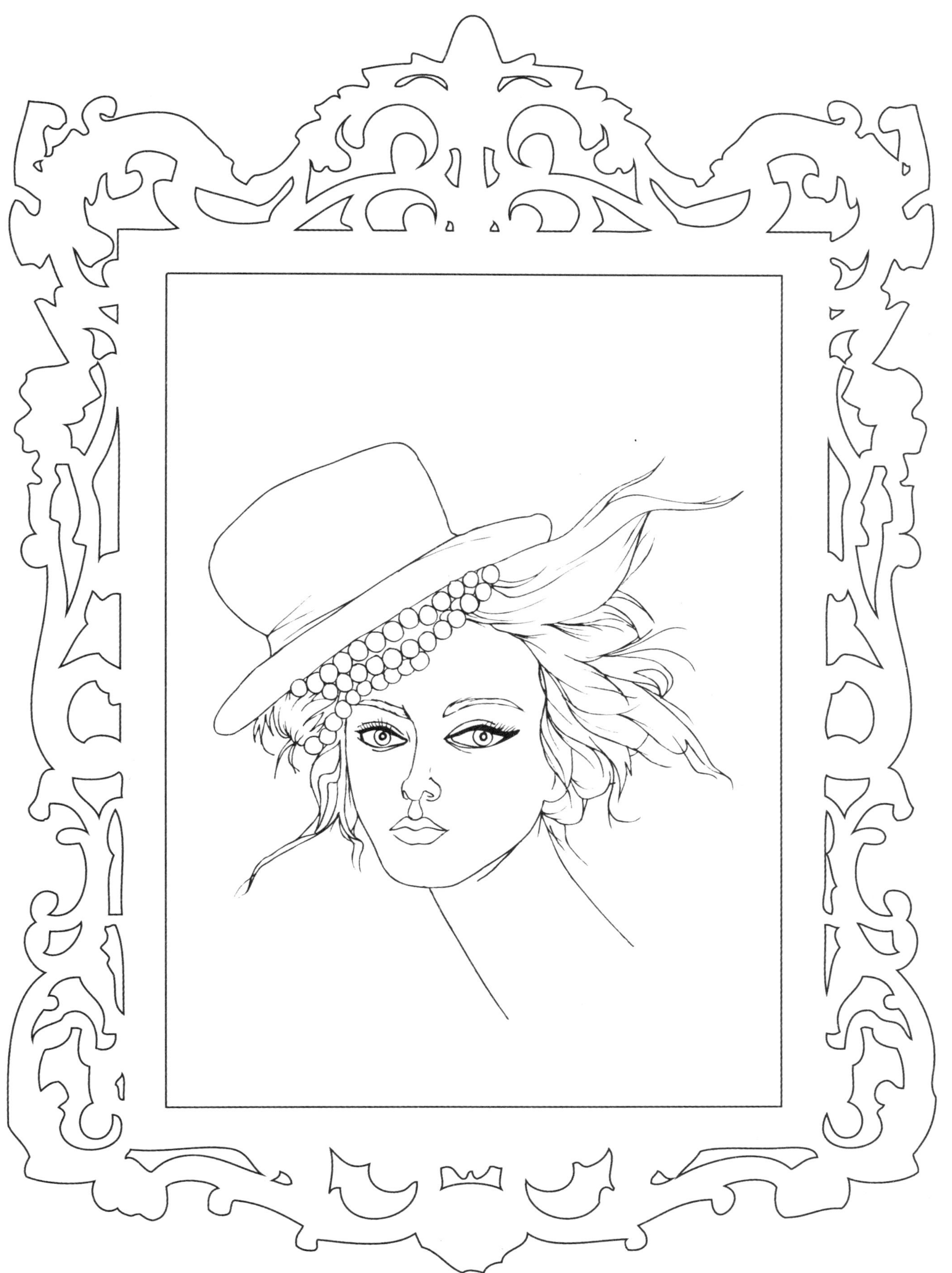

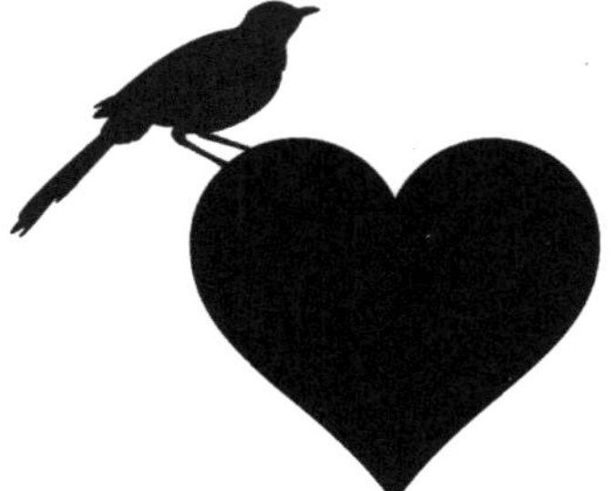

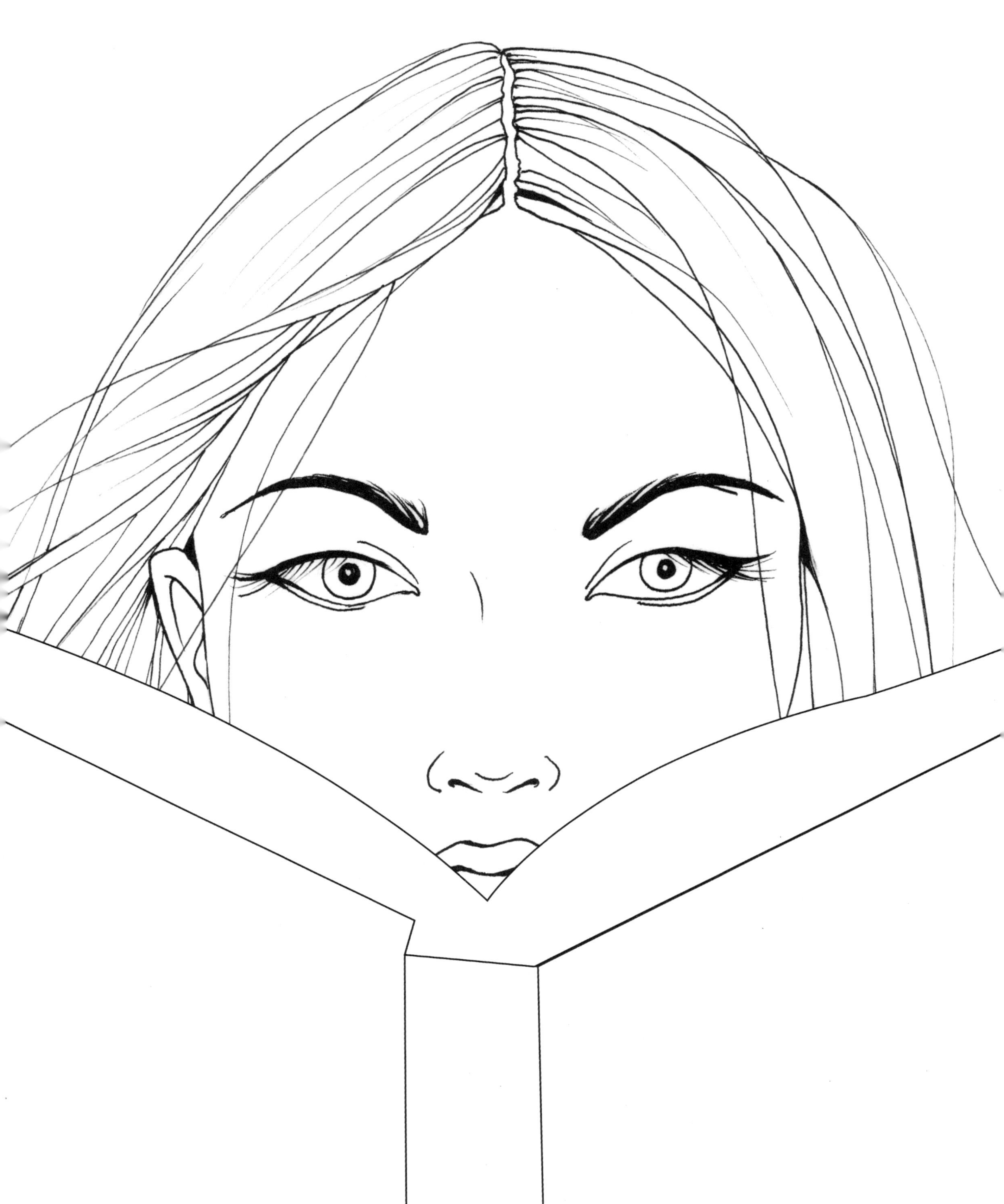

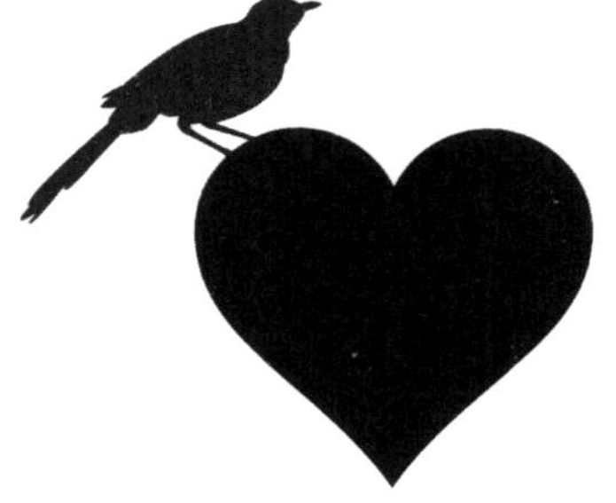

THE END

or is it?